. . . *The Joyous Patriot* . . .

THE JOYOUS PATRIOT

The Correspondence of Ralph Verney

1900 – 1916

Edited by

DAVID VERNEY

LEO COOPER
LONDON

First published 1989 by Leo Cooper Ltd

Leo Cooper is an independent imprint of
the Octopus Publishing Group, Michelin House,
81 Fulham Road, London SW3 6RB

LONDON   MELBOURNE   AUCKLAND

ISBN 0 85052 8410

Photoset by Rowland Phototypesetting Ltd
Bury St Edmunds, Suffolk
Printed and bound in Great Britain
by Mackays of Chatham plc, Chatham, Kent

In Loving Memory of Ralph and Nita.

. . . *Illustrations* . . .

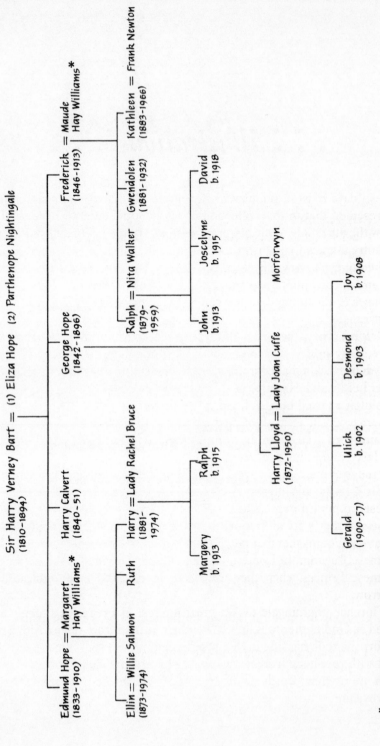

Sir Harry Verney Bart = (1) Eliza Hope (2) Parthenope Nightingale
(1810-1894)

Edmund Hope = Margaret   Harry Calvert   George Hope   Frederick = Maude
(1833-1910)   Hay Williams* (1840-51)   (1842-1896)   (1846-1913) Hay Williams*

Ellin = Willie Salmon   Ruth   Harry = Lady Rachel Bruce   Ralph = Nita Walker   Gwendolen   Kathleen = Frank Newton
(1873-1974)   (1881-   (1879-   (1881-1932) (1883-1966)
                                  1974)   1959)

                         Margery   Ralph   John   Joscelyne   David
                         b.1913   b.1915   b.1913   b.1915   b.1918

                         Harry Lloyd = Lady Joan Cuffe   Morforwyn
                         (1872-1950)

                    Gerald   Ulick   Desmond   Joy
                    (1900-57) b.1902   b.1903   b.1908

*Margaret and Maude Hay Williams were sisters

... *Preface* ...

These days it is so popular to denegrate all that the British Empire represented that in this collection of my parent's letters I have tried to show the other side of the picture: the story of a man doing his duty to his Country unquestioningly throughout his life thanks to the unique ability of the English to have a lively sense of humour, to enjoy life and to be both fair and uncorruptible, a quality which was the hallmark of those who gave themselves unstintingly to the service of their King, their Country and their Empire.

Ralph Verney, the writer of these letters, born in 1879, came from a large, close-knit Victorian family. His grandfather, Sir Harry Verney of Claydon, Buckinghamshire, had four sons by his first wife, Eliza Hope. After her death he became deeply attached to Florence Nightingale, who resolutely refused him, so he turned to her elder sister, Parthenope, and they married in 1858. Florence was a continual visitor to Claydon and became aunt to all the young Verneys, especially Frederick, the fourth son of Harry, and Ralph's father.

Frederick married in 1870 Maude Hay Williams, the younger daughter of Sir John Hay Williams. Her sister, Margie, had married Frederick's eldest brother Edmund. The relationship between these families was very close and they were all frequently at Claydon. Frederick entered Parliament as Liberal member for North Bucks and became advisor to the Siamese Legation in London and he and his wife made a home for the Siamese Princes when they were sent to England to be educated at Harrow.

Florence Nightingale took a great interest in Frederick's family and acted as Godmother to Ralph. When he returned from school with a bad report she took his side in the ensuing family row, sent him 10 shillings and with prophetic insight wrote that she 'backed Ralph'. This she did with more than words as he eventually succeeded to her estate in Derbyshire.

The Verney family had their own shorthand which enabled all members of the family to write to each other in complete confidence and which explains the freedom with which Ralph was able to express himself throughout these letters, particularly in those written from France in 1914–15.

Ralph went to school at Harrow and then to Christ Church, Oxford where he formed many friendships that reappear throughout his letters. From there he went straight into the Army being gazetted a second lieutenant in the Oxfordshire Light Infantry in 1898. He joined the Rifle Brigade on the 7th February 1900 and this story starts on the 23rd March of that year when he was 21 years old.

. . . *Chapter One* . . .

Ralph sails in the S.S. *Umbria* on 23 March, 1900, to join the Second Battalion of the Rifle Brigade in the South African War. He arrives in Durban after 38 days at sea, joins his regiment at Pietermaritzberg and goes straight to Ladysmith which had been relieved in February. From there they march to Newcastle, then on to Carolina and arrive at Helvetia just in time to take part in the battle of Bergendal Kopje.

. . . .

Rifle Depot, Gosport   March 23rd 1900

My dearest Mother,

I am very well and very fairly comfortable here for one night; we go tomorrow at 7.10 a.m. to Southampton and sail about 2.00 p.m.

Very likely you will see me come marching home again within 12 months as they are going to try and let the regiments who have been at Ladysmith have a rest in England. I saw Willie and Ellin* today and gave him the letters for him.

You were so *very* brave at my departure, mother, and it made it so very much easier for me to be brave too; but you will see me home again before very long, if I mistake not.

I shall post letters of course at our first coaling station.

* Ellin was 'Claydon' Harry's sister and had married Willie Salmon. 'Claydon' Harry was so called to distinguish him from his cousin, Harry Lloyd Verney.

. . . .

Royal Steamship *Umbria*   Sunday, April 1st 1900

My dear Father,

We are now anchored in the harbour of St. Vincent, a small town in one of the Cape Verde Islands; nearly all the population is black, and quite different from anything I saw anywhere else.

I

This morning several of us went ashore and were beset by black boys wanting 'one penny'.

Abadie, the son of General Abadie, and I went up to a Portuguese Fort this afternoon for a walk, it was a good climb up a rock, and when we got to the top they would not let us in. So we went round the other side and scaled a wall and got in, at which they were furious; but when we brought out a cigarette case and offered the four soldiers there a cigarette apiece we were all the best of friends!!

It is so very expensive telegraphing from here (2s. 9½d. per word) so we shared the telegram and sent it to Claydon knowing it will be sent on to you at once.

. . . .

Harbour of St. Vincent, Cape Verde Islands   Wednesday, April 3rd
Royal Steamship *Umbria*

My dear Kathleen,

I went to the prison the other day and talked to one or two prisoners who seemed perfectly happy; the gates were not shut or any precaution taken to keep them shut up; so I asked a black gaoler why they did not shut up their prisoners; so he said that 'the island was so very leetle, and where could they go to?' So they were no more prisoners as far as I could see than the inhabitants.

The mail only goes once a month from this place, so you may not get this for a long time yet, unless they can send it by a transport.

A few policemen walk about these streets with sort of short swords on; they are most obliging to 'Meester Offisser genleman' as they call us; if you ask where the hotel or any place is they always catch hold of a boy and tell him to show us where it is.

We have got several doctors on board going out to Africa, and I should be very sorry to fall into the clutches of the majority, who are a most bloodthirsty-looking set.

. . . .

Royal Mail Steamship *Umbria*   Friday, April 6th

My dear Mother,

Every morning from 6.30 to about 8 a.m. there is a sail spread out like a bath on deck filled with salt water; you can have almost a big swim in it; they empty it by pulling down one side of it and letting all the water run right over the deck.

2

As we sailed out of the harbour the crew of an Italian man-of-war, which had come in that afternoon, played God Save the Queen and cheered us like mad; we were not slow to return the compliment.

When she (the Italian man-of-war) entered the harbour of St. Vincent yesterday afternoon, H.M.S. *Cambrian* hoisted the Italian flag and fired a salute of 13 guns; then the Italian man-of-war first saluted the Portuguese flag with 21 guns, then saluted our flag with 13 guns; after that the Portuguese fort on shore returned the salute with another 21 guns. It was very grand, and pleasant to hear our guns making much more noise than the others all put together.

We expect to be at Cape Town next Sunday afternoon: and until we get there it is very uncertain what will be our destination. But as far as I can see, it is more likely that my battalion will be posted on the lines of communication than sent up to the front: this would be rather monotonous and harassing work.

We have had 5 deaths on board since we left Queenstown, two belonging to this detachment. The hospital used to be down below, but they have now set aside a part of the poop at the stern of the vessel for that purpose; the Army Doctors may be very skilled in their profession, but they have not much idea how to make men comfortable on board. The other night Willie and I visited the hospital and found 3 electric lights burning without any sort of shading, and they were just in the eyes of all the patients. Willie, after a good deal of persuasion, got the hospital orderly to put some newspaper in front of the light; these doctors do not think of any simple little comforts like that.

· ·

Saturday, April 14th

Today I have been very busy with packing everything up; everything has to be sorted into two heaps: one heap you take on to the front, the other heap is left either at Cape Town or Durban.

· ·

Cape Town   Friday, April 20th 1900

My dear Mother,

We came here on Monday morning and in the afternoon Willie and myself went to Maitland camp and met Toby Salmon; we have since spent many afternoons together.

3

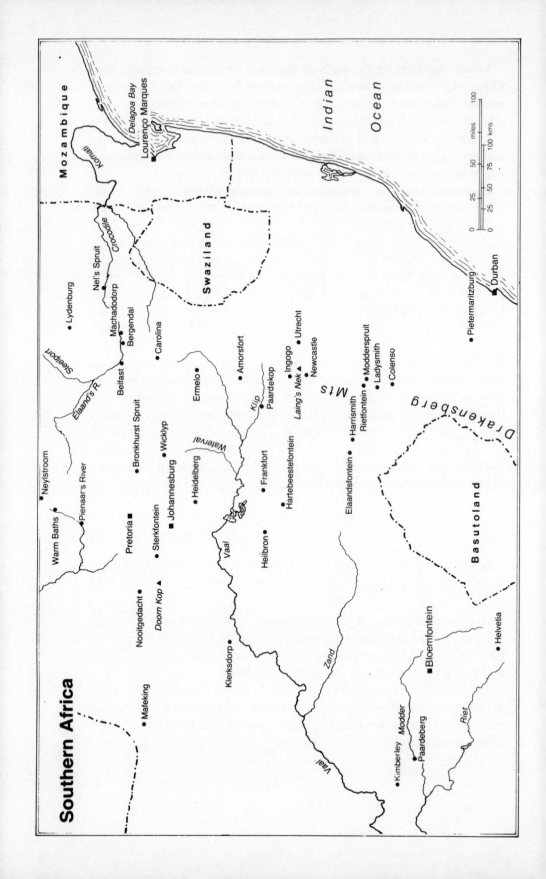

Yesterday I went with Lindsay up to Mount Nelson Hotel, where Lady Roberts* was staying; when I entered the hall, I saw two Harrow friends; one was Toby Long, the son of Walter Long, Minister of Agriculture; the other was a chap called Bastow who was at Maguire's with me.

Long was wounded in the arm, and is going home for a couple of months on Saturday. I was awfully glad to see them again.

* Lady Roberts (nee Nora Bews) was the wife of Lord Roberts (1832–1914), affectionately known as 'Bobs'. He took over supreme command of the war in South Africa from Sir Redvers Buller in December, 1899 and was awarded a Garter and an Earldom for the speed and dexterity with which he turned the fortunes of the war.

. . . .

Monday, April 23rd

Today we leave Cape Town for Durban, but stop at Port Elizabeth and East London; this will mean that we shall be another 8 or 9 days on board. Last night I dined with Leitrim at Mount Nelson Hotel, and we drank the health of the Loders Club, as they were having their first 'wine' yesterday, for this term.

. . . .

Pietermaritzburg Camp   Wednesday, May 2nd 1900

My dear Mother,

We arrived at Durban on Sunday evening about 6 p.m. but were not able to disembark until yesterday morning, which completed our voyage of 38 days!! I don't suppose I shall ever make such a long voyage again. Finally we got into a steam tug and towed a barge full of baggage alongside the quay. The *Umbria* is too large to come actually alongside the quay, so she anchored in the harbour.

We got ashore about 11.30 a.m. Tuesday, and stayed all day at the station waiting for baggage, etc. The K.R.R.* went by the first train from Durban about 4.30 p.m., but we followed on (with Willie) at about 5.30 p.m. amid scenes of great enthusiasm, crowds of natives returning from work cheering. About halfway, we stopped for the men to receive a bit of bread and some coffee which was most acceptable; we had cold meat and excellent coffee also in the refreshment room.

We got to Pietermaritzburg at 12.30 midnight and marched up to camp about a mile away from the station. When we had got the men distributed into tents (15 or 16 in a tent) it was 2 a.m. in the morning. The officers' tents are a long way from those of the men, about ½ mile. We came down

5

to our tents and found all our luggage in a heap in the middle of the road. So we had to carry all our luggage ourselves to the tents and jolly hard work it was too.

There are several tents pitched here, and we had to hunt about until we could find an empty one. Basset and I share a tent.

We had settled down and turned into our valises about 3.45 a.m. this morning; I was ordered to go on duty today and so had to be up in camp at 7.30 this morning; my night was very short though very welcome.

* King's Royal Rifles

. . . .

Ladysmith   May 9th 1900

My dear Mother,

We left Pietermaritzburg on Friday evening at 8.15 p.m. Willie left by the earlier train at 7.30 p.m. and went straight to the K.R.R. at Elaandslaagte. It was not very nice saying good-bye to Willie as he has been very good to me since we left England and I was very sorry to part from him.

We arrived at Ladysmith at 5.30 a.m. Saturday morning, and went into a small camp near the station for the men to get their breakfasts. An officer came down to us about 10 a.m. to show the way up to our camp which is nearly 3 miles from the station and all uphill. We were feeling very hot and tired, when as we turned a corner the drums and pipes of the Gordon Highlanders struck up the 'Cock of the North' and played us in to our camp amidst great cheering. I never heard such sweet music in all my life; it was very good of the Gordons to do it.

The Commanding Officer is at Durban now on leave, but Major Cockburn met us and was very nice and civil; he sent us to the mess and gave us drinks. Gradually we met all the officers who are here, about 16 or 18 in number. Colonel Walter Kitchener* is commanding our Brigade and General Lyttleton** is our General commanding the division. He

* Colonel (later Lieut-General Sir Walter) Kitchener (1858–1912) was the younger brother of Field Marshal Lord Kitchener, of Khartoum and 'Your Country Needs You' fame; the latter was Chief-of-Staff to Lord Roberts in South Africa, 1899–1900, and Commander-in-Chief, 1900–1902.
** General Sir Neville Lyttelton (1845–1931) joined the Rifle Brigade in 1865, fought at Tel-el-Kebir in 1882 and commanded a brigade in the Nile Expedition of 1898. At the end of the Boer War he succeeded Kitchener as Commander of the British Forces in South Africa.

. . . .

came to breakfast at our mess yesterday, but I did not get the chance of talking to him.

I have done a good deal of work already. On Saturday night my company (D company) was to furnish the 'inlying piquet' and has to be ready for any emergency. We all had to sleep with our boots and clothes on, and our belts, etc., at our side. Each company takes its turn.

On Sunday night from 4.45 p.m. until Monday night at 6.45 p.m. I was on outpost duty; we marched away to some trenches in the veldt about 1½ miles away and slept there all night; I had to take charge of a visiting patrol and go and visit the next piquet to ours at 1 o'clock in the morning; and also inspect our sentries. At 4.30 a.m. we sent on our scouts in front and climbed a hill called Middle Hill which is quite close to Wagon Hill and we stayed there all day, building trenches and walls to fortify the hill. I enjoyed it very much, as luckily the night was not too cold, and there was no dew practically.

I am very fit indeed and very well. There is a strong likelihood of our making a move forward soon to try and take the Biggarsburg Pass; there are only 2000 Boers holding it, and they think we could take it. Already two Brigades have moved forward, I do hope we shall not be left behind. The third K.R.R. have moved I believe; Willie may have already been in action!

The transport here is carried on in great carts drawn by 10 or 12 or 16 oxen; or 6 or 8 mules; they go along slowly but very steadily; they can do 18 to 24 miles a day.

It is most interesting being here and seeing all the hills and scenes of the battles; Harrison is my senior subaltern and was wounded on Jan. 6th; Captain Biddulph commands the Company, and was also seriously wounded on the 6th January. They are both well now. Lewis Hall, the other subaltern, was killed; the colour sergeant was wounded, and so an ordinary sergeant had to take command of the company. I have been all over the scene of that fight on the 6th Jan. where my regiment was engaged. Harrison pointed out all the places of interest to me: bits of shell, shrapnel bullets are lying about. We may receive orders to move forward at any time now. I am awfully keen to go up to the front.

. . . .

Modderspruit   May 17th 1900

My dear Mother,

Yesterday we received orders to move out of here about 11 miles from our camp at Ladysmith.

I was on outpost duty the night before last and they forgot to send any breakfast to us, so we had nothing till we got back to camp except a bit of chocolate. When we did get back, we found we had to march 11 miles, and start within 2 hours. The march was dreadfully hot and the dust was thicker than any London fog. We started at 2.30 p.m. and got into Modderspruit Camp at 6.45 p.m. We got hold of some blankets, and spent the night in the middle of the road, just where we halted. I lay down and was so awfully tired, I went straight to sleep as I was.

I got your letters yesterday written from Venice, I hope you had a good time all together. Shall you go to the Paris exhibition?

. . . .

May 19th 1900

My dear Mother,

We have moved our camp nearer water since I wrote to you last. On Monday the 21st, we start to march to Newcastle. We march 14 miles a day twice, and 16 miles a day three times, as it is to take us 5 days altogether.

This ought to make us pretty fit, and it will also get us right up to Buller's* force, where we shall see any fighting if there is any.

From there the present plan is for us to go straight on to Pretoria providing the Boers do not give more resistance than they have lately. At our present camp, which is pitched at the bottom of a hill, we have to furnish 4 outposts. Three companies are posted on different hills and are staying there for three days. The other outpost is made up of half a company as a support to some guns which are near here.

We have all just got some new thick short coats, instead of our overcoats. They call them the 'British Warm Coat'; it is lighter to carry and of course of Khaki colour; the men have also got them. The great disadvantage of them is that they do not cover the legs at all, but they are so much lighter that it rather compensates for it.

The news of the relief of Mafeking reached us yesterday. There was great rejoicing; it has not come officially yet, but we all think it must be true.

* Sir Redvers Henry Buller (1839–1908) had been appointed commanding general of the British forces in South Africa in 1899 and later general officer commanding in Natal. Owing to several severe reverses round Ladysmith, he was superseded by Lord Roberts and returned to England in 1900.

. . . .

Ingagane   May 28th 1900
4 miles from Newcastle

My dear Father,

Since I wrote last we have had several long and rather trying marches. We started from Modderspruit on Wednesday, May 23rd at 9 a.m.; we marched to Sundays River, a distance of about 11 miles. I had been on outpost duty all the night before and so started under not very favourable circumstances. The day was frightfully hot and the dust was awful, but we got in at last about 3.30 p.m.; twenty-two men fell out on the road from my company alone, so you can imagine it was pretty bad.

On Thursday we started at 4 a.m. and marched to the top of the Biggarsburg Pass; not a single man fell out the whole way out of the regiment; it was the Queen's birthday, and so they determined all to march the whole way. We bivouacked about 5000 ft. high and it was pretty cold. On Friday my company was on baggage guard; we were ordered to parade at 4.30 a.m. and to escort two naval guns.

We were waiting for those guns from 5 a.m. until 8.15 a.m. by the side of the road; but the march was fortunately a short one only 10 miles; we started at 8.15 and got in at 1 o'clock midday.

It is very trying work being on baggage guard as you have to march with the transport and there are so many delays and so much dust.

On Saturday morning we started at 8 a.m. and marched to Ingagane. The day was beautifully cool and though the march was a little long (14 miles) it was the easiest one we had.

All our tents were left at Ladysmith so we always now sleep on the ground in our valises. We cannot get any bread now at all, so thick biscuits (just like Spratt's dog biscuits) do instead. They are not at all bad when you get used to them.

There are one or two Kaffir 'kraals' near here. They are round huts made of grass, and are exactly like bee-hives, with a hole to crawl into them. We go round and try and buy eggs and chickens from them. Yesterday I went and made them understand what I wanted by crowing and flapping my arms. They are kept very fairly clean.

The Boers are said to be in great numbers at Laing's Nek, and everybody says there will be a fight here in a day or two; but I expect you know much more about it in London than we do here.

Aunt Margy will remember Colonel Campbell who commands the 1st Battalion K.R.R. and who came to Claydon about 2 years ago. He sent us 3 bottles of champagne to drink the Queen's health with on the 24th. His

9

camp was fairly close to ours, and they had kept a 'case of champagne in their mess for the occasion. We all got about an eggcupful.

. . . .

June 2nd 1900

Last Monday the Boers shelled Ingogo, or some troops near there. We could see the shells bursting fairly plainly though we ourselves were out of range. It is the first time I have seen any firing in earnest, but we were a long way off then. Anyway it gave one an idea what it would be like to be in the thick of a fight when shells were flying about like that.

. . . .

Tuesday, June 5th 1900

We got orders on Monday morning to move to the North side of Newcastle to relieve Talbot-Coke's brigade which has advanced to Ingogo. We have had our tents sent up from Ladysmith, and are now under canvas once more. Last night we had 4 companies out on outpost duty. I had to take half a company out on to the main road from here to Utrecht and to furnish an examining post. All persons not having a proper pass had to be stopped and kept till 6 a.m. in the morning.

We are now divided into two separate parts for the present; the right half battalion is bivouacking on the top of this hill, and the left half are down in the valley. We have 1½ companies out on outpost every night out of 4 companies and half a company out every day, so that we get a day off duty about every 3 days.

. . . .

June 6th 1900

This morning I went to the top of a hill about 2½ miles from here towards Laing's Nek where the Boers were shelling troops near Ingogo: we could see the big Boer gun on the top of Pugwana Hill just opposite Majuba. They fired pretty regularly from about 10 this morning until 12.30 midday, and they began again about 2 p.m. I saw several of our shells burst somewhere near the gun, but it was not damaged or put out of action. The hill where I was, was out of range, but we got a good view.

10

The news of the surrender of Pretoria and the capture of Mrs Kruger*
arrived in camp this morning.

* Wife of President Paulus Kruger (1825–1904), four times president of the Transvaal,
known as 'Om Paul'. Too old to take part in the Boer War, he went to Europe in
September, 1900, in a vain attempt to get the European powers to intervene and died in
Switzerland four years later.

. . . .

Near Newcastle   June 19th 1900

My dear Mother,

I have now been posted on the top of a high hill, between Signal Hill and
the Drakensburg mountains. We are up here for a week, that is to say my
captain and myself, as Harrison is occupying another fort with a few men
about 3 miles from here.

You would have laughed this morning if you had seen me soon after 7
a.m. with my coat off, putting up a barbed wire fence, just like the ones at
Claydon, only my fence has a lot more wire on it, and is meant to hinder
any Boers that would like to come and attack us by night. Some raiding
parties of Boers were reported to us last night by General Kitchener to be
within 15 or 20 miles of us; so you can imagine we are on the alert.

There is a farm here belonging to a Boer. This afternoon I walked down
there and found a son of his, who had fought against us in the earlier part
of the war; but now that we are up here, he has become quite friendly. He
gave me a bottle of fresh milk, and I am going to send a man down
tomorrow morning to bring up some eggs from his farm, though he swears
black and blue he has not got any. I told him this afternoon that if the eggs
were not forthcoming tomorrow morning I should have to buy up all his
hens which were running about.

. . . .

Newcastle   June 28th 1900

My dearest Mother,

So many thanks for the Shetland vests and the socks. I am keeping one of
the vests and the socks, but am distributing the rest to those who want
them. It is very cold indeed at nights here. This morning my basin was full
of ice and the water in my bucket was frozen over ¼ inch thick; but in the
daytime it is beautifully warm, about as warm as an ordinary summer day
in England.

This morning the Gordon Highlanders who are encamped next to us,
and are also in General Kitchener's brigade, had orders to strike camp

and go towards Utrecht a few miles, in order to protect the railway. I think that there is some idea that a force of Boers is coming to try and intercept the railway, by blowing up a bridge or putting up a few yards of the line near here. I wish they would come. We are quite ready for them. Their number is supposed to be 3000. Two shots were fired into Mount Prospect station last night, and that is not very far from here.

I returned from my week of outpost duty yesterday. On the whole I rather enjoyed it, as my captain used to lend me his gun occasionally, and I got some doves which are very good eating. He shot a guinea-fowl one day, and we told our servants to roast it in a big cooking pot, and not to overdo it. At luncheon that day (12.30 p.m.) we heard something frizzling away, and asked what it was. My servant said, 'It is only the guinea-fowl cooking for dinner tonight sir, and it is getting on nicely sir, thank you.' They were going to roast the wretched bird from 12.30 until 6.30 at night. We mildly suggested that it might be rather overdone by dinner-time, so we went out and pulled it out of the cooking pot; but in two hours it was back again. The servants kept pulling it out to smell it, as it smelt awfully good. However, by dinnertime it was done to a turn, and was perfectly delicious.

. . . .

Newcastle   July 10th 1900

My dear Father,

We have moved our camp now to the south-west of Newcastle and about 2 miles out of the town. The reason for this move is that De Wet* might come through Muller's Pass, and so we are encamped here on the road leading from that Pass to Newcastle, by which he must come.

Today most of the men in camp are employed in digging trenches and pits to protect us from shellfire from a hill on our left. If any guns did get up by night on to this hill, they would give us a good time of it in the morning soon after sunrise.

* Christian Rudolph De Wet (1854–1922) became general and commander-in-chief of the Orange Free State forces when the South African War broke out in 1899. See also footnote p. 152.

. . . .

Field Hospital   Tuesday, July 17th 1900
Newcastle

The Boers sent a man in with a flag of truce to give some message or other here, and he came right through Newcastle. General Kitchener thinks it is probably a ruse to gain information about us, so he has sent Gough,* one of our Captains, back to Utrecht with a letter informing the Boers that we have sent off their messenger, who came to us, round back by Delagoa Bay.

* John Edmond Gough (1871–1915) won the VC in Somaliland in 1903. Both his father and his uncle had won VCs in the Indian Mutiny. See also pp. 185–6.

. . . .

Royal Hotel   August 4th 1900
Durban, Natal

My dear Father,

I have been here since Monday evening, and tomorrow night I go up country again to Newcastle. My fortnight's leave has done me a lot of good, and I am quite fit again for duty.

The mess gave me one or two commissions to do in Durban. One was to buy a dozen laying hens. So I went into the market and inspected the hens, and picked out a dozen, put them into a couple of baskets and had them sent up to this hotel in a rickshaw, but when I get them up country I expect it will be too cold for them to lay any eggs.

Another job I had to do, was to buy 1 doz. ginger wine; so I went into a wine merchant and asked the price, which they said was 39s. a dozen. But the shop man said to me, 'Surely you are in the Service, Sir'. I admitted that he was right. Whereupon he informed me I should only be charged 21s. instead of 39s. It seems a duty of 18s. is put upon every case of wine, and officers are allowed to buy wine without paying duty; fancy 18s. duty, it seems quite enormous.

. . . .

Komati River (near Carolina)   August 16th 1900
Transvaal

My dearest Mother,

I am not going to give you a minute account of our hardships during the last 10 days, because it may only be lost labour, but as soon as we get into regular postal communication again, you shall have a vivid account. But the chief facts are these: we are on a flying column under Buller and Lyttelton, marching from Sand's Spruit northwards towards Belfast. We have had shots exchanged with the Boers every day, but the only engagement approaching a battle was at Amorsfort on Aug. 7th. The Boers were in a strong position, but before the infantry could get to them,

13

our guns had made them bolt. The casualties were 2 officers 21 men wounded (none in our regiment). We have been marching 10–18 miles every day since, and are now about 5 miles north-west of Carolina. We are staying here a few days to get fresh supplies, and to rest.

The Boers passed through this place the day before yesterday with 12 guns and 350 infantry. Two of the guns are ours which they captured at Colenso.

. . . .

Komati River (near Carolina)   August 17th 1900

In the morning on Aug. 5th I met our Brigade Army Chaplain who was on his way home to England in a hospital ship. He told me that the 2nd Battalion Rifle Brigade was under orders to move from Newcastle but he knew nothing further. I went up country again by the 6 p.m. train that night and got to Newcastle at 10 a.m. the next morning; so it took 16 hours altogether, though the distance is not quite so great as from London to Newcastle-on-Tyne.

The Railway Staff Officer there informed me that we had already gone on to Sand's Spruit another 3 or 4 hours' journey, so I went on by the same train.

At Sand's Spruit, after I had got out of the van my luggage and the basket of hens which I was bringing from Durban for the Mess, they told me that the regiment had left that morning and that I might catch them by going on to Paardekop, another hour's journey. The train was almost moving by then, but by awful threats and abuse the guard put my luggage in the van again and I went on to Paardekop.

Instead of the regiment being within a mile or two of the station as I expected, the Staff Officer told me they were nearly 10 miles away. Apparently there was no way of getting my kit carried those 10 miles and I felt in a terrible fix. They expected a battle to be fought on the next day, so of course I was awfully keen to catch them up that night. Fortunately the 'Enniskillens' were loading their wagons and were marching out to some camp or other. They are in the 8th Brigade and we are in the 7th Brigade, so I hoped we might be somewhere near. I put my kit on their wagons and decided to walk the 10 miles with the Enniskillens. We started at 5 p.m. and did not get in until nearly 9 p.m. Of course I had not the faintest idea where our camp was and it was pitch dark, but at the Divisional Hospital camp which was near they told me it was about a mile away. The Major of the R.A.M.C. in charge of the hospital very kindly gave me a couple of

Indian bearers to carry my kit, and so finally I caught up the regiment at about 10 p.m. Aug. 6th.

Everybody was asleep, and I just put my blankets on the ground and rolled myself up in them; it was almost to cold to sleep, as a very bitter wind was just getting up, but I was only too glad to lie down.

We got up next morning (Aug. 7th) at 5.30 a.m. and had orders to march at 7 a.m. Of course everybody was very surprised to see me, and the Colonel was rather pleased that I had managed to catch up the regiment. The hens were welcomed most affectionately by all, and we have made closer acquaintance with them by now, as we found it impossible to make them lay any eggs.

We started at about 8.30 a.m. in a bitter wind which lasted all day. After 4 or 5 miles we approached the Boer guns posted on a ridge.

They shelled the Gordons who were on our left, and some shells fell rather near the battalion but did no damage. My company was the left flank guard; we had to lie down on an exposed ridge for 1½ hours. I was nearly frozen. Meanwhile the battalion had moved on over a ridge to our front, and we were told to remain where we were until further orders.

After another hour, an orderly rode up and said we were to join the battalion and he would shew us the way. When we got to the place where he said he had left the battalion there was no one there, and it was already getting dark (about 5.45 p.m.)

We went on marching in the direction of Amorsfort (or Amesfoort) which was supposed to be our camp. It took us 2½ hours hard marching to get to camp, which we could only find by guesswork, but the worst was to come.

We hoped the transport would have got in before us, and that we should soon have our blankets, as it was awfully cold. The transport had not arrived when we got in at 8.10 p.m., and consequently no blankets, coats, or food of any kind could we get.

We waited till 10 p.m. then till midnight still no transport. All the water in our water-bottles was frozen solid.

The transport never arrived until nearly 10 a.m. the next morning. The cold was perfectly awful, and I should not have got over it without being sent to hospital again, unless some of the officers had not got a blanket from hospital and wrapped me up in it and kept my feet near a fire, kept alight by grass and bits of wood.

After a day's rest, we marched again on Aug. 9th to Piet Spruit; on the 10th we got to the Vaal River, and so on day by day until on the 12th we got to Ermelo which you will see on the map. We started again next day on a

14-mile march and so on until we arrived here north-west of Carolina on Aug. 15th so from Paardekop to Carolina has taken us from Aug. 6th–Aug. 15th, marching every day except one.

And now we are resting for 5 or 6 days, while our wagons get fresh supplies, to carry us on during the march ordered for the 22nd. I am very fit on the whole now, and am enjoying our few days here very much.

Orders have come for this division to be at Machadodorp by the 25th, which is about on a line with Pretoria to the east of Middelburg and just north of Carolina. It is expected that the Boers will make a stand there, and so on Saturday or Sunday next a big fight is being looked forward to, but the Boers may prefer flight when they actually see us advance. One can never tell.

I really feel very much better for our rest here, and am very glad to hear that we probably continue our march again tomorrow. Almost every farm in the country displays two or three white flags in prominent places. We have burnt five farms in this neighbourhood since we came.

Much love to all,

Ever your affectionate
Ralph

. . . .

About 14 miles north of Carolina   Friday, Aug. 24th 1900

Last night the Boers killed 1 officer and 4 men of Strathcona's Horse. There has been a lot of shelling early this morning on a ridge about 1 mile in front of us, but the shrapnel shells from the Boer guns burst too high in the air to do any real damage luckily. When a shell bursts it looks like a white puff of smoke in the air.

The Boer guns must have been withdrawn since early this morning, as they have stopped shelling the ridge in front now.

Outpost duty comes very often, I have been out 4 nights in the last week. One of the Gordon outposts was rushed the night before last, and they lost 6 killed and 7 wounded, so it shows how careful we have to be.

As we came into camp yesterday evening 6 shells fell right among our transport, and if they had burst would have done a lot of damage, but not one burst luckily, and only 1 wagon was hit.

. . . .

Machadodorp

My dear Father,

I am afraid that you all must have had a very anxious time after you had heard of our awful fight on the 27th before the list of casualties appeared. I should of course have sent you a telegram to say I was all right if it had been possible, but no private telegrams can be sent.

My last letter was from Twyfalaar, so I will start this letter from Aug. 21st the day we left there and marched to Van-Wykx-Vler. We stayed there two days and on the 23rd we marched to Geluck. In the evening I went to see a man in hospital there. As I came out I heard whew —— ew Bom!! and a shell burst within 50 yards of me, the first shell I had ever been close to. On the 26th we marched towards Dalmanutha and some bullets fell very close to me again as we were just behind the flank guard which had a small fight.

Now for Aug. 27th – a date I shall never forget. We got up at 5.30 a.m. as usual, and received orders to march at 7 a.m. After we had gone about 5 miles we were split up, my company being ordered to go on the right flank and to send out a few scouts just to keep a good lookout over a valley. We waited nearly 2½ hours here, and then General Kitchener rode up to where I was and said 'That Kopje over there must be taken today.' With my glasses I could see several Boers building up fortifications; but we all thought there were only about 30 Boers there.

An order came up from the Colonel that every man was to fill up his ammunition pouches to 200 rounds each; they usually only carry 150. We were told at about 11.30 a.m. to advance behind some guns which were on the little hill marked A. Soon after that our battery started shelling the Boer position on the kopje with the most marvellous accuracy. They burst lyddite and shrapnel all over it.

At 12.30 we began our advance. My company was in support of C Company which had the brunt of the attack. We were extended to 10 paces between every man. I was carrying a rifle just like the men. As we advanced and just as the first line was showing over the ridge a most awful fire was poured into them and whistled all round us. We threw ourselves on our faces and lay there for ½ hour, while the first line kept up a hot fire on the enemy. Bullets were flying all round us when we made our first rush of about 30 yards, throwing ourselves on our faces again. The guns were shelling the position all the time. This is the sort of noise one hears: *Whew-ew-ew-Bom*!! *pic-poc – pic-poc* (the mauser rifle); *Whi-i-ng* (a bullet

17

passing over your head); *fut*! (a bullet striking the ground close to you); *tack-tack-tack-tack* etc. (maxim); *Bom-Bom Bom-Bom* (Pom-Pom gun); the rattle of musketry fire was awful. Every time the first line advanced we rushed on about 60 yards behind them.

At about 2.15 p.m. we were 250 yards from a kopje. The bullets were like hail, so thick they were falling all round one. My captain was next to me on my left, and he shouted out, 'No one to get up yet. Crawl forward on your hands and knees.'

About 150 yards away we poured in a terrible fire on the enemy. I fired about 35 rounds myself. Then the charge came when we were 50 yards from the kopje. We fixed swords and got up and ran as hard as ever we could across the open. Then a loud cheer rose from about 3 companies and the kopje was ours!!! The Boers started to run when we fixed swords. We bayoneted several who remained till the last and then held up their hands to surrender. I can't describe to you the awful appearance of that last 50 yards over which we charged, our poor fellows lying killed and wounded. The sight in the kopje was most awful, as the shells had played havoc with them.

Lyttelton came up about 10 mins after, and said 'Bravo R.B., Splendidly done.'

We reformed as quickly as possible and some companies followed the Boers and shot at them as they rode off. My company remained as an escort to 3 guns which were shelling them. We captured a Pom-Pom, but the Enniskillens also claimed it; the question was afterwards referred to Buller who very justly said that if it had not been for the gunners it would never have been taken, 'I therefore give it to the gunners'.

Then came the awful roll call; 1 officer killed, 7 wounded; total casualties in the regiment were 85 officers and men killed and wounded.

. . . .

Aug. 28th

We got up at 5.30 a.m. and paraded at 7 a.m. and attended the burial of our poor Captain Lesley and the other poor chaps. We had encamped for the night on the ridge we had taken, and underneath a few trees the grave was dug. The Battalion was drawn up in 3 sides of a square, and the dead were brought on stretchers just as they had fallen. Lyttelton and General Kitchener with their staffs were there.

From there yesterday we intended to march to Nooitgedacht where the prisoners are, but, after we had gone a little more than half way, our cavalry reported that the Boers had all left, and had released all the

18

prisoners who could be seen coming down the line in great numbers. So we returned here last night, and have today to rest in. The regiment requires a day's rest after all the marching and fighting, and everyone is very glad to be able to get a bit of a wash.

It will remain perfectly unaccountable to my mind how I escaped without a scratch. Four of my own ½ company were hit within a few yards of me, and my face was smothered in the dust the bullets kicked up; the worst part of it was advancing the last 250 yards as there was absolutely no cover at all. It was just thin short grass we had to advance over, while the Boers were shooting from behind great rocks. We got a certain amount of loot in the shape of rice, beans, coffee, sugar which the Boers had left behind them.

Lord Roberts rode over in the morning and said to Buller, 'I believe that kopje to be impregnable with the force under your command'; but Buller said he would let the Rifle Brigade do what they could, and would withdraw them if it was too strong a position. The men behaved splendidly and they followed Biddulph (my captain) and myself who were in front, like heroes. Several men deserved the V.C. that day, though they won't get it, especially a Corporal of the Gordon Highlanders who brought a maxim gun on his back right up into the first line amid a storm of bullets, and fired away as quietly as if he was practising on the range.

The Colonel had a very narrow escape; the bullet hit the buckle of his belt, and so, instead of it going into his stomach, glanced off into his left shoulder.

It was my great wish to see a real fight, and I hope never to see another one like that; as when the position was taken, and the strain over, one felt so awfully sorry for the brave chaps lying on the veldt, that it was almost impossible to keep back the tears. At the impressive service next morning, very few men left that scene with dry eyes.

I never before realized what 'the horrors of war' really meant.

P.S. It may give you some idea of the fire if I tell you that *35,200* rounds were actually fired by the Battalion alone, and that we threw ammunition in pocket-handkerchiefs, etc. to those who were in want of it in front.

The Boers are reported to be flying in every direction. That kopje we took turned out luckily to be the key to their whole position.

Give my love to Harry and Joan, and thank Morforwyn very much for the letter she wrote to me from Clochfaen.*

* Harry Lloyd and Lady Joan Verney, whose home was Clochfaen in Wales, and Harry's sister, Morforwyn.

. . . Chapter Two . . .

After the battle at Bergendal the Second Battalion marches to Lydenburg where they stay for nearly seven months in constant contact with the Boers, and start the scorched earth policy of burning all farms.

. . . .

Crocodile River   Sept. 3rd 1900

My dearest Mother,

I have only time to write a short letter now, as I have to go out on outpost this evening, and notice about a mail going tonight has only just been given.

Your last news of me was from Helvetia. The day before yesterday we marched from there to this river; yesterday we were going to attack the Boers who were reported to be 1500 strong with 2 guns.

The Boers probably became a little nervous about 10 a.m. for they fired two shots from a Long Tom which we did not know they possessed. This made us a little more careful.

My company was ordered to escort 3 5-inch guns. We advanced in extended formation on the right flank. Suddenly a Long Tom on a ridge on our right front sent a shell very close to them, so they moved off under cover more to the left and we had to follow them.

My captain ordered me to extend the men to 20 paces apart. As we followed the guns across a piece of open ground, the Long Tom fired 3 shells at us. One burst within 25 yards of me. I heard the gun go off and then this awful shrieking of the shell coming towards us. It sounded as if it was going to hit me full in the chest, but it hit the ground 25 yards short of me. Great pieces of shell were shot 30 ft. into the air and fell with a thud unpleasantly close, but no one was hit. It frightened me horribly, and had not we extended the men to 20 paces someone must have been hit.

60 or 70 shells at least must have been fired at our force yesterday, but

the casualties were only 1 man killed, 12 wounded. We followed these guns about all day, and had to wait till dark before we could retire back to camp.

The Boers have 3 Long Toms, 1 Pom-Pom and 1 Howitzer and are in a very strong position at the head of this valley. Spitzkop is their right flank and their line of defence extends in a N.E. direction from there.

Had not that Long Tom fired those two shells early in the morning, it is the firm opinion of all of us that we should have suffered a fearful disaster, as the Devons were ordered to make a frontal attack on the position, and we were in support, just expecting to fire a few shots and quietly take the position. We were all in a terrible state of mind last night lest Buller would decide to attack the position today, but he has sent for General Hamilton's* division to turn their position on the left, and for Pole Carew's** force to turn it on the right, so the Boers are fairly caught unless they retire.

* Major-General (later General Sir) Bruce Meade Hamilton (1857–1936) was then commander of 21st Brigade. He was described by Rawlinson as 'a good fellow as generals go, though not brilliantly clever'.
** Major-General (later Lt-General Sir) Reginald Pole Carew (1849–1924) was then commander of 9th Brigade. He was Unionist MP for Bodmin 1910–16.

. . . .

Lydenburg   Sept. 5th 1900

My dear Father,

On active service, as you may know, the Commanding Officer has to send in to the War Office confidential reports on the officers under his command.

Though it is 'confidential' I don't think there is any harm in my showing its contents to you.

2nd Lt. Ralph Verney   2nd Bn. Rifle Brigade

'A very nice young fellow. Takes great interest in his profession. Quiet manners. Has great influence with N.C.O.s and men for so young an officer; only joined us in May last. When he has gained a little more confidence he will make a good officer.'

. . . .

My dearest Kathleen,

As it is your birthday today, I am going to send all the news in a letter to *you* which also brings with it many happy returns of the day and all best wishes.

My last letter was sent off from Crocodile River, and so I will tell you what happened to us there and what we have done since.

The morning after my letter had gone was full of adventure. We had breakfast at 8 o'clock and we were hoping to have a quiet day. I had just taken my second cup of coffee (without milk) when Bom: Whew-ew-ew Bom! was heard. At the first Bom everybody dropped his knife and fork; as the Whew-ew became louder everybody's face was screwed up into dreadful contortions; and when the second Bom came, we all felt momentary relief, as the shell pitched 100 yards in our rear.

During the night the Boers had dragged a Long Tom to the top of a hill which overlooked our camp about 6000 yards off. This is a very good range for Long Tom and they shoot very accurately.

The next shell was fired about 3 mins. later and pitched 100 yards too short. We all rushed to pack up our blankets, and when the third shot was fired we were already moving under cover. This third shot was a shrapnel which burst right over us, but luckily rather too high and only one man was hit. We all got under shelter in a big donga, at the bottom of which flowed a stream with good water. When we had been there about 20 mins., my company was ordered to go further down the stream. We had to walk across some open ground to get to where we were wanted, and Long Tom shelled us all the time, but, as soon as we saw the puff of white smoke from the gun, we had about 10 seconds to get under cover before the shell burst. Luckily no one was hit this time, owing to our being able to get into this donga or deep ditch before the shell arrived.

We stayed under shelter all day until 5 p.m. when we went back to camp. On the next day it was decided to take this position which was at the head of the Crocodile Valley. General Hamilton had already come up on our left and was threatening the Boer line of retreat, so that when the real attack began, they all retired without firing a shot. We were guarding the baggage and so did not start until midday, and got into camp after about 10 miles marching at 7.30 p.m. The baggage goes very slowly and we have to regulate our pace accordingly.

The next day (Sept. 6th) we marched to Lydenburg and encamped in a flat kind of basin just out of the town. We were enjoying our tea in the late afternoon after a very hot march, when suddenly this annoying Long Tom started shelling us again from a ridge about 3 or 4 miles away. The Boers had retired out of Lydenburg, but had posted 2 Long Toms on a high ridge. We were all able to sit under a small ridge, over which the shells came and did no damage to us, though they did a certain amount of harm to General Hamilton's division which was encamped on a sloping bit of ground about ¾ mile away.

On Sept. 7th we were ordered to keep guard over the town, while an attack was made on the ridge against the two Long Toms. I remained on the outskirts of the town for 5 hours, and I sent my servant into the houses near to get some food. He procured half a loaf of bread which was a great treat for me, as it was just a month since I had tasted bread.

Our time here is entirely occupied with entrenching this position and building gun-pits. We have 4 Howitzer guns with us, so we could make it pretty warm for any Boers who wish to attack us.

We can get a few eggs here but not many, and bread can be had in small quantities, but milk is absolutely unknown, either in tins or fresh from the cow.

As you have, I believe, a certain fondness for dogs, I am going to tell you two incidents which happened to our regiment at the Battle of Bergendal on Aug. 27th. One of these was in connection with a dog which belongs to a man in my own half company, and which rejoices in the name of 'Jack'. It is a brown and white spaniel. He is quite devoted to his master, and he kept close to him all the time during the battle, quite heedless of the bullets. Just before the charge, a bullet went through the dog's neck and it fell over half stunned. We had no time to wait to see if it was dead or not, and when Wood (its master) looked for it afterwards, it was nowhere to be found. We all gave it up for lost. Two days afterwards we were crossing a drift, and as we were waiting for everybody to get over I saw Jack right in rear of the Battalion, smelling at everybody. His master whistled once, and the dog came dashing up, perfectly mad with delight, and apparently very little the worse for its wound. How, after two days, during which we had marched nearly 15 miles altogether, the dog ever found us again, I don't know. The bullet apparently grazed its shoulder bone, and it must have followed us by its smell for 15 miles.

The other story is in connection with a dog belonging to a man in another company, who was killed, shot through the head. He had a little fox terrier, which remained by its master all through the fight after he fell.

General Brocklehurst* was riding by after the battle and saw this little dog nearly dead for thirst. With great difficulty he dragged the terrier away, and he has now sent it to the Queen as a present.

Another very nice incident after the battle happened about ½ hour after we had taken the kopje.

Lord Roberts, who had come over from Belfast, rode over the battle-field, and saw a man lying on the ground severely wounded, and feeling very cold. Lord Roberts got off his horse, took off his own overcoat, and laid it over the man. So delighted and grateful was the wounded man that he tried to get up and thank Roberts, but he told him not to get up, but to keep the overcoat, if he liked, for himself.

* Colonel John Brocklehurst, Royal Horse Guards, was never a general. He commanded the cavalry in Natal after the Battle of Ladysmith and, in Rawlinson's opinion, possessed neither the 'dash nor the brains for a good cavalry commander'. Another contemporary, however, described him as 'the most perfect gentleman in the British army, the kindest, nicest and most chivalrous.'

. . . .

Lydenburg   Saturday, Sept. 29th 1900

My dearest Mother,

Tomorrow morning one of our companies is going to accompany the Leicester Regiment and this force, with a few guns and some cavalry, is going to advance in a northerly direction to meet Buller. Aspinall is in command of the company that is going, and he was told he might ask for any one junior to him he liked to go with him as his subaltern. He asked for me, and so I am off at 6 a.m. tomorrow on the war path again. There are a certain number of Boers between us and Buller, and our object is to try and hold them from the south until Buller is able to attack them from the north.

Wicklyp is about 10 miles from here, and our camp was right on the top of the ridge, looking down into the Crocodile Valley, on which the Boer Long Tom was posted which shelled us on our way up. It was most interesting seeing the trenches the Boers had made. We could well understand what a beautiful view they must have had of us, advancing up the valley which is about 16 miles long altogether.

We saw exactly what the Boers wanted us to do, and what we very nearly attempted, namely to advance straight up the road right up the hill, and so receive a crossfire from 3 Long Toms, besides a storm of bullets from their trenches.

. . . .

24

Lydenburg   Oct. 4th 1900

My dearest Mother,

We started last Sunday morning at 4.45 a.m. from here, and the R.B. company formed the escort to the baggage. We passed through very hilly country about 5 miles from here called the Speckle Room. It took us until 2 p.m. to get to a kopje about 3 miles this side of Kruger's Post. Here the baggage was parked and we were told that the village itself was clear but a ridge just the other side was occupied by the Boers. The Leicester Companies were sent on to take the ridge and I was told to take a half-company on to a high and very steep hill on the left of the road, which they thought was occupied by a few snipers. I skirmished up it, and to my relief found that the few snipers had bolted so I sat tight for 2 hours holding the hill, from which I could get a splendid view of the Leicesters advancing towards the ridge about 3 miles away. The Boers made no stand, and in the evening we advanced into the village.

We were having tea about 4 p.m. when Aspinall suddenly looked up and saw a puff of white smoke from a hill in the distance, and said, 'There's Long Tom'. Surely enough we heard the well-known Bom!! and the whistle of the shell. We had no idea that the Boers had mounted guns near, all owing to the fault of the cavalry! They fired very quick, and they had 2 Long Toms, 1 Pom-Pom, 1 High Velocity. They made very good shooting indeed, unfortunately, and killed 1 officer of the Devons and wounded another very badly; 4 Strathcona's Horse and 6 South African Lt. Horse were wounded. They stopped about 5 p.m. and we hoped we were going to have a quiet night.

Taylor had looted a beautiful fat chicken for our dinner, and we roasted it in a biscuit tin. We had got fresh green peas and new potatoes! Just as the chicken was served up for dinner at 7 p.m. we heard the Long Tom again. It was quite dark which made it worse, and they must have taken aim with the gun on our camp fires. The shrapnel shells burst like fireworks in the air. We put the company behind Mr. Erasmus's house for shelter, who is now on commando somewhere still, but his wife and family are still in the house, and the shells nearly frightened them out of their lives. They fired away at us for nearly ¾ hour, until all the camp fires were put out. They wounded about 12 men altogether this time, and killed two, but no one in our company was hit, luckily. Altogether the Boers must have fired off nearly 100 shells at us, a regular bombardment. At midnight a force of 250 men went out to try and capture the guns but the Boers had withdrawn them in the night. I had not been shelled at night before, and I don't want

25

to repeat the experience; it was most unpleasant. Next day we were ordered to escort the 5-inch guns, but as there were no Boers left, we marched back here with them and got into camp about 6.30 p.m.

We were away 3 days, during which we marched nearly 36 miles and were up at 4 a.m. each morning.

I spoke to General Lyttelton at Kruger's Post and he told me that we were not going to India after all, but that we should probably stay in this country for some months more, perhaps somewhere in Natal.

About 14 prisoners gave themselves up at Kruger's Post, and we had charge of them. Of course they had to give up their arms, and ammunition. I got a very nice little Mauser Rifle from one of them, and a bandolier with 60 rounds of ammunition in it. When I come home, you will like to see it, and if we are going to do any more fighting, which is very unlikely, I shall use it instead of the ordinary rifle.

We hear very little about the General Election. I wonder if Father is standing for anywhere; I hope he gets in this time.* It will be very unlucky if he does not, and very hard on him; but all the same, I am not radically inclined, though the present Government have done badly. What a pity he could not come to some arrangement with the North Bucks Constituency, it would be much nicer for him to represent them than any strangers.

* He did not contest a seat that year.

. . . .

Lydenburg   Oct. 13th 1900

My dearest Mother,

Father has often tried to impress upon me how useful my very small knowledge of sketching will be to me in the service. Here is an instance for you!!

Last Wednesday morning General Kitchener sent to ask our Adjutant whether he could send a competent officer to make a map for him of Lydenburg and the surrounding district. I had done two small maps for the Adjutant at different times, and so he sent me.

The map is on a scale of 2 inches to the mile, and there are certain boundaries given me. I found it a much more important job than I thought it would be. They gave me a horse to ride about the country on, and they let me off all duty till it was finished. It took me 5 days to make my sketches and plans and now I am in the middle of drawing it out neatly. I shall give it to the General the day after tomorrow, and shall probably get more kicks than halfpence for it, I expect; but I will let you know the exact number of kicks in my next letter.

. . . .

Lydenburg   Saturday, Oct. 20th 1900

My dear Uncle Edmund,

In some of your letters you have asked me whether I think the Dutch farmers and Boers out here will ever be friendly to the English. Our soldiers have always got on very well indeed with the Boers who have been captured or who have given themselves up, and I think that in time the Boers will make friends with us, when Kruger and their leaders can no longer poison their minds with lies about the cruelty of the English. When I was at Kruger's Post about a month ago, one of the prisoners asked me whether it was true that we made the Boer prisoners walk from Lydenburg to Machadodorp, nearly 50 miles, with bare feet?! Somebody had gone from here to Kruger's Post just after we had come here, and had sworn to having seen this happen. He had given the names of certain Boers who had been compelled to do this. Naturally, being already prejudiced against us, and with such evidence, they believed this story and so refused to give themselves up.

But on the other hand there are several Boer women in this town who still hate the English as a nation. They are quite willing to offer one a cup of tea, and are always quite pleasant to talk to, if the subject of the war is not mentioned. I have had long talks with some of them and it is rather interesting. I asked them the other day what they thought of Kruger now that he had robbed the bank at Pretoria, paid his faithful officials with worthless cheques, and finally left them in the lurch by fleeing out of the country. All they answered was 'What has that got to do with you? We are quite satisfied with him; he has not robbed you, and if we don't complain, why should you?' We are now sending most of the Boer women out of the town altogether, because we refuse to go on supplying them with food. We are sending them under a flag of truce to a laager some miles away. They don't mind going now, but as soon as the rainy season comes on, I expect they will wish themselves back again.

. . . .

Lydenburg, Transvaal   Wednesday, October 24th 1900

My dear Gwendolen,*

I have been seeing rather a curious sight this morning early. About 50 Boer families leaving the town in carts and ox wagons to go to the Boer

Laager, about 8 miles towards Kruger's Post. We have turned out all those families whose husbands are still fighting against us; altogether I suppose nearly 250 women and children. We sent some out this morning in our own ox wagons. We took them as far as the Boer lines, and then dropped them, and told the Boers to take them anywhere they liked. We had a force posted within range, so that at the slightest sign of treachery in trying to capture any of our wagons, we could have given them snuff. Most of the women were very annoyed at having to leave their homes, and go into the veldt, and several of them said they would try and persuade their husbands to give themselves up. Our chief amusement now consists of paper chases across country on ponies. This is great fun, and I never miss one if I can get hold of a pony to ride.

* Ralph's sister.

. . . .

Lydenburg   October 26th 1900

My dear Father,

Since I wrote the enclosed letter to Gwendolen I have again been on the warpath. After dinner, the night before last, I was just going back to my house expecting, and wanting, a good night's rest, when the Adjutant told me in a subdued voice to be at the Mess again at 12 midnight for further orders. After a few hours dozing, therefore, I returned to the Mess, and found officers belonging to three other companies there also. We were told to have our companies ready paraded by 1.30 a.m. I went round and woke up my men, and fell them in at 1.30. A night attack on the Boer position between here and Kruger's Post was coming off. Four of our companies and five companies of the Devons formed the infantry; some guns and mounted infantry came too. We finally marched off very quietly at about 2 a.m. During the whole march (nearly 5½ miles) scarcely a word was spoken. The road was good, and we did it in 1¾ hours, which was very quick indeed for night marching. About ½ a mile this side of the valley, which the Boers occupied, we halted and received more definite orders in whispers from General Kitchener himself. F Company which is commanded by Alexander (whose sister Ellin knows) was to go first. Davies, one of the subalterns, was to take six men and rush the picquets with fixed swords. When they got there, there was no picquet to be found, but, after about 10 minutes, four Boers came up on ponies, evidently to be there during the day as a look-out post. They were allowed to come quite close, and then they were captured, one Boer being shot through the shoulder.

While this was happening I was extending my men along the side of a hill which commanded the road. By daylight all my company were posted, as this had to be done in the dark, and without any noise, which was a very difficult and jumpy job, because the Boers might have been watching us very close by for all we knew. As soon as it was light enough to see, a maxim opened at a few Boers, and shortly several could be seen riding up the opposite side of the valley. We blazed away at them, but the range was rather long. The Boers had not the slightest idea that they were going to be attacked, and I believe our forces had got into position without us being discovered. One reason for this was that the Boers were making merry that night as their wives and families had come out to them, though perhaps involuntarily. After blazing away for about 1½ hours, our company advanced across the valley, and then another, until three companies were on the side of the hill the other side of the valley. The Boers fled in all directions, and offered no resistance.

· ·

Lydenburg   Nov. 14th 1900

My dear Ellin,

During the last week another night attack was made on the Boers, this time in a south-westerly direction towards Spitz Kop. The first position to be taken was a ridge about 9 miles from here. The Boers made a certain amount of resistance, and they caught one of our guns in rather a nasty hole. The gun with a team of 8 horses was crossing a spruit near the top of a ridge. Some Boers who were hidden somewhere quite close fired right into them, killing 6 and wounding the remaining two. Of course the infantry was pretty close, so there was no chance for them to capture the gun. Two of the gunners were wounded very badly, one has since died of his wounds. The officer in charge of the gun, a Major Gordon, got a bullet through his helmet, which just grazed the top of his head, taking the hair off in its passage; a pretty narrow escape, wasn't it?

The last ridge which we took, nearly 14 miles from here, overlooked their laager. From this we captured 10 horses, a few waggons and tents, a complete set of telegraph instruments and a heliograph. We also got Schuman's (who is the Commandant) private portmanteau with several of his clothes, and his private tent was also found afterwards and brought back. I hope this will make him uncomfortable.

· ·

Lydenburg   Dec. 17th 1900

My dearest Mother,

All my stores were ready loaded on the railway truck on Monday Dec. 4th; but I was so enjoying myself at Lourenço Marques that I postponed my departure for two days. Everybody is most hospitable down there, especially the large merchants and store-keepers who wish to get orders from you. They will give you the best dinners and the best cigars on the chance of getting you to give an order for your mess to them. I really had some very good cigars in this way.

There was a Mrs Pretorius* staying at the Cardoza Hotel with me. She is the wife of a Boer Commandant, and so is rather an important person on their side. She is only 18 years old, but was married at Pretoria about 6 months ago, just before we got there. They were married at 4 one afternoon and he had to go away and fight at 7 the same evening, and they have never met since. But we are now sending her up to her husband who is on commando near Belfast, in the hopes that she will persuade him to come and give himself up. I had to take charge of her from Lourenço Marques to Machadodorp. We started at 7.30 a.m. on a Wednesday morning, and we got to Machadodorp at 3.30 p.m. on the Thursday. She was a very nice girl indeed, well educated and very sensible. She had a great admiration for her husband for holding out so long. I questioned her in a friendly way about her property, etc. She told me they owned a lot of farms round Pretoria; so I impressed upon her the fact that if her husband was taken prisoner, all the farms would be confiscated, but that if he gave himself up at once, he would very likely be allowed to keep his farms. I had one adventure on the way up with her, and a very nasty one while it lasted.

Just before the train gets to a place called Waterval Boven, there is a long tunnel which is often filled with strong sulphur fumes, as I think I mentioned in my last letter. We were in an ordinary covered van, just like a luggage van in England, as no carriages are now allowed on the line. It was very hot, and we had got both the doors each side of the van wide open, to admit as much air as possible. I had borrowed an arm chair for her at Koomati Poort, so she was fairly comfortable.

Well, we approached the tunnel and we entered it. Suddenly I smelt these sulphur fumes. I rushed to the doors but they refused to be shut, and we were now in the tunnel. In a few seconds the van was filled to the roof with these sulphur fumes. Mrs. Pretorius screamed to me, 'Mr. Verney, I am dying, I am suffocating.' I groped my way to her and stuffed my pocket handkerchief into her mouth, and told her to keep calm; it would be over

30

soon. I held my sleeve over my mouth, and lay on the floor of the van. I thought the tunnel would never end, and the train was going very slowly up a steep incline. At last it got gradually lighter and lighter, and as soon as we were out of the tunnel the sulphur fumes soon got blown out again. But it was really horrible for a minute or two, and the fumes were scorchingly hot. However, Mrs. Pretorius soon got over it, and insisted that my pocket handkerchief had saved her life. She was none the worse in the end for the adventure.

We had to spend most of the Thursday morning at Waterval Onda, waiting for a train to take us on. So I took her to breakfast at a small hotel there is there. At first the woman informed me she had absolutely nothing for breakfast, so I asked if she had any bread; Oh yes, she had bread and also jam. Then I said, 'Haven't you any porridge?' Yes, she had porridge.

Finally we had porridge, liver, a poached egg each, and some bacon for breakfast. This was what she called 'Nothing, absolutely nothing.'

After our meal, I asked her if there was a sitting room. She admitted that the hotel boasted of a room which did duty as a sitting room, and I found a piano in it (quality moderate). However, I amused Mrs. Pretorius by strumming on it, and whistling to it for nearly an hour.

We then continued our journey at last, and arrived at Machadodorp. She was most affectionate in saying good-bye, thanking me for all the care I had taken of her, and saying she should hope some day to have me as a guest in her house at Pretoria.

Before parting she gave me a little souvenir of her in the shape of a Kruger sovereign coined in 1900. These are very rare, and hard to get. Wasn't it good of her?

Finally we parted at Machadodorp, and she went on to Belfast. It was quite an experience having to escort the wife of a hostile general up the line for a day and a half, and as it turned out a very pleasant one, as she was so very nice herself.

When I got to Machadodorp, I had my van with the stores run into a siding and unloaded by kaffirs. Then, after a great deal of trouble, I got hold of two ox-waggons, and loaded them up with all the stores, which were as much as ever they could carry.

As there was no other officer available, I had to take command of the convoy. It took us 4 days to get up here. We started at 6 a.m. every morning and usually got to our destination for the day about 11 a.m. For the rest of the day the oxen used to graze. I had left my pony at Machadodorp so I was able to ride alongside the convoy, which consisted of 27 waggons, most of which I dropped at different stations along the road. I was welcomed with shouts of applause from the mess, as I came up with my two waggons heavily laden with stores, amounting to over £300 worth altogether. There were nearly 200 different cases containing every sort of thing from soap to sultanas, from biscuits to port. I was very lucky for not a single case was lost; everything arrived properly labelled and addressed, which pleased me very much. This was largely due to the ever faithful Taylor, my servant, who never left the waggons, lest any one should take a fancy to anything, as he expressed it. I hoped to have a day or two to myself after I arrived, but the very next day I was ordered out to go with a flying column to the relief of Nel's Spruit which was besieged. During my absence, owing to two of us having gone to the Mounted Infantry, I had been posted to a different company altogether. Lowndes is my captain now, not Biddulph any longer. We sent 4 companies, and the Devons sent 5. We paraded at 11 p.m. on last Thursday night. We had to march to Paard-Platz that night. It is only 6 miles, but all uphill, and some of it very steep. I did not get there until 4 o'clock the next morning, as I was rearguard, and had to keep behind the waggons which crawled along.

* Wife of the grandson of Andries Pretorius (1799–1852), one of the leaders of the Great Trek (1835), after whom the town of Pretoria was named.
. . . .

2nd B. Rifle Brigade   Dec. 27th 1900
Lydenburg

My dear Uncle Edmund,

We celebrated Xmas day by having a grand concert given by the regiment to the inhabitants of Lydenburg. It was most successful and there was no lack of talent. One of the most popular choruses was:

> Father has disgraced the family.
> This horrid story I should like to shirk;
> For none of us have ever done a stroke in all our lives,
> But blowed if Father ain't commenced to work!!

Next day followed the 'Lydenburg Race Meeting'. This was almost a greater success than the concert. The weather was very fine though very hot:

My pony, called 'Sackobono', came in 8th out of a pretty large field, which was as good as I expected. I managed to get Grey Friars in fifth. I enjoyed riding those two races awfully, and it was most exciting.

My pony is called Sackobono because he was such a sack of bones when I got him.

Polo is played with great zeal by all of us. We have 3 afternoons a week filled up with polo, if the weather permits. Both my ponies play, in fact they play a good deal better than their master.

Ever your affectionate
Ralph

· ·

Lydenburg   Feb. 1st 1901

My dearest Mother,

We have had rather more peaceful times here lately, as the Boers have gone to Carolina and are kicking up disturbances in that part of the country. We have surrounded this town with mines; they are very good things, but they often go off unexpectedly; perhaps a dog, or mule hits the wire, which lets it off. Then there is a terrific explosion and we have to wait to see if any Boers are about.

The wire which, if touched, will explode the mine is 80 yards long, and the wily Boer has heard these go off sometimes, and no doubt is not anxious to risk any personal experience with them.

I can't tell you what great grief was felt by the troops here when we heard of the Queen's death. She was always known to the Kaffirs out here as 'the Great White Queen' or 'The Little White Lady'. All the inhabitants have felt it very much too, but not half as much as the soldiers.

· ·

Feb. 4th 1901

A mail came in the day before yesterday, and brought me all your letters written from Claydon. I imagined you all so well, sitting at lunch on Xmas day, and Uncle Edmund getting up and proposing 'Absent Friends'. As you know, I was at Fort Howard on Detachment then, and as I was acting mess president for our mess, I got up and proposed 'Absent friends'; only we drank the toast at dinner, and you did at lunch.

I had brought up from Delagoa Bay two cases of champagne for our Xmas dinner, and so it was all done in proper style.

It was very kind of Uncle Edmund to say a few words about me.

· ·

33

Lydenburg   Feb. 18th 1901

My dearest Mother

Before Kitchener left here, the Boers had again become rather a nuisance. Botha had sent nearly 500 more up here to reinforce David
Schuman,* and had ordered him to try and capture Lydenburg again. We
were told of this by the natives. We waited for two nights and nothing
happened, but on the third night about 1.30 a.m. the Boers started
attacking or rather sniping the town. I was in the town then, but the
sniping was at the other side; they also attacked in a half-hearted way
Mission-Camp which is about 3 miles north of the town.

* He probably refers to General H. Schoeman, at that time Commander of the Boers in
the Transvaal.

. . . .

                                                            Feb. 22nd 1901

I am on detachment now at Fort Howard. It is rather fun going out in the
afternoons partly to scout and partly to shoot. 3 or 4 of us go out as a rule,
one with a rifle and the rest with shot guns. Yesterday I got two shots at a
buck, but as I only had No. 8 shot in my gun, I could not make much
impression. However, I got a quail, which though small, is excellent
eating.

   We saw two hares, but did not get a shot at them, also 7 coran, which are
big birds with black and white wings. Two wild duck came somewhere
near us, but out of shot, so that there is a certain amount of game near
enough to make it worth going out shooting.

. . . .

Lydenburg   Feb. 28th 1901

This morning about 10 a.m. a flag of truce and two horsemen were seen
coming over the ridge about 2½ miles out from here. I jumped on a horse
and was sent out to receive them. I met them about 2 miles out. They
turned out to be 2 Boers who had come straight from the Boer Laager
under David Schuman. They took off their hats as I rode up, and we
shook hands. They told me they had 4 letters to be delivered in Lydenburg, and I took them and gave a receipt. We chatted away for over half an
hour. I asked them if they had heard any news lately. They said no; so I

informed them that General French* had badly defeated Botha,** and had picked up 287 Boers dead. I also told them that De Wet had lost 3 guns. After rubbing this in for nearly 10 mins., I asked them what good they were doing to their side by going on fighting now. You are keeping your wives and children out of their homes, I said, and you are lessening your chances of getting your farms back again. I explained to them that if they surrendered in a body, probably in a year or two, if everything was quiet, they would be allowed to have a voice in the government of the country and they would be treated on an equal footing to the other people in the Transvaal. We shook hands again and parted the best of friends, and I said I hoped before long to meet them again as friends, not as enemies, and to have the pleasure of seeing their wives and children.

They did not seem particularly pleased with the news I told them and I tried to paint it as black as I could. This is the first time I have talked to a Boer who was still fighting against us, and it was rather an interesting experience.

The night before last we made an attack on Kruger's Post; my company did not go this time. We surrounded the Boer laager before dawn, and we caught them all in bed; 45 prisoners were taken with lots of ammunition and forage etc.

* John Denton Pinkstone French (1852–1925), later 1st Earl of Ypres, Field-Marshal and Commander-in-Chief of the British Army, 1914–15, commanded a cavalry division during Roberts' advance on Bloemfontein and Pretoria.
** Louis Botha (1862–1919) commanded the Boers at Colenso and Spion Kop, where-after he was made Commander-in-chief of the Transvaal Boers on the death of General Joubert. He later became first prime minister of the Transvaal (1907) and first prime minister of the Union of South Africa (1910–19).

· ·

Pokwani's Town, Transvaal   Wednesday, April 23rd 1901

My dearest Mother,

We have now been on the trek for the last 10 days. We started from Lydenburg last Saturday week and have passed through the Waterval Valley and through the country belonging to Seccoccoeni (pronounced Sekakooni) the great Black Chief.

We first of all took Schuman's Laager which was 12 miles S.W. of Lydenburg. We advanced by night, and arrived there at dawn on the Sunday morning. They all fled and managed to get away most of their cattle.

We went down from there into the Waterval Valley, which is one of the richest and most productive parts of the Transvaal. We passed any number of farms, all well stocked with mealies and poultry. We were allowed to loot any Boer farm we could but we did not touch anything belonging to the Kaffirs.

The Waterval Valley was almost entirely thick bush veldt, and the road was very bad in places, but the country was awfully pretty, and very much more interesting to march through.

After the third day we got to a place called Rietfontein. There was a Long Tom in the neighbourhood, and General Kitchener wanted to find out its position. About 4 miles to the West was a range of cliffs nearly 10 miles long; its sides were as steep as the walls of a house, and almost impossible to climb. But we were ordered to send 4 companies on to the top of these cliffs. 3 of them went round and managed to get up from the other side, but I was ordered to try and take my company up the near side. Our guides told us that they thought there would be about 50 Boers at the top and so we expected to have a fight. We started about 3 o'clock in the afternoon, and it took us 4 hours to climb this cliff on our hands and knees with our rifles slung over our backs. When we got to the top there were no Boers, and so we stopped there for the night without any blankets and with very little food. Next morning we climbed along the ridge, which ran parallel to the road. We had managed to get a few mules up one side of the cliff, and so during the day we sent them to a stream to get water. Suddenly several shots were fired and one of the negroes who were with the mules dropped, shot through the head. We got them away as quick as we could, but one was hit on the way and had to be left. We saw 3 Boers with rifles going back to a farm afterwards, and they must have been hiding somewhere near.

Then next day we came to the border of Seccoccoeni's Country which is the Steelport River. This is about 4 ft. deep nearly, and we had to wade through it. We started at 5.30 a.m. and came to the river just after the sun had got up. As we were not in any particular hurry we all took off our clothes, held them above our heads while we waded through. The stream was very swift, and the negroes stood in the water, and held a rope right across for us to hold on to.

It was awfully amusing seeing the men going across with nothing on but their belts, and rifles slung across their shoulders and holding their clothes above their heads.

We did just the same, and it was much better than marching in wet clothes all day. It was a great labour getting the guns and wagons across, but it was done all right in the end. During the afternoon, Blacker and I went round the kraals to get hens for the mess. I had inquired of the man at

36

the store what was the price of hens, and he said 1/– each, so I held up a shilling in my fingers, and said 'Chuck-a-chuck-a-chuck' and then we singled out a good fat hen and chased it till we got it in a corner and caught it.

Then we held out another shilling and went through the same process.

It was tremendous fun, and we brought back 8 good fat hens for 8/–. When we had caught a hen, which was not a very easy job, we tied it by the legs on to a ring in our saddles. Blacker took a photo of me on a pony with 8 hens tied on to my saddle.

· ·

Vaal Kop (10 miles from Pokwani's Town)   April 25th

Last night we marched to this ridge, expecting to make a large capture of cattle, and Boers. As usual the latter have gone off somewhere but we got 40 sheep, and 400 cattle. This is just a ridge with no kraals anywhere near. Today 4 of our companies have gone out to a kloof where they say 150 Boers are hiding. If so they ought to have a bit of a fight, but I have heard no shots at present.

· ·

Holnek   April 27th

We came on here the day before yesterday. The General, with the rest of the force, stopped at Vaal Kop, but we were sent on here in order to capture as many cattle and sheep as possible.

A few hours after we arrived, we started on a night march towards a laager which was placed in a hollow with no means of exit. We arrived at dawn and found white flags flying from almost every wagon. We went down, and captured several wagons, 5 Boer families, and lots of cattle and sheep.

Yesterday we made another raid, and increased our spoil. Our total bag now during the last 2 days is 1,500 head of cattle, 2,500 sheep, 219 wagons, 29 Boer prisones with their wives and children, besides several horses, mules, donkeys, etc. We have brought them all into our bivouac, and we shall take them on with us back to the General probably tomorrow.

Among the captured families are one or two whom we sent out of Lydenburg when we entered it. It was rather curious meeting them again as prisoners.

We got some more hens from these captured families, but please tell Uncle Edmund that I paid 2/–for each of them, and did not commandeer them.

37

I have been in the responsible position of Mess President for the regiment all through this trek. Capt. Stephens who is the real Mess President has gone with another column, so has Harman the other member of the Mess Committee, so I was left to run the Mess by myself. We have always had plenty of hens, and sometimes a turkey or two to eat; so I think everyone so far is very satisfied. But I have had two great mishaps; the first was just after we had left Hannan's Store. The hind wheel of the Mess wagon broke, and the whole thing nearly upset. As soon as I got into camp I took off a hind wheel from another wagon and sent it back in a small trap, and put it on the Mess wagon, and so got it into camp all right. But I did not know how to get hold of another wheel for the next day. Luckily I heard of a Boer wagon which had been deserted by them; this was 7 miles away from our camp. I got hold of half-a-dozen kaffirs and with great difficulty explained to them that they were to go out and fetch this wagon, and that I would give them 10/– between them if they brought it in safely. They started at 3 o'clock that afternoon, and they did not get back until nearly 3 a.m. next morning. I gave them 10/– and some porridge, and they were quite satisfied. I then took one of the wheels off this wagon, put it on to our own Mess wagon, and we were fixed up all right.

The other misfortune was on the way to this place. The road was rather bad in one place, and there was a steep step on one side, and of course the silly ox-driver went right off the road and the whole wagon turned right over with all 4 wheels spinning in the air. I had a basket with over 30 hens, all alive on the top; 20 of these were drowned in a stream underneath the wagon, a few bottles of whiskey were broken, but we escaped very well on the whole. We got the wagon up again, but I find the driver £2 as it was entirely his fault. The wagon used to have a hood, but that was too much smashed to be of any further use, so it came in for firewood.

. . . .

Blinkwater   May 1st

We have brought all our prisoners and cattle down to this valley, which is called the Steelport Valley. General Bindon Blood* is here, and he is going to take charge of all our captures, and send them on to Middelburg.

We brought along with us from Holnek 59 captured wagons, each with a family in them, about 2,000 head of cattle, and 2,500 sheep and angora goats. We distributed our companies all along the road, putting 3 or 4 men with loaded rifles in charge of each wagon. The rest drove along the herds of cattle and sheep. Our progress was slow, especially in rear of the column, the average pace of the sheep being 2 miles an hour.

It was most curious taking all these families along. Several of them sang Salvation Army Hymns while riding in their wagons, 'Hold the Fort, for I am coming' and suchlike were the most popular, and they did very well to march to. At night we formed all the wagons up in a square and placed sentries all round with fixed swords.

Among our prisoners is a man who belonged to the Zaaps or Johannesburg Police, who were our most formidable enemies at Bergendal. This man was on the kopje, and he says he stayed till we were within 150 yards. He had his horse shot under him as he was escaping, and he got away on foot. We congratulated him on the fine way his side fought there, and he said in rather broken English 'Yes, we defended it bravely, but we never could have advanced and attacked it; our men would not have gone, and no one could have made them.'

* General Sir Bindon Blood (1842–1940) was a descendant of the famous Colonel Thomas Blood who tried to steal the Crown Jewels from the Tower of London in 1671. In 1897 he commanded the Malakand Field Force, the subject of Winston Churchill's first published work.

....

Warm Bath   May 26th, Sunday

The West Australians had been ambushed on the third day out of Middelburg, and had had 6 killed and 10 wounded. This news reached us about 11 a.m. that morning, as we were rearguard. General Kitchener at once took 2 guns and 2 of our companies back to try and take revenge. There was a farm from which Boers had shot at them, and we shelled it for about 20 mins. Then General Kitchener came up to me, and told me to take 3 sections (about 40 men) down to this farm and capture 6 or 7 Boers who were hiding in it. I took two of the sections on with me, and told my colour-sergeant to bring on the third section in support.

I had to go down a hill for about half a mile, and I kept my men at an interval of 12 paces apart. When I got to within a few hundred yards of the farm, there were several bushes and a good deal of brush-wood through which we had to go. The men all fixed swords, and we doubled straight through it, and rushed on through to the farm. I surrounded it, and then tried the door, which was locked. I burst it open with the butt of my rifle and found only a large quantity of wool in the room, which I set fire to afterwards. After we had thoroughly searched the farm and the garden round it I sent a signal message to the General saying 'Farm all clear. Await further orders.' Until these orders arrived I turned my men into the farm, and told them to get as many hens and ducks as they could for themselves. After about 10 mins. orders came for me to return to headquarters. When I fell my company in, every man paraded with at least one chicken or duck tied on to his belt. There were 7 Boer women in the farm who were brought into camp in the evening, and the buildings were burned down.

Uncle Edmund will be perfectly horrified at my behaviour. No doubt I ought to have paid the women in the farm for every hen that my men took, and it was dreadful to set fire to the wool which was in the barn. But when the Boers had ambushed these Australians like that, it was only fair to prevent a like incident happening again. Uncle Edmund will be glad to know, however, that I did not butcher the women and children, but that they were brought to camp quite safely in a wagon, and were sent to Middelburg to the women's laager there.

My men had a splendid dinner that night, and they thoroughly enjoyed our little expedition, as I did.

. . . .

Pretoria   June 9th 1901

P.S. Mrs Pretorius, whom you may remember in connection with my trip to Delagoa Bay, is here. I am making the most of my time.

. . . .

Middle Kraal   June 28th 1901

My dear Uncle Edmund,

On arriving at Carolina I learnt that my regiment was with General Kitchener about 30 miles away at least, and that no convoy was going out to them from there.

So I signalled through to General Babington's* column to ask whether it was worth while my joining him with the object of meeting General Kitchener. An answer came back from Col. Kays who is commanding the 1st K.R.R. saying 'Come first opportunity.'

I got another team of oxen, took as many stores as I could put on one wagon, and started off one morning, and trekked for 6 days before I met my regiment which had been ordered to join Col. Campbell's Column; you will remember Col. Campbell, then a Major, at Claydon a few years ago. He came and had a day's hunting there, and I came over from Oxford also.

40

We are now in his Column and are waiting here for a day or two until a convoy arrives from Middelburg with supplies.

You would be horrified at the means he employs to finish this war. His plan is to burn every farm he comes across, and he does it very thoroughly. Regular expeditions go out with cavalry escorts with the sole object of looting and burning as many farms in an afternoon as possible, and you will probably never write another word to your affectionate nephew when you hear that he accompanies these expeditions as often as he can get leave to do so. The other afternoon I brought back 18 chickens, 2 geese and the fattest pig I ever saw, for our Mess, and I did not pay a single penny for any of them. All the women and children are brought into camp in wagons and at the first opportunity they are sent on to the women's laager at Middelburg.

This must sound a most barbarous proceeding to all who are living at home in peace and quiet, but, my dear Uncle, if we do not destroy all these farms, what is to prevent the old Boer from coming back and living in peace and plenty as soon as we leave the particular district in which his farm happens to be situated? This is proved by the number of Boers there are in this part of the country, although Buller marched straight through it last year, and French has been through it since. The order then was 'No looting, no burning of farms' and the consequence is we have to do a trek through this country again.

---

* James (later Lt-General Sir James) Babington (1854–1936) joined the 16th Lancers in 1873 and was promoted colonel in 1896 – good going at a time when it was not impossible to remain a subaltern for 25 years.

. . . .

2nd Bn. Rifle Brigade   July 5th 1901

My dear Aunt Margy,

I often think how you would laugh at the rather elementary means I employ in order to provide a few extra dainties for our mess. The other day I got hold of some flour, and was very keen to make it into bread, but the great difficulty was the total absence of any baking powder or yeast in our camp.

My cook explained to me the properties of yeast, and the way it made the bread rise; so it suddenly occurred to me that any effervescing substance would do instead, and he was inclined to agree with me. Therefore I went to the hospital and said I wanted half a bottle of Eno's Fruit Salts, which they gave me; this I used in the same way as baking-powder with the most excellent results.

Everybody said the bread was very good, and not till it had all been eaten did I inform them what it had been made of.

. . . .

Bronkhurst Spruit   July 13th 1901

My dearest Father,

We are on our way back to Middelburg, where we hope to remain for the present. We started from Elaand's River Station this morning at 8 a.m. and marched for 10 miles within a few yards of the line until we got to this station. We have been on a 3 days' trek from Elaand's River after some Boers who were reported to be at Doorn Kop which is about 12 miles N.W. of that station. We started early one morning, and were getting close to the place without having seen any Boers at all, when suddenly our advance guard was sniped at from an old ruined church, without a roof on it. A 15 lb. field gun was brought up, and they still kept on sniping us, at a range of about 2,000 yards which is of course very close range for a gun. So Col. Campbell said to the Gunner Officer, 'Just burst a shell inside that church.' The first one burst just over it, the second one went through a ruined window, took a man's head right off, who was firing out of it, and burst inside wounding another Boer.

Then three Boers rushed out of the ruins waving a white scarf on a stick as a white flag. They had had about enough of it, and I don't wonder. We camped there for all the next day, as some of us went out to bring in a few families that were in a farm near. I was on outpost all day on the top of a hill. One Boer sniped at me at a very long range and I did not even hear the bullet at all.

We marched back to Elaand's River next day, and started early this morning on our march for Middelburg.

. . . .

Masonic Hotel, Middelburg   August 12th 1901

My dearest Kathleen,

Last night Gen. Sir Bindon Blood and his A.D.C. came to dinner, also a few other guests, and we had a great feast. Ask Mother what she thinks of this for a menu:

    (i)   Clear soup, with poached eggs (floating)
   (ii)   Fish Cakes (Salmon tinned!)
  (iii)   Fillet of beef & chipped potatoes

(iv) Roast Chicken and fresh cauliflower
(v) Fruit tart and custard (tinned peaches)
(vi) Macaroni cheese
(vii) Fresh Fruit (apples and oranges)
(viii) Pâté-de-foie-gras sandwiches
Coffee. Liqueurs. Champagne.

Then we have tennis parties, with tea going on; some of the nurses don't play at all badly and we get some very good sets.

. . . .

... *Chapter Three* ...

In October, 1901, Ralph joins the Mounted Infantry and spends his time capturing Boer Commandoes until Peace is declared in June, 1902. Ralph returns home via Cairo and then spends a period with his Regiment in Cairo.

. . . .

Spruyt's Hotel, Pretoria   Oct. 5th 1901

My dear Father,

Don't think that I have somehow exchanged into another regiment, because I haven't, but I am now in the 20th Battalion Mounted Infantry.

About a week ago, Col. Cockburn got orders from Pretoria to send an officer to the 4th Bn. M.I., and one morning he sent for me to come to the Orderly Room, and he offered me the job, which I accepted.

I came here on Friday last, and am off to a place called Neylstroom (or Neilstroom) on Wednesday next. This place is about half way between here and Petersburg on the Northern Line.

There is a company of M.I. there of our 4th Bn. which came straight out from home, about 6 months ago, and which is commanded by a Captain Saunderson of the 4th Bn. The other officers in it are Jim Crighton whom I met at the Curragh, and Jenkinson who was at Harrow with Harry. They both belonged to the 4th Bn. and are now seconded.

In my opinion it is a great thing to be in the Mounted Infantry, and if ever I want to get a job in it again later on, of course I shall have much more chance of being taken for it, if I have served in M.I. out here. It is a great change for me, and it probably means that I shall not be with my regiment again for two years or more.

There is one thing I want you to try and do for me at the War Office if you will, and that is to get me seconded. The reasons why I particularly wish to be seconded are:

(i) that when the time comes for me to return to the regiment, I may get a chance of being posted to a home battalion if I want it,

(ii) that it is a better thing for my battalion to have me seconded, as then they can get another officer in my place. Whereas if I am not seconded, I still count as doing duty with the 2nd Bn. though I am not with them.

So you see for both these reasons I should very much prefer to be seconded and should be much obliged if you would try and work it for me at the War Office. I was very lucky indeed to get the offer of going, because there were two officers senior to me in the battalion who wanted to go, and had applied for it, but the Colonel gave me first choice and I took it.

I am very fit, and in very good spirits.

Yrs ever affectionately
Ralph

. . . .

36 miles N.E. of Neylstroom   Oct. 24th 1901

On the third day, we rested in camp, as we were to make a long march that night. We had received information that a Boer Commandant called Hans Botha was going to sleep at a certain farm, 18 miles back along the road we had just come and that he would not expect us to come to that farm as we had already left it 18 miles behind us. But 100 men of the M.I. were ordered to make a night march back, and to surround this farm at dawn.

We started at 10 p.m. and marched, either walking or slowly trotting, until 2.30 a.m. We then divided into two parties. One lot of 25 men, under Jenkinson, whom Harry knows, went to the South side of the farm, and at 4.30 a.m. they were to charge across some open ground straight at the farm.

Meantime we went a long way round and got on to some hills just behind and overlooking the farm. We took up a strong position there, and at 4.30 a.m. we saw Jenkinson charging straight at the farm.

The idea was that, when the Boers saw this, they would make a bolt back to the hills we were holding, and then they would catch it from us. Everything went off splendidly, except for one little point, which was that there were no Boers in the farm at all.

So we had marched nearly 25 miles all for nothing.

That was my first experience of a night attack with the M.I.

We came next day to the place where Captain Gosling and Nugent were badly hit. They were in this company, having come out from the 4th Bn. It is a place called Zand River Poort, and it is a very narrow valley with high hills each side. We got through it quite safely this time, and we rested next day to prepare for another night march, this time to take 3 small laagers, more than 30 miles away. We started at 5 p.m. and continued trekking all night, with an hour's halt about 2 a.m.

When we got fairly close, another company dismounted and stalked the laager. They waited until it was just daylight and then rushed it; we were just behind but did not take part in the actual rush.

We heard great shouts of 'Hands up' and found that all the Boers were asleep in their wagons. They were hauled out, just as they were, and we captured over 40.

We also got another small laager, and our total number of prisoners was 62; a great success and everyone was delighted as they were all supposed to be 'fighting Boers'.

We captured their wagons, and cattle, and later in the day marched back about 20 miles to meet the convoy of our wagons which was following behind us.

So we did about 100 miles trekking in 2½ days, which was pretty hard work, both for men and horses. We are now going back to Neylstroom, and what we shall do then, I don't know. We shall very likely go south, as this part of the country is fairly well cleared now.

. . . .

20th Bn. M.I.   Nov. 14th 1901
Pienaar's River

My dearest Mother,

Yesterday we came off trek, having been on the go for 18 days (and nights). We are getting fresh horses here, and shall go out again pretty strong.

They say we are going out to Neylstroom again, after a party of 300 Boers; I should much rather go south than north, unless we go right up to Petersburg.

We had one successful day on the 10th, when we got 25 prisoners. I was Advance Guard, and we were going down a very steep and narrow path. Suddenly two snipers opened fire on us, from some rocks. We got our horses under cover, and blazed away at them.

I was sent on with a sergeant and five men to a very steep kopje on our left front. We left our horses at the bottom and scrambled up. My signalling came in most useful here, as I got a large handkerchief and tied it on to a stick and sent a message down to report that the country was all clear. They had a heliograph and flashed up orders to me, so altogether it stood me in good stead.

There was a good deal of firing, but we had nobody hit. About 4 p.m. we started back to camp, which was said to be about 12 miles distant.

We were ordered to off-saddle and bivouac until daylight; starting again at 4.30 a.m. We finally reached camp at 7.30 having been on the go for 27 hours, with very little food indeed. That was the hardest day, and wettest night I have yet had with the M.I. We are all very glad of a day or two's rest.

. . . .

Modder Nek   Dec. 6th 1901
8 miles W. of Neylstroom

My dearest Mother,

We have just had a very hard and tiring trek of 14 days; quite the most tiring I have ever done.

We first went to a place called Riet Vlei which is about 40 miles west of Neylstroom. We then started on a trek without any wagons at all, in order to catch a man called Badenhorst.

For 4 days and nights we had nothing but what we carried on our horses. We lived on biscuits and tea, and were marching every one of the four nights, sleeping for a few hours during the day.

Our object was to get to a certain pass in the mountains by a certain hour, as the Boers were being driven that way by Col. Colenbrander's* column, which is operating with us.

Though we had not caught any Boers ourselves, we had driven some into the path of the 12th M.I. who captured 61 altogether, so all our work was not wasted.

* Colonel Johann William Colenbrander (1859–1918) of Dutch extraction, one of the best Zulu linguists in South Africa. In 1901 he raised and commanded Kitcheners' Fighting Scouts.

. . . .

                                                  Dec. 14th 1901

My dearest Mother,

We have had a great deal of hard work during the last week. We did 35 miles the first day, starting at 4 a.m. and getting in to camp at about 7 p.m.

47

with only one hour's halt in the middle of the day. We had to go up very steep rocky paths, and that was why it took us 12 hours steady going to do 35 miles.

We bivouacked at this place, which is called Sterkfontein, and we started on again at 3 a.m. next morning. We were told to search a large fruit plantation as there were tracks of Boers leading into it.

A very sad thing happened here. Our Adjutant, who was carrying no arms, was a little ahead of the company, and he got rather separated from the rest. Suddenly a Boer jumped up about 20 yards from him. Buxton, who was the Adjutant, shouted out to him, 'Hands up', but the Boer seeing that he had no rifle with him, fired and shot him right through the body. He only lived about 40 mins. and never regained consciousness at all. He was one of the Norfolk Buxtons, and was in the Norfolk Regiment.

We caught Badenhorst more by luck than anything else. He is a very important man in this district, and Colonel Dawkins was very pleased about it. We also got about 15 other prisoners. Badenhorst is much the most important man we have yet captured.

. . . .

Dec. 16th 1901

Since I wrote the last page, we have been on a patrol to clear some farms, and bring in all the women who were living in them.

We started at 10 a.m. yesterday morning and we reached the farms about 1 p.m. I had to take two wagons and collect the women from two farms a little distant from the others. I found a Dutch woman with 3 daughters in one farm. They were rather angry with me when I had explained that they had to pack up at once and get on the wagon, and come away with me. I told off six of my men to take what things they wanted out of the house and load them up on the wagon. I then hoisted the mother and daughters on top of their furniture in the wagon and set fire to the house.

I went on to the second farm and found a woman with 5 small children. I soon made friends with them and they rather enjoyed being lifted on to the wagon with all their chairs and tables, but the mother did not like it at all, especially when she saw her house in flames. I did not enjoy having to do this job much, but it had to be done, as the Boers were known to sleep in these farms.

We heard of some Boers, the sons and husbands of these families, hiding in a Kloof close by, so we went back with the wagons towards camp about 5 miles along the road, in order to make these Boers think we had

48

gone altogether; but we stopped in some thick bush and lay hidden until midnight. We then went back to the Kloof, and our plans were as follows: Jenkinson with 12 men held the left side of the Kloof, another officer held the right, and Saunderson with 15 men remained in the centre. Meanwhile I was to go with a guide, by a circuitous road, to the bottom end of the Kloof with 20 men. This I did, and at daybreak, about 4 a.m., climbed down the most awfully steep cliffs right into the bottom of the Kloof. Then I slowly advanced to the top where Saunderson was waiting. It was very difficult to move along at all, as the undergrowth was so thick and tropical. We had to go along in Indian file, and I made the guide go in front, though he kept saying in very broken English, 'The Boers will shoot and kill me.'

I told him I would shoot him if he did not go on, so he thought it wiser to do so. We had gone about halfway, when he dropped down and whispered, 'Dutchmen'. I crept forward and saw 8 Boers with rifles sitting on the ground. When I got close up to them, I jumped up, aimed my carbine straight at them, and shouted, 'Hands up'. It was rather an exciting moment, as I did not know whether they would fight or not, and there were only 2 other men close to me.

However, our guide recognized a brother of his and called to him in Dutch to surrender as they were surrounded. They threw down their rifles, and held up their hands, and surrendered to me.

. . . .

20th Bn. M.I.   Dec. 31st 1901
Harrismith O.R.C.

My dearest Mother,

Major du Maurier, who is commanding the 20th M.I., has taken me on his staff as Quartermaster. In ordinary infantry battalions, the Quartermaster has risen from the ranks, but in an M.I. Battalion, the Quartermaster is chosen from one of the officers of the Battalion, because when on trek he acts as a galloper to the Commanding Officer.

I am awfully glad to have got it, as I hear all that is to be heard in the way of news, and it is a very nice job, being galloper. Of course I have had a lot of work to do these last few days, as I am in charge of all the food and rations both of men and horses in the Battalion. Also I have to draw from the Ordnance Store everything we want in the way of saddlery, clothing, etc. etc. There is a tremendous lot to learn, but luckily for me Deedes, of the Yorkshire Light Infantry, who is now Adjutant, in place of Buxton who was killed, was Quartermaster before, so he helps me very much.

. . . .

Heilbron, O.R.C.

My dearest Mother,

It is a long time since I have written, but we have been continually on the go, ever since the date of my last letter, which was posted at Harrismith, which we left about 10 days ago. We had a big attack on a Boer laager one morning in conjunction with Colonel Rawlinson's column. He marched 30 miles during the night, and then we had a long gallop over the veldt before we found where the Boers were.

Colonel Dawkins himself, Major du Maurier, and about 5 other officers including myself, were some way in front of any other troops, owing partly to our better horses, and partly to our being in the centre. We saw some sheep about 300 yards in front of us, and we went straight for them. Quite suddenly when we were 150 yards only from them, Bang! Bang! two Boers calmly stood up and fired point blank at us. This was the first intimation we got that there were Boers so close to us. We went at them as hard as ever we could, as it was only by that way that we could hope to escape a bullet. They each fired once more at us, but they were frightened and their aim was wild. They then jumped on their horses and fled. We saw quite 50 Boers behind them escaping down a road. We rushed on to a small bluff with rocks on it about half a mile on, and lay down and opened a tremendous fire on them. But some more Boers were waiting for us, about 1500 yards away in some rocks, and they knew exactly what the range was. We were 5 officers and about 4 men, and before we had been there five minutes, one of our officers was hit right through the heart and was killed at once. The bullets were cracking on the rocks all over the place, and for about a quarter of an hour we had quite a hot time of it, but soon the Imperial Light Horse got round on our right and turned the Boers out, but it was very unpleasant while it lasted and we lost a very good officer, called Bretherton of the Royal Fusiliers. We captured about 5000 head of cattle but only got 15 prisoners altogether, chiefly in my opinion owing to the centre, where we were, going on so much ahead of the flanks; but as Colonel Dawkins galloped on, we had to go with him, otherwise he would have been by himself. However, it was a badly managed show, and we got badly punished for it.

Since then we have taken part in a great drive across the O.R.C. after De Wet. We started from Harrismith and went to the Frankfort district. Colonel Rawlinson's columns were on the left of us, Colonels Byng and Eliot were on our right. We extended in a long thin line right across the country, and swept on about 25 miles a day. Heilbron, where we are now, was the place against which we were driving them. They could not get away from there, unless they broke through the Blockhouse line.

For three nights running we were all on outpost watching lest they should try and rush through our line and break out.

They tried every night, and there was very heavy firing, and consequently very little sleep; but the third night was the worst, and there was continuous firing right through from dark till just before dawn.

Yesterday was the last day, and we found Boers hiding in the grass, which was rather long, all over the place; and we came across a small laager of 40 Boers in the bed of a river. Their horses were there, and their rifles. When they saw us coming, they all came out and waved a white shirt, to signify they surrendered. The total number of captures during the 4 days drive was 290, as far as we know at present.

. . . .

Klip River   22nd Febry. 1902

My dearest Mother,

We have been on the move every day, except one, since I last wrote, and I have a good deal to tell you. We left Heilbron on February 12th, and marched for 2 days in the direction of Heidelberg. On the third day we came in contact with a small commando of Boers. We had been expecting to meet them, but not until some miles further on. We were therefore not taking any particular care about keeping extended, but were standing together in a bunch rather ahead of the men; there were several rocky kopjes not 300 yards from us, and we were just going to send a few men on to them to keep a lookout.

We had been standing there five minutes when half a dozen Boers, who had crawled up into the rocks, blazed at us all of a sudden. Colonel Dawkins was with us, and the Boers must have spotted him, for they fired very close to us. However, they managed to miss us, and we did not give them another chance. We jumped on our horses and went straight at the kopje, but the wily Boers had already gone, and were 1000 yards away before we could get a good shot at them.

We then went into Klip River Station for the night. We had no blankets, as the wagons had gone a different road.

. . . .

Rifle Brigade   1st April 1902
Pretoria Club, Pretoria

My dearest Mother,

I have a good deal to tell you this week, so I will start from March 24th on which date we started out on a patrol after De la Rey[1] and Kemp.[2] We set off at 6 p.m. on the evening of the 24th, Generals Walter Kitchener and Kekewich,[3] Colonels Rawlinson[4] and Grenfell[5] all taking part.

We knew that there was a Boer laager at a place called Hartebeestefontein, about 20 miles W. of Klerksdorp, but our orders were to march straight by, and pretend not to see it. We did this and marched straight on for another 20 miles. We did quite 40 miles during the night and at daybreak we all spread out in a long line and started to drive back to Klerksdorp. The idea of going so far during the night was to make the Boers at Hartebeestefontein think we were doing an ordinary trek, and were not going to molest them.

We started back at about 6, perhaps a little later, after having galloped a good five miles to catch 4 ox wagons, which we did in great style.

For 10 miles we saw no sign of any Boers. Rawlinson's column was the centre one and Kekewich was on our left, and Walter Kitchener on our right. After three hours march or more, we saw a convoy in the distance which we took to be our own, which was to come out from Klerksdorp to meet us. At midday this convoy was about 5 miles from us and was going the same way as we were. We could see no infantry with it, and at last we came to the conclusion that it was a Boer convoy. Our horses had already done a good 60 miles since 6 p.m. the night before, but we started off at a fast canter to get round this convoy. At about 2 p.m. we were very close to it, only about 3 miles from it. Only we were on the hills to the left of it, and the convoy was trekking in the plain, with an advance guard out, exactly as we do. We were quite uncertain whether it was one of our convoys or not, as it was going along so quietly and calmly.

But soon we saw them make for a 'nek' about two miles in front of us. We galloped forward and got there a few seconds in front of them. We were even then not quite certain whose convoy it was, until some men came to the top of the small pass which we were guarding and halted about 1500 yards from us.

We fired a volley at them, and they turned about and went for all they were worth back again.

Then the fun began. The Boers were just like rabbits. They tried to find an opening everywhere near us, but always met with a volley.

Kekewich on our left was quite close to us, and so there was no chance of getting between us. They started off to go south, straight to where Walter Kitchener ought to have been; but somehow or other he had lost touch, and to our horror the Boers broke back, though they had to abandon the convoy, 4 guns and 2 Pom-Poms.

We all made absolutely certain that we had got them, and it was simply sickening to allow them to get away like that.

We pursued till dark, but only got 170 roughly out of 600.

For 26 consecutive hours the horses had their saddles on, and never once got a bite of anything to eat. You can imagine that they were nearly dead. I suppose we covered close on 100 miles. We were quite exhausted, and just slept on the ground as we were.

[1] Jacobus Herculaas De la Rey (1847–1914), farmer, politician and soldier; Assistant Commandant-General of the South African Republic 1900–2; Senator for the Transvaal 1910–14.

[2] Vecht-General Christoffel Greyling Kemp, then only twenty-nine years old.

[3] Major-General Robert Kekewich (1854–1914) conducted the defence of Kimberley from 15 October, 1899, to 16 February, 1900.

[4] Henry Seymour (later 1st Lord) Rawlinson (1864–1925) was besieged at Ladysmith 1899; on Lord Roberts' staff 1900–02; thereafter a successful column commander.

[5] Lieutenant-Colonel Harold Maxwell Grenfell (1870–1929) was in command of a regiment of Brabant's Horse, though only a Captain in his own regiment, the 1st Life Guards.

. . . .

Field Force, S. Africa   21st April 1902

My dear Gwendolen,

We are all very excited about these peace negotiations, and I think that they ought certainly to come to something, and, if peace is made now, I hope to be able to come home at any rate in about 6 months' time. They may give each battalion of M.I. a district and make them do a sort of police work, until the country has completely settled down.

. . . .

20th Bn. M.I.   2nd May 1902

My dearest Mother,

I was out shooting with Colonel Brazier-Creagh* who is Senior Medical Officer to Rawlinson's columns. We had gone some way from the columns in search of game, and there were two chaps in the I.L.H. with us. There were a few Boers on a distant skyline whom we saw early in the day, but we did not keep our eyes on them, and finally forgot them altogether.

53

We had just walked upon a small mealie patch and had secured 3 brace of partridges, and so we mounted our ponies in order to catch up the column again, which was nearly 3 miles ahead. We saw three men at a farmhouse which we had just left, not more than 900 yards from us, and I said to Brazier-Creagh, 'I suppose those are our men,' and he said, 'Yes, they belong to Brigg's column, and that man on the grey pony is in the I.L.H.' He had just spoken, when to our horror we heard 'poc-cum poc-cum' and two bullets whizzed over us. In two seconds we had separated and were galloping as hard as we could go. There were 6 Boers altogether and they gave us a very hot time of it. The ground was quite open, and as soon as we got to the top of a rise and over the other side the Boers galloped after us, and sniped until we had got over a second ridge. The bullets came uncomfortably close, and often hit the ground between us.

* Colonel George Washington Brazier-Creagh (1858–1942) was an explorer who had led expeditions through little-known regions of Eastern Persia and Baluchistan.

. . . .

20th M.I.   14th May 1902
Mafeking Line

My dear Father,

We have just finished one of our 'drives' and the total number of prisoners is 352. Most of them belonged to Kemp's commando, and were genuine fighting Boers, who said that they were not going to surrender, even though all these other commandos [have] come in. So that is the reason for our making a drive over to this Western part of the Transvaal, where the water is very scarce, and when found, is very black.

We had no fighting at all, but every night there was a tremendous lot of firing all along the line. The Boers were evidently trying to get through, as one was picked up in front of the Imperial Light Horse quite dead one morning. This column did not catch very many, but they mostly seem to have run up against Col. Thorneycroft,* who got 250 in a bunch.

We saw a great many buck, in the bush country, which is about 20 miles wide, and extends up to within two miles of this place. We got four altogether in the battalion, but though they are very tender, they have not got much taste about them.

* Fuller details of the career of Major-General Alexander Thorneycroft (1859–1931) and his Mounted Infantry may be found in Vol. iv of Lord Anglesey's *History of the British Cavalry*, p. 70.

. . . .

54

20th Bn. M.I.   21st May 1902
S. Africa

My dearest Mother,

We are now on our way back to Klerksdorp, and are having a very dull and
monotonous time of it, as we are not allowed to try and capture any Boers,
as all their leaders are away at this Peace Meeting. Lord Kitchener said
that no hostile operations would be carried on between the 10th and 31st
of this month, as the Boers did not want to let their commandants go away
for Peace Conferences unless we agreed not to molest them during their
absence.

Personally I have rather enjoyed it, as I have devoted every day to
shooting. I got 100 cartridges off an officer in the I.L.H. at Devondale
Siding, and have had great fun. Today I got 1 hare, 1 large coran, 1
partridge and 1 black coran; not very much, but still enough to keep the
pot boiling and game is rather scarce, and very wild.

· ·

20th M.I.   June 3rd 1902
Klerksdorp

My dearest Mother,

You will have heard long before now the great and joyful news that Peace
was signed at Pretoria last Saturday night. On Sunday morning we were
sitting in our tent, having just finished breakfast, when, like a thunderclap,
we heard a great burst of cheering from the direction of Church parade,
which we did not attend on that morning. We rushed out to hear the news,
which we had guessed already, and which Colonel Rawlinson had
formally given out as soon as service was ended. He had received a
telegram from Lord Kitchener, which he read out on parade. Each
different camp took up the cheering, which lasted for nearly an hour. We
could hear General Walter Kitchener's columns cheering nearly 3 miles
away, and the Imperial Light Horse had taken it up from us in the next
camp. Sports and impromptu smoking concerts have been the order of the
day (and night) ever since. On Sunday night, du Maurier, Deedes and
myself dined with Col. Dawkins to celebrate the occasion.

· ·

Elaandsfontein   26th June 1902

My dearest Mother,

I have just come back from Pretoria where I went to get stores from the
Ordnance for the Battalion. I went to see Vernon, in the Rifle Brigade,
who is Staff Officer to Gen. Alderson,* the Mounted Infantry chap. He
showed me a printed order to this effect, 'After July 15th any unit must
have half its establishment of Officers, the remainder can have 4 months'
leave.' So there is a possibility of my coming home in about 3 weeks, which
seems much too good to be true.

I went to call on General Lyttelton at Pretoria and had a nice little chat
with him. My great friend Freddy Blacker came up from the 2nd Bn., as I
wired to him to tell him to do so. We went to pay our call together.
Lyttelton talked a good deal about the early part of the war, and said, 'Of
course you were at Bergendal, and I never want to see a hotter fight than
that was.' I entirely agreed with him!

* General (later Lt.-General Sir) Edwin Alfred Harvey Alderson (1859–1927) was
  Inspector General of Mounted Infantry in S. Africa 1900–02.

. . . .

Rifle Brigade, 20th M.I.   11th July 1902
Elaandsfontein

My dearest Mother,

The only piece of news that I can give you for certain is that this Battalion
of M.I. is going to be very shortly broken up. Deedes will go back to his
company which is in the 3rd M.I. and I shall wend my way back to old
Middelburg again to the 2nd Bn. When I arrive there I shall settle with
Maitland the Adjutant about my leave, and so don't expect me to give you
a definite date for another 3 weeks at least.

. . . .

20th M.I.   July 23rd (1902)
Pretoria Club

My dear Father,

I have just come back from a visit to the 2nd Bn. at Middelburg. Du
Maurier gave me a few days' leave, and so I thought I would go and see
them all again. On my way, I stayed two days at Groot Oliphant's River
with Freddy Blacker, who is on detachment there. We went out shooting

one day to a farm about 11 miles out. Stephens, who is a Major in the 2nd Bn. and a great friend of mine, came too, so that we were three guns altogether. We rode out on ponies, and took three pointer dogs with us. Our bag at the end of the day was 9½ brace of partridges, 4 coran, and 2 snipe. We had great fun, and took out a large lunch in a cart, which we out-spanned at a farm belonging to a Dutchman who was building it up again. We gave him some lunch and some whisky, and we became the greatest friends. He wanted us to come out and stay with him for two or three days to shoot. Stephens and Blacker had never been to this farm by daylight before, but they had been there 5 times by night to try and catch this man who was lunching with us. Rather curious position, wasn't it? We laughed a good deal over it, and the farmer enjoyed the joke too, especially as he had not been caught, but had surrendered. He was as happy as a king, and had started working his farm again, and building up the remains of his house.

Please let Uncle Edmund know of this picnic, the Dutch farmer and British Officers having lunch together on the former's farm in perfect harmony!

. . . .

20th M.I.   8 August 1902
Elaandsfontein

My dearest Mother,

The latest news from the 2nd Bn. is that they are going to Cairo during the next trooping season! That would be very jolly, and Cairo is always talked of as a good station. After my 4 months' leave, I might have to join them at Cairo instead of coming out here again, which I should much prefer.

Your letters arrived this morning, full of the wonderful doings at Claydon for Harry's coming of age. How I should have liked to have been there; he seems to have established quite a reputation already as a speaker. I am so glad he mentioned me in his speech.

. . . .

2nd Bn. Rifle Brigade   Sept. 9th 1902
Victoria Club, Maritzburg

My dear Kathleen,

As it is your 18th (?) birthday, I am writing my mail letter to you. I arrived at this place at half past three this morning with my company of M.I. from Harrismith. We had a telegram this morning from the Embarking Officer at Durban saying that the transport *Malta* left Cape Town on Sept. 6th and would embark the 2nd Bn. Rifle Brigade for Cairo. So, instead of staying here for a month or 6 weeks as I thought we should do, we are very possibly off tomorrow or the next day. I was going on leave home almost at once, but I have decided to go to Cairo first with my regiment for this reason. If I get 4 months' leave as soon as I arrive it will only take me 5 days to get to London from there, and 5 days back. That is only 10 days altogether off my leave, instead of three weeks from here.

As soon as I get to Cairo, I shall get leave for certain, and shall be able to tell you all about the Suez Canal into the bargain.

. . . .

Peninsular & Oriental Steam Navigation Coy.   Sept. 25th 1902
S.S. *Malta*

My dearest Mother,

We embarked at 6.30 this morning, and we sail this afternoon.

. . . .

2nd Bn. Rifle Brigade   Oct. 9th 1902
SS. *Malta*, The Red Sea

My dearest Mother,

Some of us went ashore at Aden yesterday for a few hours, while the ship was coaling. A steam launch belonging to the P. & O. Company took us off, and of course I went too.

We visited the club in force, in spite of a large notice to the effect that members only were admitted. While sitting in easy chairs on the veranda, a nervous looking individual came up and apologized for his presence there to us, but asked if he might come in, as he was a passenger on board a steamer that was coaling there! We of course said that we were delighted to see him, and hoped that he would make himself perfectly at home.

In his gratitude to us for our kindness and hospitality, he offered us refreshment of a liquid nature, and we became great friends. We explained to him just before we left that we were also passengers on board a steamer that was coaling, and had walked in uninvited. This seemed to upset him a little, and I could not quite understand what he was saying, as he was a foreigner, but it sounded rather more violent than good-bye.

We came back on board again about 4.30 p.m. and very soon after weighed anchor, and started for Suez, which we ought to reach on the 12th inst.

. . . .

. . . Chapter Four . . .

After a spell in Cairo and then as a lecturer in England, in December 1906, Ralph rejoins his regiment in Shahjahanpur in India. He goes on leave to Singapore and Rangoon and hears of his appointment as A.D.C. to Lord Chelmsford,* the Governor of Queensland. He arrives in July, 1907, and begins life in Government House. He learns the duties of an A.D.C., does a spectacular tour through Queensland and enjoys the social life.

---

* Frederic Thesiger, 3rd Baron and 1st Viscount Chelmsford (1868–1933) was Governor of Queensland 1905–09, of New South Wales (1909–13) and Viceroy of India 1916–21.

· ·

H.M. Transport *Rewa*   December 27th 1906

My dearest Mother,

We have just left Malta and I had a very nice time there after handing over my draft to the 4th Btn. I lunched with them before we started and saw many friends including Capt. Digby who wished to be remembered to you all and hoped that you had forgotten the incident of his ringing the fire alarm instead of the front door bell. It was a great pleasure getting your letters. I thought James would go and see you and give you the latest news of me.

It is much calmer now and also much warmer which I like. We get to Port Said on Sunday when I shall post this. I took some photos of the Grand Harbour at Malta which I shall have printed in Bombay. I am in command of 177 men now whom I take right up to Shahjahanpur with me. I had to take charge of nearly £300 in cash today which is to pay them during the voyage and also bundles of documents, so it gives me a good deal to do.

George Lindsay who was the only subaltern senior to me in the regiment has gone as adjutant to reserves so I am now the top and obviously the next for promotion. I will add a few more lines later. I was much interested to hear about the Education Bill today but I did not hear of any fresh changes in the cabinet though they seem to think Burns* will get promotion.

* John Burns, (1858–1942) Labour MP for Battersea, 1892–1918, was President of the Local Government Board from 1905 to 1914. He did not, therefore, get promotion.

. . . .

2nd Battalion Rifle Brigade, Shahjahanpur

My dearest Mother,

I arrived here yesterday morning at 5 a.m. We came up here from Bombay as fast as we could, leaving there on Wednesday evening at 6 p.m. and travelling day and night till Saturday morning. We were only two hours in Bombay so I had no chance to see Yarr or cousin Antonia. The *Rewa* got into Bombay harbour about 6 a.m. but we did not disembark until 4 p.m. as my draft had to stay onboard in order to clean up all the troop decks after the rest had left.

On the way up here we stopped at various places for meals. We halted for only 1½ hours every morning, for half an hour in the middle of the day and again 1½ hours late in the evening. It was hot in the train during the day and quite cold at night. We came by Deolali, Jhansi, Cawnpore, Lucknow to Shahjahanpur.

My bearer, who used to be with Capt. Digby when he was in India, met me at Bombay and looked after me very well on the way up here. It is of course all rather strange at first, and I have not yet settled in my bungalow as there's no furniture of any sort there. I am staying for the first few nights in Talbot's room while he is at Agra.

. . . .

2nd Bat. R.B. Shahjahanpur   January 22nd 1907

My dearest Mother,

I have settled into my bungalow now and am very comfortable. I have spent some of your Xmas presents to me in buying some most beautiful rugs and tablecloths from Cashmere. We can get them very cheap out here compared to what you would have had to pay for them at home. They are all embroidered by hand.

Basset who is adjutant of this bat. is going away on 3 weeks' leave and I am to do adjutant to the bat. while he is away so I shall be pretty busy. I also have to look after the 180 men I brought here with me as they are kept separate from the rest of the bat. for a whole month for fear of any illness they may have brought with them from Bombay though we were only there such a very short time.

Basset had a letter from his people last Sunday saying that the notice in the gazette that I am promoted to Captain. We have not heard anything about it here yet, but may do so by next Mail on Sunday. If I have been promoted I suppose I shall be sent off again almost directly.

. . . .

Jan. 31st 1907

I am trying to get a month's leave towards the end of Feb. to go and pay a visit to Singapore to stay with Ned Coke.

Your ever affect.
Ralph

. . . .

Shahjahanpur   N.D.

Next Sunday I am going to Hardoi, a place where we shot 200 duck a fortnight ago. We only had 12 guns then. We are trying to get about 20 this time. The geal or lake is so very big that it takes 20 guns to keep them on the move. There are large numbers of geese there but they are very shy and difficult to get near. The water is simply black with coots like the ones at Claydon, thousands of them but we do not shoot them in this country. Only the natives eat them.

We shall go to Hardoi Saturday night and stay in a dak bungalow or rest house. There's always one of these in every large village. We take our bearers and our sheets and blankets and perhaps beds also. If you go and stay with anybody in India you always take your own bedding and your own servants and your own bed.

Your very affect.
Ralph

. . . .

Shahjahanpur   February 12th 1907

My dear Father,

Just a line to say that the following telegram was sent to Lord Chelmsford by Harman, 'Verney accepts A.D.C. letter follows. Harman.' He showed me the letter before he sent it off and in it he said, 'I do not think you could get a better man for the post of A.D.C.' so unless Lord Chelmsford had made other arrangements I suppose he will write to me on receipt of that letter and apply for me to the War Office.

His A.D.C. gets £340 a year, and all his food and lodging paid for as he lives with him. He also gets a free pass over all Australasia including New Zealand. So I think I shall certainly do well to take it if I can. I shall hope to find a letter from him on my return from Siam. I wrote to the Crown Prince the other day to tell him that I was coming out and so I hope that he or somebody else will put me up. I sail from Calcutta at daybreak on the 24th and hope Harman will come up to Bangkok with me before going on home, at any rate for a bit.

Your ever affect.
Ralph

· ·

S.S. *Bharata*   March 4th 1907

My dear Father,

I am having a most interesting journey and arrive at Singapore tomorrow morning where I hope to meet Ned Coke. Harman is with me and after staying on the rubber plantation for a few days we hope to go on to Java, which is two days from Singapore. I had hoped to go up to Bangkok but that takes five days to do and I haven't the time to spare for it, so Java will be instead of Bangkok probably.

We hear that Ned Coke's plantation is 18 miles from Johore which is 1 hour's journey from Singapore. It is a very wild district and hardly anyone lives there, so we shall have to rough it a bit I expect. We shall try and persuade Ned Coke to come to Java with us. I believe it is a country well worth while a visit and we hope to have time to go up into the interior.

Your ever affect.
Ralph

· ·

Lai Sang Rubber Co.   March 11th 1907
Gunong Pulai

My dearest Mother,

I have been here for the past week and am staying here till Wednesday when I return to Singapore for a day or two and I hope then to go up to Java if I can get a boat. Harman is here too and leaves for England on the 16th. We have had a most interesting time and have seen over the whole estate and have been initiated into the whole business of rubber planting.

We live in a house built of grass and bamboo and we have 2 or 3 Chinese servants. We get up about 6.30 a.m. and start the coolies working till about 8 o'clock when we come in for breakfast. We are then out again till 11 a.m. when all work is stopped for a couple of hours. The work is started again at 1 p.m. until 5 p.m.

In the evening we go out to shoot pig which come out of the jungle to feed on the tapioca. They are very difficult to get and though we have seen a good many we haven't been able to shoot one yet but hope to do so before we leave.

· ·

Hotel Europe, Singapore   March 14th 1907

My dearest Mother,

Just a few lines to say that the boats to Java do not fit in with my plans very well so I am going to Rangoon on the 16th and am going up to Mandalay for a trip which I believe is perfectly lovely. I shall have from the 20th till the 29th in Burmah and hope to go up by train and return by boat all down the River Irrawaddy. I can catch a boat again from Rangoon to Calcutta arriving there on the 2nd April which will suit me very well.

· ·

Rangoon Hospital   April 8th 1907

My dearest Mother,

I have had a very bad go of malaria fever which I must have caught in Johore. I am practically all right again now and hope to leave here next Monday to rejoin my battalion at Chaubattia. I haven't had any letters from home since Feb. 18th so I do not know in the least what you have all been doing. But I shall get them in Calcutta.

Your very affect.
Ralph

· ·

Rangoon   April 14th 1907

My dear Father,

Yesterday I received a telegram from our Adjutant saying that Lord
Chelmsford had written to ask if I can be in Australia by July 20. I wired
back to him this morning saying that I could, so I suppose I shall have to
leave India about the end of June. I have written to him explaining that I
have had fever and that therefore I have not yet got his letter, but saying
that I conclude from his telegram that he is kind enough to wish me to
come on his staff and that I will write again as soon as I get to India where
his letter is waiting for me.

Your very affect.
Ralph

· ·

2nd Bat. R.B. Chaubattia   May 20th 1907

My dearest Mother,

I am today sending 2 big boxes to Bombay by luggage train and I hope they
will be there by the 25th June so that they can come by my boat; fancy
taking 20 to 25 days to get from here to Bombay! I have written to Dr. Yarr
to tell him I shall be in Bombay for three days before I sail but I am afraid
he will be in a hill station and so I shall not have much chance of seeing
him unless he can come to Bombay.

I am much better now and yesterday had dinner in the Mess for the first
time.

Please do not trouble to answer all my invitations to dances. I do not
know either of the 2 hostesses whose invitations you mention on your last
letter and I do not think it the least necessary to inform them that I am in
India.

Your very affect.
Ralph

· ·

2nd Bat. R.B. Chaubattia   May 27th 1907

My dearest Mother,

I have been appointed acting adjutant from tomorrow until I leave for
Australia. I am very glad to be doing this as I shall be able to ride instead of

walk on field days etc. and I am not yet strong on my legs and so have not been able to go out on manoeuvres so far. I shall be very busy as the training of Companies and musketry is in full swing.

I have received a very kind invitation from Lord Lamington* to go and stay at Government House, Poona, with him before I leave India. Before he became Governor of the Bombay Presidency he was the Governor of Queensland so that I hope he will give me a lot of information about the country and hints about the people which will be most useful.

Your very affect.
Ralph

* Charles Wallace Alexander Napier Cochrane Baillie, 2nd Baron Lamington, (1860–1940) was Governor of Queensland 1895–1901, Governor of Bombay 1903–07.

. . . .

Chaubattia   June 4th 1907

My dearest Mother,

This morning in the orderly room I received a telegram from the War Office that my appointment as A.D.C. was sanctioned so that is now settled that I sail from Bombay on the 25th.

. . . .

The Manal Palace Hotel, Bombay   June 20th 1907

My dearest Mother,

I left Chaubattia last Sunday afternoon directly after lunch. On Saturday night I was given a farewell dinner at the Mess and the Colonel very kindly came up to dine in the Mess. The band played that night instead of Friday night and we had champagne. The Colonel proposed my health and said a lot of nice things about me which made me feel horribly uncomfortable. I got up and returned thanks in a very few words and at the end the band played 'Auld Lang Syne'.

Next day I bicycled as far as Kerna, 18 miles from Chaubattia, but this will surprise your least when you hear that it was all down hill all the way. Unfortunately I punctured as the road was rather bad and had to do the last 4 miles on a flat tyre. I slept the night at a small hotel near Naimi Tal kept by an old soldier who had been 35 years in the army. Next morning I went up to Naini Tal which is at the top of a very high mountain and called on Sir G. Hewitt, the Governor, who asked me to stay the night with him. I did not see him as he was ill in bed with a bad throat, but I saw his military secretary. The house is most beautiful just like a large country house in England and the drive was bordered with a mass of hydrangeas which looked quite lovely.

I went to Kathgodam in the afternoon, leaving there by train at 4 p.m. I slept that night at Bareilly, starting off next morning at 6 a.m., passing through Lucknow and finally arrived at Bombay about 6 p.m. yesterday evening.

I do hope your dance was a great success. It sounded as if it ought to be with 14 people giving dinner parties for it. I know you will like Capt. Harman very much, but do not think you will get him to dance.

· ·

Government House, Kirkee   June 23 1907

My dear Father,

I have been here since last Friday and have had a very nice visit. I leave again tomorrow morning early for Bombay. Lord Lamington asked to be remembered to you. I like him very much and it has been very interesting staying here and seeing how the Lt. Governors live out here.

They certainly do themselves very well and live in great state. There's a private band which plays every night at dinner. Before dinner everybody assembles in the drawingroom and when H.E. comes in he is announced by an A.D.C., everyone standing up in silence. The native sentries in most beautiful uniforms stand at the front door and the servants are all in scarlet and gold.

· ·

S.S. *Delhi*   June 26th 1907

My dearest Mother,

We sailed from Bombay at 10 a.m. yesterday morning and so far we have had a good passage. I get to Colombo on Friday morning and leave again by the S.S. *Himalaya* on Sunday morning.

I find that I call at Fremantle and at Adelaide before I get to Melbourne which will be interesting. I might go from Adelaide straight to Brisbane as a friend of mine in the R.B. is A.D.C. there and I wrote to him to meet me. I may stay a night there at Gov. House with the Northcotes if I have time. My friend is Stephens their A.D.C. and a brother of the people I stayed with at Rangoon after my fever.

· ·

Galle Face Hotel, Colombo   June 19th 1907

My dearest Mother,

I arrived here yesterday morning at 7 a.m. and came to this hotel which is
most delightful. But I was anxious to see some of the interior of the
Country so I started at 2 p.m. and went 70 miles inland to a place called
Kandy which is 1500 feet above sea level.

I thought the country perfectly beautiful, the palms and bananas and
coconuts were magnificent and it was fairly cool as they have had a lot of
rain here. I stayed the night at a hotel up there and returned here this
morning starting at 7 a.m. and calling at the P&O for my letters on my way
from the station.

. . . .

S.S. *Himalaya*   July 10th 1907

My dearest Mother,

We arrived in Fremantle last Tuesday morning at 7 a.m. I went up the
river to Perth in a steam launch that left at 9 a.m. It took about 1¼ hours.

I liked Perth very much but it is at present so new, all the houses are
built of red brick which makes one notice it all the more.

There's a theatrical company on board here and a man called Hoyle
and his wife and nephew called Burton are the chief people in it. The
latter dances very well too and tap dances, what you're so fond of. I have
been having lessons every day on it and am picking it up very quickly so he
says, in fact I am considered a genius at it.

. . . .

Melbourne Club   July 15th 1907

My dearest Mother,

I have just arrived and have been made an honorary member of this club
which is the best in Melbourne. I leave here for Sydney this afternoon,
arriving there tomorrow morning. Stephens is going to meet me at the
station. I got a letter from Brooke the A.D.C. at Brisbane asking me to
come up as quick as I could as there was rather a lot of work waiting for me
to do at the beginning of next week. 500 invitations to be sent etc. etc. so I
expect I shall be pretty busy.

I am to get the household evening coat on my way through Sydney and get my uniform pressed and brushed up ready for immediate use on arrival. I have no time for more now.

Much love to you all ever your affect.

Ralph

. . . .

Union Club, Sydney   July 15th 1907

My dearest Mother,

I arrived here this morning early and have been made an honorary member of this club at which I am staying. I lunched today with Sir. H. Rawson* the Governor of N.S.W. and am dining tonight with the Northcotes** at Gov. House so I am getting to know them pretty soon.

Admiral Sir H. Rawson was quite charming and he is coming up to Brisbane in a fortnight's time with his A.D.C. to shoot with Lord Chelmsford in Queensland so I expect I shall be going out with them. I have been this afternoon to a tailor to have my evening coat made for me, a dark blue one with white facings and brass buttons.

* Admiral Sir Harry Rawson (1843–1910) was Governor of New South Wales from 1902 to 1909.
** Henry Stafford Northcote, 1st Baronet and 1st Baron (1846–1911) was Governor-General of the Commonwealth of Australia 1904–08. He was Governor of Bombay 1899–1903, during which appointment the D.N.B. remarks that he 'efficiently dealt with plague and famine, and preserved the fine Gujarat breed of cattle'.

. . . .

Government House, Brisbane   20th July 1907

My dearest Mother,

I arrived here last Friday night. I like the Chelmsfords very much indeed so far. I am rather appalled at the amount of work the A.D.C. has to do, but I suppose I shall get into it in time. Brooke, I am glad to say, is remaining on for a fortnight to show me what to do.

H.E. opens Parliament on Wednesday and I shall have to be in attendance on him, full uniform I expect. Yesterday I went with him to see a lacrosse Match, Canadians v N.S. Wales. I haven't seen this game before and was immensely taken with it.

. . . .

68

Government House, Brisbane   July 21st 1907

My dearest Gwen,

Many thanks for your letters which I found waiting for me here both from
you and Kathleen. I am at present much alarmed at the amount of work
there is for me to do.

These are a few of my duties. Look after the servants and pay their
wages, look after the stables and pay the wages of the coachman etc. and
all the bills for the horses' food etc., arrange for H.E.'s public engagements like opening agricultural shows and attending public dinners etc.,
arrange the Government House dinner parties, about 2 a week at this time
of year and also be in attendance on H.E. whenever he goes out anywhere
at all officially, and generally make myself useful in entertaining guests
staying here. In fact I think I shall be very busy indeed, at any rate until I
get used to do the work systematically.

But I like both Lord and Lady C. very much so far which is a great
comfort. They are both exceedingly kind and very homelike. We have
prayers every morning at 9 a.m., read by him and then breakfast im-
mediately after. I go to Lady C.'s writing room after breakfast and she tells
me if she wants me to arrange a dinner party or anything else she wants me
to do. Then I go to Lord C. and see what he wants me to do, and also tell
him what engagements are coming up for him.

I think I shall like the work very much when I get more used to it but at
present I feel inclined to pack up my box and return to India by the first
boat!

. . . .

Government House, Brisbane   July 28th 1907

My dearest Mother,

We have had a very busy week. On Wednesday H.E. opened Parliament.
It was a very pretty ceremony and it was my first official ceremony. Capt.
Newton, his private secretary, and myself drove with him in his carriage
with an escort of mounted police. Guns were fired as a salute when we
started. Newton and I walked just in front of H.E. up the floor of the
House and sat just behind him while he read out the Governor's speech.
In the evening I went with him to a big meeting at the school of music here.
Lady C. came too and gave away certificates to those who had passed a
certain exam in music.

On Thursday I went with H.E. and Lady C. to a place called Lockyer where he opened an agricultural show. It was quite a big affair and I enjoyed it very much though it took over 3 hours to go there by train. We had his special saloon carriage, however, which was very comfortable indeed and we took a well-filled tea basket with us. Lord C. is a very good speaker indeed I think and speaks very clearly so that everyone can hear what he is saying. I can see that he is very popular in Queensland, more so perhaps than Lady C., who is handicapped by being very short-sighted which is rather a pity. But I think I shall like them both very much.

On Friday we took the *Lucinda* which is the Gov. House yacht and went a trip into Moreton Bay. It was a birthday treat for Andrew, the youngest boy. We took provisions on board and landed for about 2 hours on an island called Bridie Island. We started at 9 a.m. and got back at 6 p.m. There were 5 children, Fred who is at school at a place called Southport about 2 hours by train from here. He is the eldest and is 10 years old, then comes Joan, Queenie and Bridget and lastly Andrew. I like them very much indeed and they are a very happy family.

The other night Lady C. wanted to have a practice after dinner so we took up the rugs in the hall and danced for about an hour. I danced with H.E. to show him how to do the twostep and the waltz as he is not in very good practice. We had great fun and I got Lady C. to say we might have a few very small dances later on of just a dozen people or so.

Your very affect.
Ralph

. . . .

Gabbinbar Toowoomba   August 4th 1907

My dearest Mother,

We have come up here for a few days for the agricultural show. H.E., Mr. Villiers, Brooke and myself rode the whole way from a place called Ipswich 20 miles out from Brisbane. We took three days over it staying the first night with a Mr. and Mrs. Cotton who have a large farm at a place called Hidden Vale and the second night with a Mr. Armstrong who is a member of the legislative assembly which is the House of Commons in Queensland.

The show is on Wednesday and we return to Brisbane on Wednesday evening. I have the right to go into the House of Commons here whenever I like and sit on the Speaker's right in a sort of box. I went there the other day for a couple of hours. It is very interesting as I know most of the

70

1. Ralph in 1898.

1 = Where our first Battalion are
2 = Majuba
3 = Laing's Nek, the road over the pass
4 = Boer gun position on Pogwana.

Sketched on outpost on top
of hill facing Laing's Nek.
June 7th 1900

2. Sketch drawn by Ralph (see letter of 6 June, 1900).

3. 'With Sir Redvers Buller: Capture of a position
by the Rifle Brigade after a brilliant bayonet charge.'
(see letter of 31 August, 1900).

4. Fighting near Machadodorp, 27 August, 1900.

5. Kopjes held by the Boers on the road to Bergendal.
(see letter of 31 August, 1900).

6. Ralph sitting in the waggon in which he travelled to Machadodorp.

7. 'Sackobono.' (see letter of 27 December, 1900).

Ministers now – the Balfours and C.B.s [Campbell-Bannerman]* of Queensland and they come out and talk to me in my box which is very interesting. I shall go there a good deal when I have more time and can let H.E. know what is going on there as he is not allowed in the House and is glad to hear what they are doing there.

* Mr. Balfour was Prime Minister of Great Britain from 1902 to 1905, Sir Henry Campbell-Bannerman from 1905 to 1908.

. . . .

Government House, Brisbane   August 10th 1907

This next week is a very busy one. Tomorrow we have a garden party here and I have to stand and present all the guests to H.E. and Lady C. In the evening I have to go to meet Sir Harry Rawson who arrives at 9.30 p.m. I have to do that in uniform. On Tuesday we go to the Agricultural Show here in the afternoon just to see the judging. In the evening we go to a dance given by the Murray Priors who are very nice people indeed.

On Wednesday we have the official opening of the show by H.E. and there's another dance that evening. Thursday night we have a dance here at Government House and on Friday morning we start off to Delalah for the duck shoot and we shall be away a week. I went to a very good dance on Friday night last given by the Naval and Military officers here. I went with H.E. but he left at 10 p.m. and allowed me to stay on, so I returned at 2 a.m. next morning having danced hard and enjoyed it immensely.

I went on Thursday morning to return the call on Capt. of H.M.S. *Challenger*, Bridson by name. It was rather fun. They sent a boat off for me and I was received on board by the Captain as I was calling on behalf of H.E. I stayed on board about ½ hour and then came back. It was rather fun but very hot as I had to go in uniform and spurs are much in the way going up and down 'companions'.

. . . .

Government House, Brisbane   August 23rd 1907

Our dance on Thursday night was a huge success, so everybody said. We had about 20 sailors from H.M.S. *Challenger* to decorate the House inside and out with flags. I stood at the door leading into the Ballroom and announced everybody as they came in, about 500 altogether. It took nearly an hour and I was glad when everybody had arrived. We started dancing at 9 p.m. and it finished soon after 2 a.m.

At the shoot our total bag was 608 ducks. I enjoyed it immensely and it

71

did me a lot of good as I was very tired after our dance and our last busy three weeks. Sir Harry Rawson leaves here on Sunday morning and returns to Sydney.

Your very affect.
Ralph

· ·

Government House, Brisbane   Sept. 8th 1907

P.S.   You will probably have seen in the papers what excitement we are having out here about the new Tariff which has been put on almost everything coming into the country. I cannot understand who is going to benefit by it. There are hardly any manufacturers in this country at all, at any rate there are not enough to supply the country with what it wants and therefore practically everything has to be imported and will have to be imported for many years to come.

The very few manufacturers that exist in Australia are all in Victoria and of course they have put up their prices to just below what one has to pay for imported goods. Take kerosene for example. As soon as the new tariff came out they put up the price of kerosene 25%. It was then discovered that nearly two years' supply of kerosene is at present in the country, because the sellers of kerosense are getting 25% more for it now, though they have not paid duty on what they will be selling for the next 2 years. It has certainly increased the cost of living taking it all round by 25% and nobody will benefit by it except a very very few manufacturers and I suppose the Government Exchequer.

· ·

Government House, Brisbane   Sept. 14th 1907

My dearest Mother,

Yesterday afternoon we went to see a wool sale which is a most interesting business. I went in the morning to the wool sheds where all the wool is laid out for inspection or at least samples of it. Those who want to buy it go and have a good look at it. Then at the sale all the buyers stand round the desk at which sits the auctioneer. The room is like a very small speech room at Harrow. As soon as the auctioneer says 'Lot 1' everybody who wants to buy it shouts out at the top of his voice the price they would give for it. It is a regular pandemonium and it is like a lot of dogs barking rather than anything else. Whoever catches the auctioneer's eye first gets that lot of wool. Most of the buying had come all the way from Sydney or Melbourne to buy this wool so that the competition was great.

. . . .

Government House, Brisbane   23rd Sept. 1907

My dearest Mother,

On Friday afternoon 37 members of the Legislative Assembly out of a total of 72 sent in a petition to H.E. asking him not to dissolve parliament. However, he could not see any other way out of the difficulty so he has announced the dissolution and we shall have a general election in about 6 weeks. The new parliament will meet again in February probably.

H.E. has been quite knocked up by it all and he was in bed all yesterday afternoon and is still resting upstairs, but I hope he will be all right again tomorrow.

. . . .

Government House, Brisbane   Sept. 28th 1907

I have had rather a hard week sending out about 400 invitations to the official evening party on Nov. 13 for the King's birthday. I had to get it done this week as we shall be away from Brisbane from now until Nov. 10th except for 2 days between this northern trip and going to Sydney and both these days we have engagements Oct. 9th and 10th.

We have also had this last week the last of our dinner parties for the present which I am rather glad of. It went off all right and we had our usual number, 26.

. . . .

State Government House, Sydney   Oct. 13th 1907

My dearest Mother,

Since last writing to you we have travelled a good deal. We had a most successful trip to Townsville and Charters Towers and had a calm passage the whole way there and back. We are now staying here till Friday with the Rawsons. We arrived yesterday morning and in the afternoon went to the races which I enjoyed awfully.

The Royal box is a most luxurious place with a large dining room attached.

On Friday evening we go to Melbourne and on to Admiral Bridges* till the Monday, then return to Melbourne to stay with Sir J. Madden,** the Deputy Governor. The Rawsons sent their own railway carriage for us on our way there from Wallangarra, the station on the border of Queensland and N.S. Wales. It had real beds in it, a bath in each room, also a dining room and sitting room, it was most delightful travelling in it. It was built for the Prince of Wales when he came out here so you can imagine it is pretty comfortable.

* Rear-Admiral Walter Bridges (1843–1917) joined the Royal Navy in 1856. Australian by birth, he retired there in 1899.
** Sir John Madden (1844–1918) was Chief Justice of the Supreme Court of Victoria 1898–1918.

. . . .

Government House, Melbourne   November 3rd 1907

My dearest Mother,

We came here on Friday morning and that afternoon there was a garden party here at which nearly 2000 people were present. It was fairly fine though the rain only kept off until just after the last guest had left. All the people assembled on the lawn and at 4 p.m. we formed a procession and with an Army of A.D.C.s leading the way all the Governors and the Gov. General with Lady Northcote came out on the lawn to the strains of the National Anthem.

Yesterday we went to the first day's racing here and drove down the course like the King does as Ascot. It was great fun. I was in attendance on my chief and Lady Edeline Strickland* as Lady C. was tired and did not come. We were the red carriage in the procession. We lunched there in the Gov. General's private room which is beautifully decorated with a grotto and fountain at the end of it.

* Lady Edeline Strickland (1870–1918), daughter of the 7th Earl De La Warr, married Gerald, 1st Baron Strickland (1861–1940) in 1890. He was Governor of Tasmania 1904–09, and of Western Australia 1909–13.

. . . .

Government House, Brisbane   November 12th 1907

My dear Father,

We have just had an extraordinary political block here during the last few days. Mr. Kidston,* our Premier, wished to do away with the Legislative Council which is our Upper House. As H.E. would not allow this, he handed in his resignation and that of all his Ministers. H.E. sent for the

74

leader of the Opposition who agreed to form a ministry. In the afternoon he asked the Premier to adjourn the House for a week in order to give him time to form his ministry. But the Premier said if he was going to form a ministry he must feel that he had the confidence and majority of the House behind him, so that he had better propose the adjournment of the House himself.

This he would not do as he does not have a majority of the House with him. At last after some few minutes' delay in the House the Speaker went on with the ordinary business as no one had proposed the adjournment. At last the Premier got up and said he would put the motion forward tomorrow that the House still has complete confidence in the present Government or rather in the Government which resigned office this morning. If this is carried I suppose Mr. Philp,** the leader of the opposition, will come back to H.E. and say that he cannot form a ministry and Mr. Kidston will continue in power.

The Labour Party in the House can turn the scale one way or the other as Kidston and Philp are more or less equal in numbers. It is rather a curious position and I went at the request of H.E. to the House this afternoon to hear it adjourned but had to come back and say that Kidston refused to do so and that Philp could not do so.

* William Kidston (1849–1919) was born in Falkirk and emigrated to Australia in 1882 where he established himself as a bookseller. He was Premier of Queensland 1903–07.
** Sir Robert Philp (1851–1922) was Premier of Queensland 1899–1903.

. . . .

Government House, Brisbane   22nd November 1907

My dear Father,

This political crisis in Queensland has been worrying my chief frightfully during the last week. We are at the present moment in the curious position of the Government being carried on by a ministry with Mr. Philp as Premier who has a distinct minority in the House, and therefore he can get no bills passed or business done at all.

H.E. has decided to dissolve Parliament and have a general election. This will be communicated to the House this afternoon. The situation is really owing to having a third party, the Labour party, in the House, who refuse to side with Philp or Kidston, who was Premier a week ago, but support one party on one bill and support the other party when it suits them to do so. There has been a certain amount of unpleasant discussion in the House; some members even strongly hint at the want of impartiality shown by H.E., so they say.

I do not think he will resign but at one time it was touch and go whether he would cable home his resignation, and now it depends on what reply he gets from Lord Elgin* as to whether he stays on as Governor. He feels it is very difficult to remain on in his position if responsible members of the Parliament here question his impartiality with regard to one political party or another. I think he has been treated very badly by his ex-ministers, who appear to feel hurt that when their resignation was offered, he took them at their word and accepted it, and sent for Philp, the other leader of the Opposition, to form a ministry.

I had to take my first message to both Houses the other day. It was the first appearance of the present ministry, the House was packed from roof to floor. I had to go in full kit right up the floor of the House, salute the Speaker, hand him His Excellency's message, which was his assent to various bills, and then with another salute retire, and do the same in the Upper House. It was rather an ordeal, but it went off all right.

* The 9th Earl of Elgin, (1849–1917) was Viceroy of India 1894–99 and Secretary of State for the Colonies, 1905–08.

. . . .

Gabbinbar, Toowoomba   29th December 1907

My dearest Mother,

We had a very fairly good Xmas day. We all drove to church in the morning and we had our Xmas dinner in the evening to which all the children came except Andrew the youngest who had eaten too much mango at lunch and was not therefore in a fit condition to be at the dinner table.

We all dressed up for the dinner. H.E. was got up most awfully well as a caricature of a parson at Brisbane who is well known as a very vain man. I was dressed up as 'Louisa' by the housemaid of that name, who has been with the Chelmsfords for some years. I wore her dress and apron but could not get her cap to stay on my head as my hair was too short. But I had a big hat on with feathers which seemed to have amused the children immensely.

After dinner we danced and I sang 2 songs to my banjo, one of which was 'Oh Ma! I'll never do it again' which has a very good chorus which the children love. Tomorrow is our garden party and the weather does not look too promising for it, but we shall not put it off whatever the weather as it has been put off for the last two years. I expect to have nearly 250 people if it is a fine day.

· ·

Government House, Brisbane   16th February 1908

My dear Father,

I think I told you last week that the election had resulted in a big defeat for Mr. Philp and a great victory for Mr. Kidston and the Labour party. The former resigned yesterday and the latter will be sent for tomorrow morning and asked to form a ministry. It all depends how he behaves whether H.E. stays on as Governor or resigns almost at once. I have been making all enquiries about a boat arriving here at the end of this month so as to have everything ready. But I am quite sure that Kidston, now that he has come back with a big majority, will be only too anxious to do anything to make things run smoothly.

H.E. has written out a letter which he will give to Mr. Kidston saying that he and his ministers have said many times during the last 2 months things which have reflected on H.E.'s impartiality and demanding that a written withdrawal of all these imputations should be published by Mr. Kidston; otherwise H.E. says in his letter it will be impossible for him to remain on as Governor. It is a strong line to take but I do not think for a moment that Kidston will refuse to do as he is asked. What I hope may possibly happen is that Philp's party who are absolutely out of it if Kidston and Labour combine may come over to Kidston in a body in order to defeat the Labour and Socialist party. The members in the House are

Kidston	25
Labour	24
Philp	22
Ind.	1
	72

· ·

Government House, Brisbane   16th February 1908

I have been working very hard this week at typewriting. I have never done much of it before but H.E. wanted a copy of all the secret despatches he has sent home since he came out here and as this could not be done by a clerk I did it nearly all myself. I have been doing it about 4 hours a day and can now do it pretty quickly. It is a useful thing to be able to do though personally I should never use it for letter writing as Uncle Edmund does. I wonder if Harry* ever sees the secret despatches from here. I think some of them are quite excellent.

* 'Claydon' Harry was Lord Elgin's Assistant Private Secretary.

. . . .

Gabbinbar, Toowoomba   21st Feb. 1908

My dear Father,

Things are not going as well as they might from the political point of view just at present. H.E. sent for Kidston on Monday morning who was very anxious to do everything he could to make things go easily but yesterday he refused to sanction the public money expended during the regime of Mr. Philp on the ploy that it had not been sanctioned by Parliament. This has upset H.E. frightfully and Lady C. refuses to go to Sydney on Monday so I have had to cancel our arrangements for that and Fred is going there with Miss Du Cane without us. If Kidston persists in this line of country and tries to bring Mr. Philp up at the Bar of the House for spending public money without authority of Parliament as he once threatened to do it will be extremely unpleasant for H.E. who of course would refuse to sign the warrant as he took the advice of Mr. Philp himself and dissolved parliament in spite of a vote of supply not being granted.

. . . .

Since my letter to Father the other day H.E. has received a very nice private letter from Lord Elgin saying that he quite understood what a difficult position H.E. has been placed in during this political crisis and saying that he hoped he would not think of resigning. This letter has pleased H.E. very much, though as it was marked private he of course cannot make use of it. But probably something official will come by this next mail.

. . . .

Melbourne Club   29th March 1908

My dearest Mother,

It is great news that you have taken Botolph House* for a year and I am very glad indeed that you have done so. I know you will like being so near Aunt Margy and the girls seem delighted. I do not remember the inside of the house much or how much garden there is. I think it is an excellent thing to take it for a year; it will give you time to find out if you all care for it sufficiently to buy it if there is a question of it being possible to do so.

I hear that parliament in Queensland is to be closed in a few weeks and opened again in September. If this is true it will enable H.E. and myself to do that tour to the Gulf of Carpentaria in June which will be the cool weather up there.

*   The Agent's house on the Claydon estate.

. . . .

Government House, Brisbane   April 17th 1908

I have fixed up our garden party for May 27th so that we can get that over before we start for the Northern tour which we do on June 13, returning on Aug. 4th.

I am wondering what Harry is doing now that Lord Elgin is no longer Colonial Sec. Perhaps Lord Crewe* is taking him on. I believe Lord Dudley** will call here on his way to Sydney in September, if so we shall go out to meet him in the *Lucinda*.

*   Robert Crewe-Milnes, 1st Marquess of Crewe (1858–1945), was Secretary of State for the Colonies 1908–10, Secretary of State for India 1910–15.
*   William Humble Ward, 2nd Earl of Dudley (1867–1932), was Lord-Lieutenant of Ireland 1902–06 and Governor-General of Australia 1908–11. In 1924 he married the actress Gertie Millar.

. . . .

Government House, Brisbane   25th April 1908

My dear Father,

The boat that brings this letter also takes home our Premier, Mr. Kidston, who will be in England for about 3 or 4 months. I do not know whether you would care to meet him but if so I should think you could easily do so by asking at the Queensland Agent General's (Sir Horace Tozer's) office wherever they are. It might interest you to have a talk with him about this country though you will not find that he is given to talking much. He was originally one of the Labour party and has a quite useful organ, also Mrs. Kidston. He came here this morning to say goodbye to H.E. and they parted on very good terms.

I should rather like you to meet him and to hear what you think of him but I am afraid you will not find it too easy to make him talk about affairs out here, but have a try.

. . . .

Government House, Brisbane

July 31st 1908

My dearest Mother,

We got back from our tour last Tuesday morning and I am glad to say all went off without a hitch anywhere. I must now try and give you an account of our tour from the beginning to the end as I know you will like to hear about it.

We left Brisbane on June 13th and had a very good passage up to Cairns, stopping for the day at Townsville. We passed through Cairns by train to Kuranda where we stayed at a delightful hotel close to the Barron Falls which are quite one of the sights of Queensland.

Colin Bell and I went out shooting in the afternoon and we got some pigeon and two scrub turkeys. The bush here is much more like jungle than anything I have yet seen in Queensland. We went on from there next day to Irvinebank where there are some large smelters of a copper mine 1250 feet deep which we went down. Mr. Moffat, with whom we stayed, has been here for 30 years and has built the whole thing himself.

We branched off the main line at Boowmoo and had to go in a small train with a gauge of only 2 ft. 6 ins. H.E. had a very good reception there but I think the morning we spent going round the works there was the most tiring we had all through our tour. It was very hot indeed and it took us quite three hours going over the whole show, the smelters, crushing machines etc. We then left for Chillagoe where we stayed with a Mr. Bach and saw the caves there which are supposed to be very beautiful but they are not nearly as fine as the caves I saw in N.S.W. called the Jenolan Caves last March.

We went from Chillagoe by train to Mount Surprise where we took to our buggies and started the driving part of the tour as that was the end of the railway. I was quite astonished at the amount of luggage that can be packed onto a buggy which is a four-wheeled trap with the ordinary driver's seat and another seat just behind it. We had two of these buggies and we did the whole 810 miles driving in them without a single breakdown.

The first buggy was driven by Mr. Bell, the Minister for Lands, with 6 horses and the second had 4 horses. I drove this one for a great many miles during the tour as I was very glad to have the chance of learning to drive 4 horses. The first day we did about 35 miles and stayed at a place called Ambo for the night.

We went on from there to Georgetown where we stayed two nights and had a ball given in H.E.'s honour. From Georgetown we went to Forest

80

Home where we stayed for the Sunday with Mr. and Mrs. Wilson. He is the manager of the station which is about 1500 sq. miles in size. We had a very good duck shoot there one morning standing on screened platforms in the middle of a big lagoon. We got about 100 duck in 2 or 3 hours' shooting. On this station they have about 30,000 head of cattle altogether which gives you some idea of the size of the farms out here though this was not the largest place we stayed at.

From Forest Home we went to Croydon in one day which was 65 miles. Before we got to Georgetown we had to cross the Newcastle range which was frightfully steep with a bad road. A great many people drove out 5 miles from Croydon to meet us and escorted us into the town which was decorated with flags and Chinese lanterns. The night we arrived there we attended a smoking concert which was really a sort of supper where I had to make my first speech in responding to the health of the visitors. I had to speak three times altogether although it is not strictly etiquette for me to speak in the presence of H.E. Croydon is entirely a mining town and we were taken down the mine sitting on the edge of buckets and holding onto the rope which let us down. H.E. and I went like this but the two Bells shirked it. The mine was frightfully wet and very rough walking underground but it was very interesting.

We had another dance at Croydon which we enjoyed immensely. These dances were more like servants' dances at home, the D'Alberts being the favourite dance in the programme also 'Varsorrana' and the Schottische, with always a Master of Ceremonies to direct the dancers what to do next.

From Croydon we went by train to Normanton which was not so flourishing a town by any means, but we had another duck shoot there which ought to have been very good but was badly managed and so we hardly got any duck at all. From Normanton we took to buggies again on the road to Burktown and we then began our camping out. We took two tents, one for H.E. and one for the Minister for Lands, and I fixed up a big tarpaulin over the two buggies which made another one for Colin Bell and myself. We had about 11 nights camping out altogether.

On the way to Burktown we stayed at a place called Inverleigh with a Mr. Cobbold and we had some excellent pigeon shooting in the evening. They were small brown birds called flock pigeon and they were very difficult to hit as they flew very fast indeed. At Burktown we had another small concert and another duck shoot. After five days' driving we then arrived at Rocklands which is a large station right on the western border of Queensland. It is about 3000 sq. miles in size. We crossed the border

81

fence and went into the Northern Territory which is really part of South Australia and is under the government of S.A.

The boundary fence is a strong post and rail fence with rabbit wire. This rabbit wire is now completely round the whole of Queensland in order to keep out the rabbits which have done so much harm in Australia so that it is quite impossible for a bunny to come into Queensland at all now and where the railway crosses over the border in the south big pits have been dug which the rabbits cannot cross. Mr. Glissan was our host at Rocklands and we had a little more duck shooting there.

We only stayed at Camooweal for two hours on our way back from Rocklands. There are only about 60 inhabitants in Camooweal altogether. They gave us a lunch, after which we continued our journey in the buggies towards Cloncurry. We had to camp out every night of this part of the journey as there were no stations we could stay at. The road was pretty good until the last two days and then it beggars description! The road in this country is any track along which a wheeled vehicle has passed and the only way in which roads are made is by the wheels of the buggies passing over it. We had to cross rocky beds of rivers which had had nothing at all done to them to make them easier for driving over. We also had to go through sandy river beds, the sand sometimes being many inches deep and it was all the horses could do to pull us through. People in England would think it quite impossible to drive over or through the places which in this country are not thought to be anything out of the way.

In fact the road we came over is the ordinary route and the only route for the Mails reaching Camooweal and in time of floods the people there have to go without letters for months together.

When we got to within 7 miles of Cloncurry we were met by about 50 of the principal people and I have got a photo of that which I will send to Gwen when my others are ready. We had another smoking concert there the first night and a ball the next evening and in the afternoon we were taken down the Great Australian Mine. The manager of this mine was a charming man called Allabaster who had been in the Royal Artillery in S.A. He was married and his wife was also very nice.

We had now finished the driving part of the tour, having done 810 miles over some frightfully rough roads without a breakdown of any sort or kind. Though we all enjoyed it immensely we were glad to see the railway once more. We started by special train from Cloncurry at midday on July 23rd. We arrived at 1 p.m. at Townsville the next day where we embarked onboard the *Bombala*, arriving back in Brisbane early on Tuesday morning.

This is the longest tour that had ever been made by any Governor in Queensland, taking into consideration the number of miles we had to do by driving as there's no other way of doing it at present. The whole tour was about 3300 miles. I took about 6 doz. photos altogether and I shall send those that come out well to Gwen during the next fortnight.

Ever your affect.
Ralph

P.S.   I haven't told you how we managed about our horses which was one of the most important arrangements to be made. We used about 275 horses altogether which we hired from different people. From Mt. Surprise to Croydon the man who drives the coach with the Mails furnished our horses which were posted along the road at distances of about 15 miles. From Normanton to the other side of Burktown the same arrangement was made until we met Inspector McGrath who came out to meet us from Cloncurry over 300 miles with 45 horses. Those we were not using were either driven in a mob by black boys behind our buggies or sent on very early in the morning and we picked them up and so had a fairly fresh lot about the middle of the day. The same teams of horses did as a rule about 20 miles and then we had a change. On the whole they were a very good lot of horses and wonderfully quiet. I had a lot of practice driving 4 horses and enjoyed it immensely.

· ·

Government House, Brisbane   August 16th 1908

My dearest Mother,

I am glad to say that this week has passed off very well. Our dance on Tuesday was I think a great success though we had 750 guests which was a great crush at first. On Wednesday morning H.E. opened the Brisbane show and directly after lunch I put on a straw hat and short coat and drove his pair of horses round the ring in one of the events. I got first prize and after the judges had tied the blue ribbon onto the horses' necks I picked up H.E. and drove him round the ring. There was a great crowd of 48000 people that day and the weather was absolutely perfect and has been so during the whole week.

· ·

83

Government House, Brisbane   Sept. 6th 1908

My dearest Mother,

I started out at 7.45 p.m. and drove to Pinkenbah to meet Lord Dudley. I
went on board and had breakfast with him and Ruthven, his A.D.C. At
10.30 H.E. came in the *Lucinda* and we took Lord Dudley up the river
back to Brisbane just for the trip. We then went back down the river and
out into Moreton Bay and put him on board the *Powerful* which takes him
to Sydney. I liked him very much indeed.

On Wednesday the Northcotes arrive and stay with us till Friday. We
have a large garden party here for them on Thursday and a banquet in the
evening given by the Mayor.

. . . .

Government House, Brisbane   Sept. 12th 1908

My dearest Mother,

The Northcotes have come and gone and I think their visit was a great
success. On Thursday we had a garden party here of about 1200 people
altogether. We had a perfect day for it and I think everybody enjoyed it
very much. They left yesterday evening by special train to Pinkenbah and I
went with them on board the boat to say goodbye. I was the first of the staff
to welcome Lord Dudley and the last to say goodbye to the Northcotes.

. . . .

Government House, Brisbane   Sept. 19th 1908

My dear Father,

In the Colonial Office Mail this week came a despatch from Lord Crewe
asking a lot of information about the education in Australia to answer a
question by you in the House. I took the despatch in to H.E. who was
much amused and told me I must really stop my father from asking these
questions as they give a lot of bother to answer. Of course he was only
chaffing. It was rather funny to get a letter from Lord Crewe asking for
information in order to answer the question put in the House by 'Mr.
F. W. Verney M.P.' I do not know whether you will get the required
information but I have forwarded on the letter to our Minister for
Education.

. . . .

Union Club, Sydney   November 8th 1908

My dearest Mother,

We returned from Melbourne this morning and I have enjoyed the week quite immensely. The Dudleys were most charming in every way and though they keep up greater ceremony than the Northcotes did on state occasions yet it is a most comfortable house to stay in.

On Wednesday we played golf in the afternoon and there was a full dress ball at Gov. House in the evening which began at 9.30 p.m. Their Ex's came down at 10 p.m. and we formed up in procession. I led the procession with Capt. Rome. We walked in at the bottom of the Ballroom and then walked right up to the dais at the top. It looked very impressive with all the uniforms. The Governors were all in their uniforms too, Sir George Le Hunt, Sir Harry Rawson and my chief were the Governors staying in the house. The first is Governor of South Australia.

On Thursday we drove out racing again and in the evening I went to a most delightful dance given by the Armitages. I only got home at 5.30 a.m.!!! On Friday there was a big garden party at Government House and another dance in the evening to which I went and enjoyed it immensely.

I do not think I have ever enjoyed a week so much in my life. Tomorrow we return to Queensland. I am sending you a group of the House party at Government House for the book. I will send it to Gwen next week.

Lady Dudley very kindly asked me to go and stay with them for as long as I like when my chief goes home next April, so I hope to be able to pay them another visit then.

When we went out to the Club races on Tuesday we had a very smart turnout indeed. With outriders, postillions, two A.D.C.s mounted as equerries, we drove down the course the same as last year.

. . . .

Government House, Brisbane   14th November 1908

My dearest Mother,

This week we had a big official dinner party in honour of the King's birthday. We sat down 33 altogether, it went off very well except that the Military Commandant never turned up for it. At first I thought that I must have forgotten to ask him but on looking through the acceptances I found his among them. He had forgotten all about it and came in full uniform next morning with an abject apology.

Today we have had a big review of about 2000 troops in the Domain at Government House, also in honour of the King's birthday. It was quite imposing and there was a very large crowd to watch it. The only contretemps was that during the royal salute our cows escaped and came galloping down the line which delighted the crowd hugely. The band, which was at that moment playing the National Anthem, saw these cows and were so amused that they could not play. The big drum was the only instrument that finished the National Anthem that time!!

. . . .

Government House, Brisbane   November 22nd 1908

Lady C. is very keen about the pure milk question now. A report came out a few months ago to say that about 1000 babies die every year in Queensland chiefly owing to bad milk and so Lady C. is having a big drawingroom meeting on Wednesday to discuss the possibility of establishing a depot for supplying pure milk in Brisbane. I think I ought to know a good deal about the method of educating and feeding children at all ages pretty soon as I attend meetings with Lady C. of the Child Study Assoc., the Greche kindergarden and now the Pure Milk Depot!

. . . .

Gabbinbar, Toowoomba   19th December 1908

My dearest Mother,

H.E. very kindly asked me today whether I should like him to bring out one of my sisters with them next October. It is a great help to Lady C. having a girl living in the house in many ways and since Miss Du Cane went home we have had no one. I think Kathleen would be most useful and I am sure she would like it. She would be away from home for at least 6 months, perhaps a year and would leave England next September.

It is very kind of the Chelmsfords who of course proposed it without my suggesting such a thing. I should like to have an idea by the next mail whether you would approve of the plan though do not write to H.E. or Lady C. about it but arrange it when you see them at home next May.

I have suggested Kathleen instead of Gwen as she is stronger and more able to stand long journeys.

. . . .

Gabbinbar, Toowoomba   January 31st 1909

Our plans are very uncertain. There is no harm in my telling you that it is
more than probable that H.E. will be given the Governorship of N.S.W.,
as when you get this letter it will have been settled a long time. This will
mean our leaving Queensland altogether at the beginning of May. I shall
therefore have to wire to you to put off Kathleen's coming, as the
Chelmsfords will go home for 6 months in October and we shall be too
busy to have her out here at first. She might perhaps return with them in
March of next year but that is supposing I stay on with him in N.S.W.

. . . .

Government House, Brisbane   27th March 1909

My dearest Kathleen,

We are very interested to hear that Sir W. MacGregor* is to be my chief's
successor here as Governor. Batty** told me he wrote and asked Harry to
appoint somebody young and with a sense of humour with the result that
somebody over 60 years of age and a man of science has got it!! However, I
think that in many ways the appointment will be popular out here as he is
well known in N. Guinea.

* Sir William MacGregor (1847–1919); Governor of Lagos 1899–1904; of Newfound-
land 1904–09; of Queensland 1909–14.
** The Rt. Rev. Francis Batty (1879–1961) was Domestic Chaplain to the Archbishop of
Brisbane, 1904–15; Dean of Brisbane Cathedral 1915–25; Coadjutor-Bishop of
Brisbane, 1930–31; Bishop of Newcastle N.S.W. 1931–58. He was a great personality
in Queensland. When asked to say Grace, he was apt to come out with:
            Rabbits young and rabbits old,
            Rabbits hot and rabbits cold,
            Rabbits tender, rabbits tough;
            Thank the lord, I've had enough!

. . . .

Government House, Brisbane   April 3rd 1909

I got a letter from Harry in the C.O. bag this mail. I think our plans are
fixed now. Lady C. will go home with Joan and Anne in November. I am
afraid that my chief's appointment to N.S.W. had nothing to do with the
many alterations to our plans in January. The telegram giving us the first
information of any change was received by me at Gabbinbar and so I knew
the possibility before H.E. as a matter of fact. I wonder if Harry codes the
telegrams that come out to us. It would be rather curious if he sends them
and I decode them here as I always do when Capt. Newton is away.

. . . .

Government House, Brisbane   28th April 1909

My dearest Mother,

I must give you an account of our visit to Thursday Island which we left a week ago today. I think it was one of the most interesting trips I have ever done in my life. We arrived there at 8 a.m. on Tuesday, April 13th and were met at the wharf by Mr. Hugh Milman, the Government Resident, who introduced the principal men of the place to H.E. when they came on board to meet him. We then went up to the Residency where we met Mrs. and Miss Milman.

In the afternoon H.E. held an informal levee in order to give everybody an opportunity of meeting him. When that little function was over we went out in a steam launch to get some coral. Thursday Island is practically part of the Great Barrier Reef which extends up the East Coast of Queensland from Rockhampton and is one of the most dangerous reefs for navigation in the world. In half an hour we got the most wonderful collection of coral you can imagine of every size, shape, colour and description.

The natives who came out with us in the boat get into the water which was only a few feet deep and simply picked it up in armfuls. It was of course nothing out of the ordinary to them but to us it was most wonderful. Some of it was like little blue flowers, some like big green vegetables, some like white heather and so on until we had got the boat nearly full of it. That evening we dined at the Residency.

On Thursday morning we started off with Mr. Hockings on a 2 days expedition to an island called 'The Prince of Wales Island' which is close to Thursday Island only much bigger, being about 69 sq. miles in size while Thursday Island is only about 3 miles across. We rode after wild pig and got 7 altogether. We took dogs with us and when a pig was sighted the dogs gave chase and caught the pig and hung on to its ears until we came up and tied it with rope. We were riding but the grass was very long, often over our heads while we were riding and the ground in some places was very boggy so that it was impossible to get along very fast. We met the launch again the other side of the island and then steamed round to a nice sandy beach where we camped for the night.

In the evening we dug in the sand for turtles' eggs. There are a great many turtles here and they come out of the water on to the sand in order to lay their eggs. They leave great tracks in the sand and when they have got above high-water mark they dig a big hole in the sand, lay their eggs and then cover them up again, but they are very clever about hiding the place. They will often dig 2 or 3 holes before they lay. The way we found out

88

where the eggs were was with the help of a pointed stick which we dug into the ground and then looked to see if there was any mark of egg in the point. In one nest we found 86 eggs which were exactly like ping-pong balls in size and colour. I put these altogether and took a photo of them.

Besides turtles there were any number of crocodiles and though we did not actually see one we saw their tracks in every direction. Where we camped next day we went out to a lugger which was at work with a diver onboard. This was most interesting but I will explain later on about that. We returned to Thursday Island on Friday afternoon and in the evening we went to dine with the officers of the garrison.

On the way to the Mess we had a most amusing accident. There was only one cab on the Island and that was driven by an old man called Joyce. H.E. and I were sitting one side of the cab and Mr. Milman was the other. It was raining hard and we were in evening dress. I was wearing a stiff evening tail coat. About half-way there without any warning Joyce upset the cab into a ditch 5 feet deep full of running water. We were going over a plank bridge and he drove over the side as it was very dark. Luckily we were not hurt.

I got out first by climbing over H.E. and Mr. Milman on top of whom we had both fallen and out through the box of the cab. H.E. followed me but Mr. M. who is quite an old man and rather peppery would do nothing but sit there and growl out, 'Stupid old ass, the silly old donkey'. However, we got him out in the end and arrived very late for dinner and very untidy but that did not matter much.

On Saturday morning the Mayor and about 30 other people came out with us to see some diving and to show as much as possible of the pearl fishing industry. The pearl shell is what the divers go down for and not the pearl itself as I had always thought. Of course the pearl itself is valuable but the shell is what makes the industry profitable as they very rarely find a good pearl.

The diver is nearly always a Japanese as it is too hard a life for the native man. They remain down for perhaps two hours at a time and if they find 30 shells in a day it is a good day's find. The shell is not easy to find as it is usually almost hidden in the sand and covered by weed and coral. It is about 10 inches in size and it is opened with a big knife and the fish which is like a big oyster taken out of the shell and carefully examined to see if there's a pearl in it, but as I said before this is very rare.

On the Friday afternoon, the diver on board the boat we went on found 5 shells while we were there, but this time the diver went down more for the sake of showing us how it was done. I had been very keen indeed to go down myself and did so on Saturday morning.

I watched the Japanese diver first most carefully to see how he dressed himself etc. I had to take off all my clothes and put on very thick underclothing with long stockings and a big jersey. I was then helped into the rubber diving dress which is all of one piece from the foot to the neck. A metal shoulder plate was then screwed on to the rubber dress by means of thumb screws, on to which the helmet was fixed by a many-threaded screw. My diving boots were heavily weighted with lead and each boot weighed about 16 lbs. I went to the side of the ship and got over onto a rope ladder which was hung over the side. Big lead weights were put on my chest and back, each of 56 lbs., and were tied on with cord. My helmet was then screwed on and I was told exactly how to regulate the tap in it which controlled the escape of air so that by tightening it I could keep the air in and make myself lighter or by opening it I could allow the air to escape and I should become heavier.

When I was ready the front glass was screwed on to the helmet and I was absolutely cut off from all communication with the outer world. I then dropped off the ladder and down I went. The life line was tied around me. This is used to signal up to the 'tender' who is a man holding the other end of the line on board the boat and who is responsible for one's safety. A diver will choose his tender very carefully as of course his life depends on having an absolutely reliable man.

The pain from the pressure going down was intense on the drum of the ears but by swallowing 2 or 3 times the pain was relieved at once. But for a few seconds while going down the pain was pretty bad. When I got to the bottom I was not able to do much at first. The water that day was rather thick. In fact it reminded me of a London fog and I could only see a few yards in front of me. After a little I was able to walk about. The bottom was all sand and there were no shells at all. It is usual for a beginner to go down in 3 or 4 fathoms but it was deeper than that where I went down. It was 6¼ fathoms. After 5 minutes I was getting to feel quite at home when I felt a pull at my life line which meant that I was to come up so I returned the pull and was hauled up again. I struggled onto the rope ladder and leaning over the side of the ship my helmet was taken off and I got quite a hearty reception! H.E. was beginning to get a little nervous about me and told them to pull me up. I was photoed in my diver's dress and will send a copy to Gwen as soon as I get it. It was certainly one of the most interesting experiences I have ever had.

On Monday we had a big corroborree of all the natives from the surrounding island. They came dressed up as devils and all sorts of things and did several of their peculiar dances. But they were much better in the evening when they did it all again round a huge bonfire when they looked most weird. One dance they all carried models of seagulls on the top of long sticks and, as they all came dancing slowly into the arena, all these gulls wings waved about, they were so very cleverly made.

In the evening the Inspector of Police came up to me and said one of the chiefs wanted to present me with one of these gulls, so he was brought up and solemnly presented it to me. I shook him by the hand and thanked him very much for it. A lot of spears and maskes etc. were given to H.E. which we have brought back for the children.

This letter is already becoming a very long one but I do not feel I have half told you about all the interesting things we saw. One thing was delightful and that was the number of coconuts. There were many coconut plantations which we visited and where we saw the natives run up the trees without any help to bring the coconuts down for us. They were wonderful at it and simply ran up the tree with bare feet and hands as easily as possible. I took some photos of this which I hope will come out. I brought about 20 big coconuts back for the children.

I am very fit and well.

Ever your affect.
Ralph

. . . .

Government House, Brisbane   May 22nd 1909

My dearest Mother,

We shall leave this house at 3.30 p.m. next Wednesday afternoon in 2 motors and as soon as H.E. steps on board the *Cooma* she will start. The streets are already being decorated and I think there will be a great send off. Tomorrow night H.E. is being given an official dinner at Parliament House by the Ministers. I shall not be there as Mr. Forrest, the President of the Queensland Club, is giving me a farewell dinner party there. Batty is coming to this. I am not looking forward to it as I shall have to get up and make a short speech.

On Tuesday we lunch with the Commandant and in the evening the Queensland Club is giving H.E. a big dinner to say goodbye. I think there will be over 100 there that night dining. On that afternoon H.E. receives a farewell address here at Government House and the Mayor and Aldermen come up and say goodbye.

Tomorrow H.E. and I go to the races and lunch with the Committee. On Thursday last a special train left Brisbane with 11 horses, 4 carriages and 136 large packing cases. It was nice of them to arrange it for that night so that I could have one more dance before leaving Queensland. These dances are much the best in Brisbane.

. . . .

State Government House, Sydney   May 29th 1909

My dearest Mother,

H.E. and Lady C. had a most splendid send off from Queensland. I took the children down to the *Cooma* in the first Government Motor a few minutes before they came in the 2nd motor with Capt. Newton.

We left the people on the wharf at Brisbane to the tune of Auld Lang Syne, many of them in tears, and I felt quite chokey myself! I have had a very happy two years there and I have had work to do which I really liked and I think have done successfully. Whether I shall be able to say the same after two years here I do not know.

. . . .

... *Chapter Five* ...

In May, 1909, Lord Chelmsford is made Governor of New South Wales and takes Ralph with him as his Secretary. Ralph marries Miss Nita Walker and they return to England on leave. The Chelmsfords also return to England and come back with Ralph's sister Kathleen to Sydney. Kathleen marries an Australian, Frank Newton, and Ralph and Nita go on leave to New Zealand before returning to England via Eastern Asia and the Trans-Siberian Railway.

. . . .

State Government House, Sydney   June 1909

My dear Father,

H.E. offered me this morning and I accepted it the job of his private secretary at the end of this year. I shall still be officially his A.D.C. as the War Office does not recognize the job of private secretary as a military appointment. But H.E. will get somebody else out from home to be extra A.D.C. under me and I shall be private secretary. I shall have to be responsible for the A.D.C.'s work as well as that of private secretary, but I shall have someone else to do the drudgery of the A.D.C.'s job which will be much nicer for me.

. . . .

State Government House, Sydney   June 13th 1909

My dearest Mother,

My great news this week is that I have bought my motor car. I have got a 9 horse power Renault which will hold 2 people or 3 without much of a squash. I have already driven H.E. out to the golf links and I went to the pier near here yesterday to fetch Lady Poore who came to lunch. I had a man up here for an hour on Thursday morning and also in the evening to teach me something about its inside. But I really know nothing at all about it but have been quite successful so far in starting it and driving it and I am very careful.

· ·

State Government House, Sydney   August 2nd 1909

My dearest Mother,

I have been staying for the Sunday at a most lovely place called Yaralla with a Miss Walker*. It is only about 8 miles from here and I went in my motor. Miss Walker is a lady of about 45 or more, she is very rich and has this lovely place which is just like a country house in England. We played tennis hard all day and played the pianola hard nearly all night!!

* Dame Eadith Walker, the daughter of the founder of the Bank of New South Wales, was Nita's aunt. Nita's father, Senator Hon. James T. Walker, was one of the six senators who drew up the Australian constitution. It was he who chose Canberra as the site of the Federal Government.

· ·

State Government House, Sydney   August 13th 1909

My dear Miss Nita,

Here is another lesson in shorthand. Our dinner party went off very well this evening. I have written to Miss Knox saying that I will come to tennis on Thursday afternoon, though I may not be able to be there until about 12.45 p.m. when we get back from church. Perhaps I might come early in the afternoon and we could do some shorthand in the garden before any visitors come.

· ·

State Government House, Sydney   August 16th 1909

My own darling Nita,

I can't go to bed tonight without writing a few lines to you first. Is it real or is it a dream? That is what I feel at present. Can it really be that these last weeks of worry and mental strain are over, and that you care for me? It seems to me almost too wonderful to be true. You helped me to speak today Nita because if you had shown the least coldness, or had seemed to me the least bit angry with me I could not have spoken. I WAS in a funk, and no mistake!!! Oh Nita how happy I am, and how I will try and be all that you deserve in the way of a husband! I always wondered what it would be like to be engaged, but now I know, and so long as I am with you, I am absolutely content.

. . . .

State Government House, Sydney   August 19th 1909

My dear Mrs. Walker,

I am longing for your return on Monday to tell you something that I think you have known for some little time.

Nita is also writing to you today, and we do hope that you and Senator Walker will give your consent as soon as you return.

We have not said a word about it yet, even to Sissie, but I don't suppose she has been blind during the last few weeks!!

. . . .

Nita to her Parents

Wallaroy, Sydney   August 19th 1909

Dearest Father and Mother,

This is to prepare you for Ralph's letter which I think he is writing this mail. Do you think you could consent to our engagement? It would make us both so very very happy. Ever since Ralph asked me to marry him last Monday I have been living in a dream wondering if any one ever felt so happy before. We thought we would wait and ask you when you came back but poor old Ralph is in such a state of anxiety and so hates acting in front of everyone as if there was nothing between us that he rang up on the telephone this morning and said he could stand it no longer but was writing to you then.

You know we have known each other for six months now as we met first at Sutton Forest when he was staying with the Rawsons last February and then I saw him several times before he went to Queensland. If you remember he wrote to me when up there and I answered, well even then he liked me very much.

Ralph is very like you Father in some ways, he doesn't care for racing, cards or gambling. He is just a clean-minded honest Englishman whom any girl would be proud to love, honour and obey.

Ever your loving daughter,
Nita

. . . .

State Government House, Sydney   August 19th 1909

My dearest Mother,

I have got some news for you this week which will cause intense excitement in the family. I do not think I have given you a hint about it up to the present. I am engaged to be married!!!!!

At the last Melbourne Cup I saw but was not introduced to Miss Nita Walker the second daughter of Senator and Mrs. Walker, both of whom Uncle George and Aunt Margy knew in Brisbane 40 years ago. I was introduced to her by Capt. Wilson when I was staying with the Rawsons at Hill View last February and we met several times in Sydney when I came back from my fishing trip. During the last 2½ months we have been seeing each other almost every day and though we have only known each other just over 6 months we have quite made up our minds.

. . . .

State Government House, Sydney   August 24th 1909

My dear Father,

I think H.E. is writing to you by this mail to tell you that he is really pleased about my engagement and that Nita is a girl whom you will really approve of in every way. I do not think that I said in my letter to mother that Mrs. Abel Smith who I think is a cousin of ours knows Nita and was very kind to her about 2 years ago when she was in England.

I only told my chief about this last night and he and Lady C. were quite perfectly charming about it. I found them sitting up in the drawingroom when I came back after dining with the Walkers and H.E. took me into his room and said 'My dear boy, there is only one girl in Sydney nice enough for you, and she is Miss Nita Walker'. Wasn't that nice of him? He told me he would write to you without my suggesting it at all and said he could honestly congratulate you all about it.

. . . .

State Government House, Sydney   Aug. 29th 1909

I shall hate not having any of you at my wedding but unless I do this I shall not be able to come home for perhaps 18 months or more. H.E. was very strong in his advice to me to go home for a trip as soon as I am married and you will get to know Nita and she will get to know you all. I think I shall like being here as a married man and H.E's private Secretary very much indeed.

I would not ask him for this because I thought he might not care to keep me on as a married man and he would not offer it to me because he thought I would rather leave his staff altogether, but we finally discovered that we both really wished for the same thing and so that is settled, providing everything else can be settled alright.

. . . .

State Government House, Sydney   Sept. 5th 1909

My dearest Mother,

I am to be married on Nov. 11th which is a Thursday. We go to a beautiful place near here called Yaralla belonging to Miss Eadith Walker, a cousin of Nita's, from the Thursday to the Sunday when we go to Melbourne where we stay for Monday night and then we embark onboard the *Orontes*, sailing from Melbourne on Nov. 16th. We shall arrive in London on Dec. 19th by getting off the boat at Naples and coming overland from there.

If you're going to Claydon for Xmas we will come there for a few days, if they will have us, though our time in England will be so short that we shall not be able to stay for more than a few days.

. . . .

State Government House, Sydney   Sept. 19th 1909

H.E. and Lady C. are giving me a silver breakfast dish and two silver meat dishes as a wedding present. It is kind of them. They are not ready yet as he is having a crest put on them.

Capt. Gilliat in the R.B. is to be my best man. You will remember him coming to lunch at home and singing, 'Sing me the songs of Arabee' in the drawingroom afterwards.

. . . .

State Government House, Sydney   Sept. 27th 1909

My dearest Mother,

Lady Dudley has given Nita the most wonderful wedding veil you ever saw. It is of very old Honiton Lace and quite exquisite. It really is most kind of her and she wrote such a charming little letter beginning 'my dear Nita' and ending up 'your affect. Rachel Dudley'. Wedding presents are beginning to come in.

. . . .

State Government House, Sydney   October 19th 1909

My dearest Mother,

Your letters are full of the Budget. I must congratulate Father most
awfully on voting with the Opposition. I do not give up all hope yet of
turning him into a real good old 'Tory'. Now that he has broken the ice I
hope he will do it again.

Lady C. will arrive in England on Dec. 12th. She will go and stay for 10
days at an hotel and then go up to Cumberland for Xmas, so you must try
and see her as soon as she arrives. Old Lady C. will know at what hotel she
is staying.

. . . .

State Government House, Sydney   24th October 1909

My dearest Mother,

This week we are off to Melbourne to stay with the Dudleys for the
Melbourne Cup, and we shall meet Napier there. I am so amused about
that cable and Harry telling you about it, which we sent home for another
A.D.C. I wrote that cable myself and was wondering at the time whether
Harry would see it. How little did you think what the real reason of it was.

I think that there are nearly 400 acceptances for the wedding already.
Nita has asked a great many children and at the tea afterwards we shall
have a big table for all the children.

Lady C. found such a very pretty pendant the other day in Sydney. It is 5
tourmalines set with diamonds. She wanted H.E. to give it to her but he
would not, so I got it as my present for Nita. I know it must be in good taste
if Lady C. liked it.

. . . .

Nita to Ralph's mother

Walloroy, Sydney   November 2nd 1909

My dear Mrs. Verney,

Words fail me when I start to tell you how deeply I feel the sweet welcome
you have given me. All the kind letters I have received this mail have made
me very happy. I only wish Ralph had been here in Sydney when I got
them. This is the first time since we became engaged that we have missed
reading the home mail together.

98

I wish I could tell you how much Ralph's love and companionship means to me. I only hope that in the years to come he will ever find me ready by his side to share in his sorrows or pleasures. I know how you must be longing to be with Ralph on his wedding day. It seems hard that your boy should be married so far away from you, and Ralph too feels it very much.

It was very kind of Lady Verney to send me the Verney memoirs. I have been wanting to read them for some time, but could not get them out here.

With love from your affect.
Janette Walker

. . . .

Government House, Melbourne   3rd November 1909

My dearest Mother,

No words can say how happy your letters by this mail have made Nita and myself. I knew you would be pleased but did not quite expect you all to enter into my happiness quite so splendidly as you have done. Nita sent me a telegram yesterday simply to tell me how very very happy your letters had made her. I am so longing to show her all your letters on Saturday. How pleased you will all have been when you get my letters announcing that we will be coming home for Xmas.

. . . .

R.M.S. *Orontes*   December 5th 1909

My dearest Mother,

It was such a pleasure to us to get your letters at Colombo and such a bundle arrived. We had a delightful day ashore there, we went to a place called Mt. Lavinia for lunch and were able to stay onshore until 7 p.m. We hope to be able to stay some time at Botolph House though we shall probably be in London for one day on our arrival as Nita has never seen the shops in town decorated for Xmas and is most anxious to do so.

If it is convenient we shall be bringing a maid with us to Botolph House as she is staying on with Nita as long as she is wanted. If you cannot put her up in the house, could you make some arrangement for her to sleep close by? Please tell Gwen that there is no need to get us a maid during our first fortnight or so in England. MacDonald the present one is very Scotch and very nice indeed.

. . . .

Ralph to Mrs Walker

Claydon House   29th December 1909

My dear Mummy,

Here we are, having a very happy Xmas, and Nita has been made quite one of the family party, and has of course captured the hearts of all my family. Many thanks for your very generous present which Macdonald gave me on Xmas day. It was very naughty of you to do it and had you told me beforehand I should not have taken it, but I cannot scold you properly at a distance of 12000 miles!!

We had a very jolly stay in Paris for two days, and went to see Sarah Bernhardt in Joan of Arc; we had neither of us seen her, so we were very anxious to. My father met us at Charing Cross and we stayed 2 nights in London, before coming down here. We arrived at Verney junction here and were met by all the Verney family at the station, and we drove in procession back to Botolph House.

Lady Chelmsford is coming to stay here next week and so is her boy Fred. I think very likely my sister Kathleen will be coming out with her in March.

We have had some village festivities here, such as a tenants' tea and party, servants' Xmas tree, and tomorrow is a workmen's dinner. At all of these functions Nita has been the chief attraction, being taken in and introduced to them all by my Uncle.

My father is in the middle of his election, which ends on Jan. 19th the polling day; I think he is certain to get in by a good majority. Harry, from here, is standing for S. Wiltshire, and I am going down there for the polling day and the declaration, but shall not take Nita.*

Your affect.
Ralph

* Standing as a Liberal for Buchingham, Ralph's father gained 6055 votes, only narrowly defeating his Conservative opponent, Hon. T. Fremantle (5944 votes). The result of the South Wiltshire election was: C. Bathurst (Con.), 4541; H. C. W. Verney (Lib.), 3894.

· ·

The County Hotel, Salisbury   January 21st 1910

My own darling Nita,

We have had a very delightful day's motoring, although it has been a long one. We did 130 miles altogether; it was very cold to start with, but I was well wrapped up. I don't think Harry has much chance from what I can see, but it may be a close fight. I am going into the counting room with Harry, as Ellin is not going to the declaration at all, as it is sure to be pretty rowdy; but Harry and I are going to get away somehow about a quarter of an hour after the declaration. The police know this and I don't think we shall have much difficulty in doing this with their help.

. . . .

Nita to Ralph's Mother

Grand Central Hotel, London   February 4th 1910

My dear Mother,

I hope you won't mind my writing thus but I feel I can no longer call Ralph's mother Mrs. Verney. You were so very sweet and kind to me and it is perfectly delightful to know that I have a mother at both ends of the world. I enjoyed those first few days I had alone with you all at Botolph House so much getting to know Ralph's parents and sisters.

It will be a very very great joy having Kathleen out there, and I hope she will always realize that Honiton is always ready for her whenever she wants to come. I am so glad that she will see our first home and only wish that you could be there too, we must try and take some good photos of it and send them home.

Ever your affectionate
Janette Verney

. . . .

R.M.S. *Orsova*   February 9th 1910

My dearest Mother,

We have been very lucky indeed in the weather. The Bay treated us very well and we have not had it at all rough the whole way. Yesterday we landed at Gibraltar but only for an hour but we enjoyed it immensely. We drove in a cab to Point Europa and the dry dock. Nita was immensely interested in the place as she had never been there before.

. . . .

23rd February 1910

Dear Mr. Walker,

I feel confident that you will agree with me in thinking that money matters would not occupy a principal place in love making a marriage. And yet it must be considered by the older people. In most cases all the arrangements are of course made before the marriage takes place, but owing to the shortness of time, and the gap in distance, this has been impossible in the case in which we are so much interested.

In order to largely lighten the burden of succession duty which must be born by those who come after me I have lately insured my life for a very heavy sum (£10,000). But owing to various increases in parliamentary and other forms of expenditure, for which provision has to be made, it is very doubtful whether it will be possible for me to keep up the large annual payments for premium which have been made by me for the past two years. Before coming to any decision on this subject I should be glad to know what your daughter's fortune is likely to be, if you are perfectly willing to give me this information confidentially.

I have transferred to my son stocks yielding about £350 a year, and propose to add to this a sum which will bring his income up to £500 a year. He will some day have £700 a year under the Will of his great Uncle as well as a considerable income, perhaps some £2000 a year, from mineral property which I now have. But this is a fluctuating amount dependent on the coal trade, and also is a wasting property. It was only possible for me to insure in this way some two years ago, and, at my age, the premium is necessarily a very large one. It is payable in November of each year. By writing to you now there is therefore plenty of time to send me any information which you may think well to give before it is necessary to decide whether any and what modification must be made in the arrangement that now obtains. I have a horror of the younger generation being burdened by the debts of those whom they succeed, and although death duties cannot be classified as 'debts' they sometimes weigh heavily on married people who may have growing families to provide for. Sometimes the difficulty of providing cash for payment of these duties is a very serious one, although the annual yield of an estate may not be large.

Believe me sincerely yours,
Frederick Verney

8. A Pom-Pom taken near the bridge over the Crocodile River.
(see letter of 3 September, 1900).

9. 'Long Tom.' (see letter of 3 September, 1900).

10. Fortifications built by the Rifle Brigade at Lydenburg.

11. A Boer Fort at Mafeking.

12. 'A waggon being pulled up out of the Steelport River. It has to be double-spanned owing to the steepness of the drift.' (see letter of 1 May 1901).

13. Guns crossing the Vaal River, March, 1902.

14. 20th Battlion, Mounted Infantry, Elaandsfontein,
June, 1902. (see pp. 54–57).

15. Ralph some time after the Boer War.

Honiton, Sydney   March 20th 1910

My dearest Mother,

We are in our own home and we have had a frightfully busy time opening everything. We arrived in Melbourne on Monday and stayed the night there in order that I might be able to see Mr. Miller who was on his way home. We left there on Tuesday evening and I found I should have to stop on the way for most of Wednesday at Hill View, so Nita finally had to come on to Sydney by herself.

When I got out of the train at Moss Vale I found H.E. on the platform to meet me. We motored up to the house and I was there till 3 p.m. in the afternoon.

Napier has resigned and a chap called Capt. Dumaresq in the R.B. is coming out as A.D.C.

Nita has been working very hard at this house in order to get it quite ready by the time Kathleen arrives which is next Thursday as she is coming round all the way by sea. I shall meet her in my little motor and take her straight up to Wallaroy where she will be at first.

I do not think we shall be able to get into Government House for three months yet. We can get the old part of the house ready but not the new reception rooms; owing to the strike they could not get the bricks delivered, so that caused endless delays. The children are going to stay up in the country for some time yet though H.E. and Lady C. will come here for a few days at a time for functions; they will both be here from Monday to Saturday next week for the races which Kathleen will go to. After that I expect Kathleen may go up to Hill View for a bit.

> Your very affect.
> Ralph

. . . .

Nita to Ralph's Mother

Honiton, Sydney   29th March 1910

We have already had visitors to dinner twice. The first were the Chelmsfords which of course put the Australian maids into quite a fluster, but our old Australian cook was a trump and only failed in the Barley water which was as stiff as blancmange! We have the two maids only and the cook is laundress as well and does most of our washing and all the cooking for £1 a week. Rene keeps the whole house as clean as a new pin and does parlour

103

maid work as well for 15/- a week. Clarke the head coachman at Cranbrook has a very nice boy of 12 who comes up every morning for an hour before going to school to clean the knives and boots and another hour in the evening to chop wood and clean Ralph's motor. Saturday mornings he cleans windows and verandas. We are very amused as it turns out he teaches the violin in the evenings. I don't think even His Gracious Majesty the King can say his boots are cleaned by a violin master!!

Kathleen and my family came to dinner last Saturday night. It is so nice having her out here; she does enjoy everything so thoroughly. One day I sent Ralph off with her in the motor to see the surf bathers which amused her immensely and yesterday of course she was at the races. The two Government House parties combined for lunch and tea so it was very jolly. Ralph and I also dined with them in the evening. There is to be a very jolly dance with Cotillon figures next Thursday, Kathleen's first dance here so we were having a small dinner of 8 first of all as the house is quite close.

Ever your affect.
Janette Verney

. . . .

Hill View, Moss Vale   April 17th 1910

My dearest Mother,

We have just got over our Federal elections and the Labour Party have won the day in a remarkable manner. We shall probably have a Labour government now for some time to come. This party is a protectionist party out here and so perhaps for once father and I shall agree in regretting their victory. Senator Walker is not coming up for election this time as Senators are elected for 6 years and only half go out every 3 years but he will be amongst a small minority in the Senate which is a disappointment to him.

The Chelmsfords go back into residence at Gov. House at the beginning of next week. The new reception room will not be finished but I hope the rest of the house will be ready for them.

. . . .

Honiton, Sydney   May 8th 1910

My dearest Mother,

We heard the very sad news of the King's death at 10.30 yesterday morning which was not more than ¾ of an hour after it actually happened, which was very quick. In fact we knew it probably before you did if you were asleep and did not get the news till you woke up next morning.

I was kept very busy yesterday with telegrams coming in all day. This morning Nita and I went to the cathedral where we had a very impressive sermon from the Archbishop. H.E. has cancelled all his engagements till after the funeral.

The news made a profound impression here in Sydney as it was really so unexpected and it came as a great shock to everybody.

I am afraid that Harry* will miss the King very much I do not know whether it makes any difference to him in his position as deputy master of the household. I hope not.

* Harry Lloyd Verney had been Deputy Master of the Household to King Edward VII
  since 1907.

. . . .

State Government House, Sydney   May 15th 1910

My dearest Mother,

Our thoughts every day this last week have been at Claydon. I was sitting working in my office on Tuesday morning about 10.15 when the orderly brought me a cable with the four words 'Uncle Edmund died yesterday' and as it was not sent off from Botolph Claydon till 7.45 p.m. I suppose he died on Sunday though whether abroad or at Claydon we do not know yet. I wired to Kathleen who was in or near Brisbane and wrote to her the same day. It gives me great pleasure to think that Nita should have known him and we shall always remember his great kindness to us last Xmas.

. . . .

State Government House, Sydney   June 1st 1910

My dearest Mother,

I returned yesterday from our trip to Norfolk Island. We had a most interesting time and the inhabitants are quite unique, their history is quite interesting, they are descended straight from the mutineers of H.M.S. *Bounty* under the command of Lt. Bligh, R.N., in the year 1788. These mutineers settled on an island in the Pacific called Othaite Island and afterwards transferred themselves and their native wives to Pitcairn Island where they lived for many years very happily. When they became too numerous for the small island they were brought over to Norfolk Island by the Government.

All of them have black blood in them of course and they are a most curious mixture of black and white. We left here on Monday and arrived there on Thursday morning. It was too rough to land at the place we had intended so we had to go round the island to a more sheltered side and even then had to be landed in a surf boat by the islanders themselves steered by a man in the stern with a long oar. We had the usual public reception on arrival and the next morning H.E. held a public meeting at 10 a.m. at which anybody who had a grievance might come forward and speak. H.E. is absolute King of this island, quite different from this country. We had to investigate many questions and receive many deputations at which I was present taking in shorthand a brief summary of the subject and H.E.'s reply. Sometimes I had to take it down word for word as fast as I could. We also were shown over the Pacific Cable station and the Melanesian Mission which has its headquarters there.

Your very affect.
Ralph

. . . .

State Government House, Sydney   June 14th 1910
My dearest Mother,

But now your letters make me realize what a change it will be to come back to Claydon and find Harry in possession. I got a charming letter from him this week and I seem to feel more like a brother to him than ever. I feel sure he will be a second Sir Harry and I am sure like Grandpapa he will be as much loved and respected by all his tenants as I hope he will for many years represent them in the House of Commons.

I shall never be the sound Liberal which father would like me to be but after all politics fade away into insignificance when it comes to sticking together as a family. Poor Harry must have had a very trying time of it during these last few weeks and must have found it very sad to have to take up the management of Claydon which has been so wonderfully done by Uncle Edmund during the last 17 years.

We had the opening of our parliament today. Nita came up with Lady C. I had to present the King's speech to H.E. after advancing and bowing three times in rather an absurd manner which was rather an ordeal and then doing the same thing when retiring backwards!! I have sent all your letters on to Kathleen who is still visiting in Queensland.

Much love to you all, ever your affect.

Ralph

. . . .

State Government House, Sydney   June 21st 1910

My dear Father,

H.E. has just heard from Sir Charles Lucas that the Colonial Office will not give him leave to be away from Australia while Lord Dudley is in England next year. Lord C. has had therefore to cancel his plan of going home in April and will be acting Governor General for 6 months. I shall probably stay on with him and act as his private secretary during that time.

This might postpone my return to England for 6 months or so but it will be well worth while. H.E. and his family will be going home in October of next year for 6 months and I may stay on here till he returns bringing back with him another private secretary.

. . . .

Honiton, Sydney   July 10th 1910

My dear Mother,

I find as usual that I have only left myself very little time to write mail letters. I have had an exceptionally busy week as I am helping Lady Dudley with a huge matinee in aid of the District Bush nursing scheme, i.e. our King's memorial fund for the whole of Australia. At present if anyone is taken ill in the Bush there often is no doctor or nurse within a hundred miles and the poor patient has often to be driven across rough country before he or she can obtain relief.

This scheme proposes to divide the less civilized country into hundreds of districts and provide a thoroughly proficient nurse with practical knowledge of every branch of nursing and the necessary medical supplies and appliances for each district. She will probably have to carry a tent about with her as many of the homes perhaps consist of one room, a shanty as they call it and is the living room of an entire family.

. . . .

State Government House, Sydney   August 22nd 1910

My dearest Mother,

Kathleen returned to us last week in blooming health, having escaped all those terrible dangers of the Bush which you were so afraid of. She has had a really very interesting time and I think she would not at all mind settling in Australia but I do not think you would approve of that at all. However, her trip has been a huge success and I cannot help thinking that

107

now that she has returned safely from it you must be glad that she should have had so great an experience.

It is splendid Harry getting into the County Council with so big a majority for Brill. Much love from us both, we are very fit and well.

. . . .

State Government House, Sydney   October 17th 1910

My dearest Mother,

The great event with us this last week has been the State election which I am sorry to say has resulted in the defeat of the Wade ministry and the return of the Labour Party to power with a small majority of 2; all the returns are not in yet from the far country districts. The Labour party will probably elect the former Speaker to the Chair which will take away one vote from the Liberal party so that they may have a majority of 3.

We expect Wade to resign next week when H.E. will send for Mr. McGowan the leader of the Labour Party who will be asked to form a ministry. I am most awfully sorry for Wade. He has done splendidly as Premier under very difficult circumstances with 3 bad strikes. He could have appointed himself Chief Justice the other day but preferred to stick to his party. He has now been beaten in spite of having worked tremendously hard during the election.

Very much love from us both ever your affect.

Ralph

. . . .

Honiton, Sydney   Nov. 12th 1910

My dearest Mother,

Last night we had the new Labour ministers and their wives to dinner at State Government House and though the ladies were dressed in rather peculiar clothes we liked them all very much. The Minister for Mines took in Nita; he has been a miner all his life and his son is now working as a miner. I sat next to Mr. Griffiths who is minister for public works and is therefore of great importance to us as we cannot get any improvements done to Gov. House without his consent. I tried to be especially charming to him!!!

Your very affect.
Ralph

. . . .

State Government House, Sydney   18th December 1910

My dearest Mother,

I am hoping that if you sent the cable from Botolph Claydon that you did not go to Buckingham for the declaration of the poll. I can so well imagine Harry's triumphant return to Claydon House, I expect the bells would be ringing and the flag flying and there must have been tremendous rejoicing, so very different from your return the last time in S. Wilts!! I do so want to know all the details. Was father in the counting room? Was Harry's opponent nice about it afterwards? Was there a row at Buckingham when the poll was declared?

Your very affect.
Ralph

. . . .

S.S. *Marama*   26th February 1911

My dearest Mother,

We are on our way back to Sydney and I will try and give you a short account of our trip to N. Zealand which has been a great success. We spent the first few days at Auckland.

We went from Auckland to Rotorua which took us all day in the train. We first of all stayed in the Wakka hotel which is 2 miles from Rotorua and right in the middle of all the sights of geysers and boiling mud holes etc. I thought Wakka was a most interesting place. There were boiling streams running there side by side with cold streams so that one can put one foot into very hot water and the other into very cold at the same time. Nita and I had a spout bath of naturally hot water which was very nice. I took some photos there which I am sending to Gwen by this mail. We did also a certain amount of fishing at Rotorua but it was not good as there has been such very little rain in N. Zealand during the past year.

From Rotorua we went to Lake Taupo.

Nita and I shared one tent in camp. Lady Graeme had a tent and young Graeme who is about 32 and very nice. We took a boy from Rotorua to cook for us but Nita did a good deal of cooking. We were really too early for the fishing this year owing to the very little rain there has been this year. But still we managed to catch some, our best day was 21 fish averaging about 9 lbs. which is not bad for rainbow trout. Nita was not successful at first but one morning when Graeme and I went up the river Nita put on her waders and went to the mouth of the stream with my light 10′ 6″ rod which I bought years ago from Hardy's and she caught two fish, one of 9½ and the other of 9¼ lbs. with this rod which was really wonderful of her as it is very difficult to catch big fish on so light a rod. Graeme and I caught nothing that morning at all so she was awfully pleased. I send a photo of Nita with these two fish in her waders. She caught another one of 9¼ lbs. that evening.

It really was much more like salmon fishing than trout fishing and the rods I had were much too small for this sport. I shall know better if we are ever able to go there again. Graeme who has fished a great deal had beautiful salmon rods which were much more suitable. My best day was 8 fish weighing altogether 75 lbs. We used to get up very early about 4 a.m. and fish before daylight every morning. We then all came back to camp for breakfast, fish till lunch, rest during the afternoon and then fish again in the evening. We hired a boat and used to fish sometimes from that.

We returned from Taupo back to Rotorua partly by motor coach and partly by ordinary coach. There is no train yet between these two places. From Rotorua we went by train to a place called Tamaranui which is at one end of the Wanganui river. We went down this river by water, the first part we had to do in a sort of steam canoe, the river was most awfully low and we kept bumping along the bottom. We took three days over it instead of only two which was annoying but still the scenery was most wonderful. The river runs in a very deep gorge nearly all the way about 175 miles. The mountains each side are covered in tree ferns and some palms and are perhaps 500 feet high and very steep. We stayed one night on this boat and the second night at a very good hotel at a place called Pippiriki. We got to Wellington by train from Wanganui the third night.

. . . .

State Government House, Sydney   April 5th 1911

My dearest Mother,

It seems extraordinary to think that H.E. will have left here today three weeks. I do not think I shall go to Adelaide with him as I have so much to do here, probably Capt. Dumaresq will go. Yesterday we had the official launching of H.M.A.S. *Warrego*, the first man of war to be built or rather put together in Australia. It all went off very well but she looks a small and insignificant ship to have made a lot of fuss over.

. . . .

Wallaroy, Sydney   June 5th 1911
My dearest Mother,

Sydney is very perturbed at present as the Labour party have announced
their intention of turning Federal Government House into a free library
and museum directly the Dudleys leave next month. Federal Gov. House
really belongs to our State Government and at the time of the commonwealth they let it for 10 years to the Federal Government for the use of the
Governor General, and 10 years are up next month. Mr. Holman and
party refuses to renew the lease which has put the federal people into a
great quandary as they have no house in Sydney to offer the Denmans.* It
will be some years before Yass Canberra the Federal Capital will be ready
to receive the Governor. I do not think they have even started to clear the
land yet. If the Labour Party insists on carrying out this scheme Lord
Denman will not be able to come to Sydney at all; he will have to spend all
his time in Victoria instead of 6 months there and 6 months in N.S.W. as
all former governors have done.

   Of course this move on the part of the Labour gov. will make them more
popular than ever with the Labour caucus and will probably secure them
more votes at the next election from a certain class as there is a class in
Australia which grudges every penny spent on the English representatives
and whose one cry is that local men should be made State Governors.

                        Ever your affect.
                        Ralph

* Lord Denman (1864–1954) was Governor-General of Australia 1911–14.
· ·

State Government House, Sydney   June 6th 1911

My dearest Mother,

I was glad to get your letter this week about Kathleen's engagement.* You
may be quite sure that I fully sympathize with you and understand your
feelings about it. In the very early days of the Greeks and Romans we read
of how mothers in those days rejoiced to send their sons out to fight and
how they recognized that 'pro patria mori' was the greatest honour that
could happen to them.

   You may comfort yourself that you are going to give to Australia one of
the best things it is in the power of any one to give her and also one of the
things she at present stands most in need of namely a really good and
healthy lady immigrant. I know it is frightfully hard for you to get used to
the idea and still more difficult for you to feel glad about it but I am quite

sure that Kathleen is going to lead the life she is most suited for and in the end the life which will be happiest for her.

About Frank's coming home I very much hope he will be able to manage it but if he does you must remember this that he will not show up at his best in the Claydon surroundings. Frank has been used to this country all his life and to see him at his best you must see him out here. You will probably think him rather unpolished and in fact quite Australian. I know, however, that you will not allow this to influence you and as soon as you know him you will recognize at once what a good chap he is.

* To Frank Newton, Lord Chelmsford's Secretary in Brisbane.

· ·

State Government House, Sydney   August 1st 1911

My dearest Mother,

I have had a very busy week indeed as we have just been through a political crisis. The Labour government resigned but as no other party appeared to have a working majority in the House Mr. Holman, the acting Premier, had to be asked to withdraw his resignation till after 2 by-elections were decided on the 16th of this month.

The Lt. Governor has written a long description home about it which I have had to type out. It has been a most interesting crisis in view of the fact that the Premier asked H.E. to prorogue parliament to help him over a difficult time which was of course refused at first. However, parliament , has been prorogued now till the 22nd August and after that it is very much feared we will have a dissolution.

· ·

Nita to Ralph's Mother

Wallaroy, Sydney   August 22nd 1911

My dear Mother,

To everyone's horror they have practically bribed one of the Liberals to accept the position which now gives them a majority of three. There has been a frightful uproar in the Liberal camp over this treachery. When the House meets tomorrow Mr. Willis will be elected Speaker but before he can be elected the Liberals and Independants are going to give him a very very bad half hour. They will be able to say anything they like as there will be no Speaker to keep order and to interrupt a politically abusive speech with the Labourites and Liberals will be bawling at each others' heads. It is not at all uncommon out here for one member to challenge another to fight him with his fists in the House. Of course the Speaker has always insisted on an apology but tomorrow one wonders what will happen if such a suggestion is made.

Your loving daughter,
Nita

. . . .

State Government House, Sydney   October 4th 1911

My dearest Mother,

Kathleen had just had that telegram from Frank to say that he had got land. Of course it is very much out of the way from our point of view but still it is high up and not low on the coast and this is a great thing. Frank writes to me that he hopes to have the house ready by Xmas though he does not expect Kathleen till the beginning of April.

Your very affect.
Ralph

. . . .

Nita to Ralph's Mother

Wallaroy, Sydney   November 15th 1911

My dear Mother,

We were very excited over our home letters this week, mostly about Harry's engagement. Lady Rachel* sounds quite charming and quite the right wife for Harry. She has certainly succeeded in making Aunt Margy most awfully happy. You mentioned that you thought the wedding would come off Dec. 7th or thereabouts.

I think the Denmans are going to be very popular. She is very natural and unspoilt and he is so tactful. We are wondering how Lady C. will like Lady Denman. I am afraid they will rather clash. Lady C. dislikes women who smoke and knows and cares nothing for horses and racing, Lady D.'s two pet topics. Of the two Lady D. is decidedly the more broadminded and has the more catholic tastes. However, she has tact and will probably avoid subjects likely to rub Lady C. up the wrong way.

Much love from your affect. daughter,

Nita

* Lady Rachel Bruce (1890–1964) daughter of the 9th Earl of Elgin.

. . . .

State Government House, Sydney   February 12th 1912

My dear Father,

I have received your letter about Kathleen's marriage settlement it has not come by this Mail but I shall expect it next week. Just about the day when you get this letter we shall be welcoming Kathleen and her party in Sydney. They are due on March 14th.

I am glad to say that Brisbane is very much quieter than it was a week ago. The strikers have been beaten all along the line and the men have gone back to work by hundreds in the face of the orders of their leaders. 1300 railwaymen came out on strike at Ipswich near Brisbane. The railway authorities gave them till the following Monday to return to work or have their names crossed off their books. 1297 returned to work on Monday morning!!

The Labour party in S. Australia have suffered badly at the general election here last Saturday. There was a Labour Government in power but now there is a Liberal majority of 6. I think the strikes in Queensland had a large effect on the voting in S. Australia.

Fisher the Labour Prime Minister actually subscribed to the strike funds. What do you think of that?!!! He also refused to allow the military to be called out to keep the peace so the better class men in Queensland came to Brisbane from the country in large numbers and formed a strong voluntary defence force. They brought their own rifles and food and they patrolled the streets for over a week under the orders of the Chief Commissioner for Police, thus doing the work of the soldiers whom Fisher would not call out as he was afraid of the Labour Caucus.

People in S. Australia as all over Australia are realizing that it does not do to have the country ruled by the Labour Party during a crisis. The consequence is that the Labour majority in S. Australia of 4 has been turned into a minority of 6!!!

Your very affect.
Ralph

. . . .

State Government House, Sydney   19th February 1912

My dearest Mother,

Yesterday Nita and I went over to Yaralla, Eadith Walker is going to send her motor for Aunt Margy and take them over there for lunch or dinner

114

one day while they are in Sydney. Mr. and Mrs. Want were here yesterday she is a sister of Frank's and they are both quite charming. Personally I think Mrs. Want is the best of the family. She had a long talk with Nita and she said she was making all the curtains for Kathleen's new home with her own hands. She was full of sympathy with you in having to send your daughter all the way out here to marry a man you have never seen.

Her admiration for Kathleen is boundless. She told Nita that she could not think what Frank had done to deserve such a girl as a wife.

> Your very affect.
> Ralph

. . . .

State Government House, Sydney   March 17th 1912

My dearest Mother,

Aunt Margy, Gwen and Kathleen have been and gone and I think their visit to Sydney was a very great success. Their boat was late, not arriving here till about 6.30 p.m. on Thursday evening.

I went in my own motor to meet them. Nita did not come with me as she wanted to be ready dressed for dinner so as to give up her room for them to dress in. You can imagine my excitement as the boat came alongside and what a long long time it seemed to be in getting up the gangway.

However, I was first on board the ship and of course we had been waving to each other. I found them all three very well, Gwen was especially well much stronger looking than I have ever seen her in spite of her rough voyage out. Aunt Margy and Kathleen went up to Wallaroy in a taxi and I took Gwen up in my little motor. Mrs. Walker and Nita were all ready to welcome them and at 7.45 p.m. we had a family dinner party, Eadith, the twins, Mr. and Mrs. Llang Want making up the rest of the party.

Much love from us both your very affect.

> Ralph

. . . .

State Government House, Sydney   March 26th 1912

My dearest Mother,

This is my last week's Mail from this address. I can hardly believe it. Last night the Denmans gave a farewell dinner party for us and a little dance afterwards which was very nice of them and great fun.

I am quite bewildered at the number of people who have come to say goodbye to me and the very nice things they say about me. We had a very jolly weekend at Yaralla. Lord and Lady Masserene and Ferrard who are staying with the Denmans came up here on Sunday afternoon.

On Thursday evening I am dining with the members of the Masonic Club and I am afraid this will be rather an alarming affair. On Friday there is a dinner party for us at State Government House and on Saturday we are having a family dinner party quietly at Wallaroy. I am afraid Mrs. Walker is dreading our departure.

We have such happy letters from Brisbane. Gwen writes that she likes Frank and already feels quite at home with him. We have the invitation to the wedding which although we cannot accept but we are putting it in the family album as the closing of the chapter on Australia!!

Very much love from us both every your affect.

Ralph

· ·

S.S. *Mataram*, near Rockhampton   April 6th 1912

My dearest Mother,

We left Pinkenbah at 9.20 p.m. on Thursday evening. During the evening we went over to Woodhill where Kathleen was helping Frank with his packing. We had tea there and then brought them back to town in the motor. We said goodbye to Kathleen outside Mrs. Hart's house and I wonder when and where we shall see her again. We lunched that day with Aunt Margy and Gwen at Montpelier and said goodbye to them after lunch. We were left the Government House motor for the afternoon and we went to Pinkenbah in it which was much nicer than going by train.

... *Chapter Six* ...

In October, 1912, Ralph and Nita return to Regimental life in Rawalpindi in India. In April, 1913, Nita goes back to England to have her first child, John, just as her father-in-law dies. In July Ralph is given compassionate leave to sort out his family's affairs and does not return to India until after John's Christening.

Nita to Ralph

12 Connaught Place, London   25th April 1913

My own darling,

I am spending the afternoon with your family trying to cheer them up; they sadly need it. This last week has been such a very very sad one for them, first the anxiety before your father's operation and now the dreadful knowledge that it was quite unsuccessful. Your poor mother has been most wonderfully brave, though she knows the worst and can have but the faintest hopes she keeps up in the most marvellous fashion. Your father sometimes asks for her and I think she feels it would never do for her to show him anything but the bravest face.

Yesterday Harry and Joan met me at the station and took me to Rutland Gardens. Aunt Margy had filled the house with old ladies and so could only give me a room on the very top floor. This Joan thought would be very bad for me, so, like an angel, turned Harry out of his dressing room and made it into a most charming bedroom. They all gave me the warmest welcome; the two older boys are still having holidays. When I got to the house I found your mother waiting to welcome me; we had a long talk and then she went home. I came here about half an hour before lunch and we talked and chatted about you and even laughed several times though we all know how very superficial our lightheartedness was.

This morning your mother broke down for the first time. Your father's

117

letters upset her. One came offering him a seat, another the chairmanship on some Bucks Council. It made her realize so forcefully that even if your father recovers he will never to able to attend to all the things he is so interested in. He has been spared much pain, which is a great blessing, but of course if he lives he may suffer great agony. Cancer at any time is quite a dreadful disease but in the intestines it could hardly be worse.

I cannot tell you what we all feel for your mother. She is almost superhuman in her efforts to be brave and unfortunately Aunt Margy is down with flu, otherwise she would have been such a help to them both.

. . . .

Ralph to Nita's Mother

2nd R.B., Kildana   27th April 1913

My dearest Mummy,

I got a cable this morning saying my father is dangerously ill; it is Sunday and so the Post Office is now closed; I can get no further news till tomorrow.

Monday morning
My father died yesterday; my one comfort is that my mother is well, and also Nita, who sent me a cable from Rutland Gardens where she is staying with Joan.

I am going home in July on leave.

Ralph

. . . .

Nita to Ralph

1 Rutland Gardens, London   April 27th 1913

My darling,

You must be worrying darling about your mother and her health, she is quite wonderful and so is Gwen. They both realize how merciful it was in sparing your father's long and painful illness. He could not have had a more peaceful end and quite free from pain, and I do not think conscious that the end was near. However, he must have been prepared for such a contingency because he wrote some letters to your mother which he gave to Aunt Margy to give to her if anything should happen.

Gwen rang us up last night while we were having dinner to say there had been a relapse and he was rapidly losing ground. We went to bed with very sore hearts thinking of your mother and Gwen. This morning early a telephone message reached us that all was over. I wanted to go round at once after breakfast but Joan and Harry would not let me. Young Harry* told us through the telephone that your mother and Gwen did not wish it.

The two Harrys were to go and spend the whole morning making arrangements for the funeral, etc. We were so glad that your mother has decided not to be present. She felt that it was more than her strength could stand. Your father will be buried very quietly at Claydon; only the two Harrys will be there. Aunt Margy is still seedy and is looking after Rachel who has had a threatened miscarriage apparently.

from your loving little wife
Nita

* Claydon Harry

· ·

Nita to Ralph

1 Rutland Gardens, London   April 28th 1913

My darling darling Ralph,

You cannot imagine how happy your cable made us all today. When it was brought in to me at breakfast this morning I could not realize it. To think that I should see your dear face again in two months instead of nine, oh it is too good to be true. I telephoned at once to No. 12 and Harry took my message. Later on in the morning I received a wire from your mother saying how much it had cheered her. I did not go round there today your mother asked me not to until Wednesday.

Tomorrow the funeral takes place and I am afraid she is at last beginning to break down, at least Gwen and Harry think she is. She has been almost too calm today. She spent the morning shopping with Gwen. I am more than thankful she is not going down to Claydon tomorrow. Harry Lloyd and young Harry will be the only representatives of the family. Willie may be there but he is at present doing a walking tour. All the papers had something about your father in them. The Times and Westminster Gazette were longer than the others. The Liberal papers I have not seen. I shall try and get hold of them to send to you.

Much love from Nita

· ·

Ralph to Nita

Kuldana   28th April 1913, 3 p.m.

My own wife,

I think after that cable yesterday I knew what was coming; I went up to the telegraph office here when it opened, and actually read the news on the telegraph instrument as the man was writing it down. Yesterday was a whole day of suspense, but it partly prepared me for the cable this morning. Of course I am at present in the dark as to what caused his death; I can only imagine that his digestion failed suddenly and completely at the end.

The Colonel came for a short stroll with me this morning, and really was sympathy personified; he asked me to go and stay with them for a few days, as he felt sure that the other chaps in the Mess would be a nuisance. Mrs. Shute has written me a charming letter, but I prefer to be here alone to fight it out. I have lunch late in the Mess after the others, and am going to have my dinner in my own room today and tomorrow; it was a horrid effort dining in Mess last night.

Of course my whole thoughts are with you three; tell Gwen what a huge comfort it was to me that she put in her cable that mother was well; and then your own cable arrived at the same time as the other one, so I knew that you were well, and at Rutland Gardens.

I miss you now more than ever but I want you to be with my mother, as I know you will do all you possibly can to comfort her, and that is the best way to comfort me. I have written to her this morning saying that I am coming home in July; I told the Colonel this morning that I would stop on till all my Company training and musketry were over, but that I must get home after that; he was quite sure I should have no difficulty about it, and he would ask Cox himself to grant me leave.

. . . .

Nita to Ralph

1 Rutland Gardens, London   30th April 1913

Darling Sweetheart,

On the Saturday afternoon he said to Gwen, 'This is not the sort of illness one recovers from quickly. I must be patient and keep to my bed for some time'. He said it very slowly and with great emphasis. Gwen felt he wanted her to repeat it to her mother which she did. This rather comforted your mother who had been wondering if he realized the end was near. Apparently he did but he wanted to spare your mother that knowledge. However, the Nurses told them next day how at 7 o'clock he said to them, 'You have done everything you possibly could, thank you'; he became unconscious almost as he said thank you and never recovered.

Nita

. . . .

Ralph to Nita

May 19th 1913

All my other letters came this morning. My darling I cannot tell you what delightful things the whole family say about you. My mother says that you have been of the greatest possible help to her and Gwen says that you know exactly when to talk and when not to talk and that your sympathy has been of the very greatest comfort to mother and to her. I feel absolutely glad to be without you myself, knowing what you are doing for my mother and Gwen. I feel they would have had a much sadder time of it had you not been at home and this is exactly what I wanted to be told, though I knew perfectly well that if you were fit enough you would do all you could to make up for my absence.

Now I want to tell you a little about the business part of the whole thing. This is the side of the question which I dislike immensely.

As far as I can make out after reading F. Smith's letter very carefully and also the statement he sent me we should have about £2500 a year during my mother's lifetime, not counting the Pleasley* Colliery which brings in about another £5000 a year. Now this will at first seem to you as it seems to me to be enormous. But I feel very strongly that as the colliery is not everlasting we ought to put by a large part of that income in order to start a sinking fund for when the colliery ceases to function. Also I have got to pay about £20,000 death duties and with £10,000 paid out of the Insurance money for which my father insured his life, this will leave me another £10,000 to pay. So you see that for some years yet we shall have to be fairly careful. Neither you or I are extravagant in our tastes I am glad to say. You are such a splendid little manager that I am sure we shall be able to get along alright. I do not go in for racing or any other very extravagant amusements.

My mother will have a clear income for the rest of her life of £2000 a year, Kathleen will have £600 a year and Gwen £480 a year during my mother's lifetime. I think my father was most awfully good about leaving his successors an absolutely free hand. He has not put any conditions on those who were to follow him.

Good night my own darling and God bless you.

Ralph

* Pleasley estate was left by Florence Nightingale to Frederick Verney.

· ·

Botolph House   5th July 1913
Plumb's wedding day (The Gardener)

Darling Ralph,

The preparations began yesterday. Your mother and Gwen decorated the sitting room downstairs and the dining room most beautifully with masses of white flowers. This morning directly after breakfast Gwen made the wedding bouquet and then she and mother laid the table and decorated it with white and silver. I gathered strawberries and picked 210 which I had to stack and arrange on 26 small plates, 8 strawberries for each person. Your mother provided a beautiful tea and plate of beef and ham was in front of each place and the rest of the table was groaning under the weight of jellies, blancmange, cakes, strawberries and sweets, there were two wedding cakes.

We had to have our lunch on trays wherever there was room. Your mother had hers on a small table in the diningroom, I had mine on a chair in the sitting room and Gwen had a stool. I did not go to the church but your mother and Gwen drove off about 2.30 and after the wedding party had passed the servants hung the streamers from the windows to the street and I put finishing touches to the strawberries, my special charge. Then I walked up to your father's seat and watched the bride and bridegroom driving back. Whitstone as best man sat on the box and was so excited when he saw me and waved most frantically much to my amusement. Gwen and mother picked me up in Wiggin's trap and we drove to Claydon. As we passed this house we could see the bride and bridegroom receiving in the hall. It was raining all the time unfortunately but cleared up about 3.30.

Your mother told me it was a fascinating service, the funniest she had ever been to, there was no music and the bride's father would insist on standing on the wrong side of the bride. Then when they went into the vestry they could hear Mr. Gordon telling Mr. White how to spell his name. By the time they reached the 'Min' on Benjamin, Gwen said she felt quite hysterical with suppressed laughter. There were such long pauses between each letter which conjured up a picture of the old man breathing heavily as he very laboriously made the letters. The silence in the church as there was no music was terrific, nothing to be heard but Mr. Gordon's voice saying 'no no not M E N but M I N'; they all gave a sigh of relief when they reached the 'I T E' of White.

We did not get back till after 6.30 and found the wedding party had just departed. At 7 p.m. the bride and bridegroom the best man and three bridesmaids all drove past in the village fly to the station. We three stood on the doorstep and waved, Whitstone again got carried away and waved back in the most frantic fashion. Less than an hour later he was waiting on us at dinner, the respectful obsequious family butler once more. We were all very sleepy and tired out and are going to bed early. However we found time over and over again to remind each other during the day that next Saturday you will be leaving India.

From your little wife
Nita

· ·

Taj Mahal Hotel, Bombay   11th July 1913

My own darling,

I had quite a good journey from Pindi, though the first part of it was frightfully hot. I had a carriage to myself the whole way up till 11 p.m. last night when to my disgust I was woken up by somebody getting in.

After a good shave and a most refreshing bath I went and had an excellent breakfast sitting at the same table we had when we arrived. I then went to Cox and Co. and found that I was sharing a cabin with somebody else, so I exchanged it for another one in the 'A' grade, I feel horribly extravagant having done this but everyone says we shall get it very rough between here and Aden and I think it is worth the extra £10 for the return ticket.

Your own husband
Ralph

· ·

Nita to Ralph

Botolph House   July 12th 1913

Dearest darling,

Your mother, Gwen and I were very busy all Thursday afternoon sorting Florence Nightingale's letters, your mother kept every one she ever wrote to your father or her. We helped her to put them in order as Aunt Margy is going through them and hopes to bring out a little book. Some of the allusions to you were so very nice, you were evidently a great favourite of hers. One marked private to your father is all about your character, you had evidently come back from school without any prizes and she writes so nicely to your father that she has not much faith in clever boys, the best men have often been proved the worst workers at school. She finishes 'I back Ralph and would like to give him 10/–'.

. . . .

Nita to her Mother

Botolph House, Claydon   July 1st 1913

Darling Mumptykins,

It seems too good to be true that I am writing this with Ralph actually in the same room. When I wrote to you last week he was not expected in England until Monday but after posting your letter a cable arrived to say he would reach London on Saturday.

He takes his mother for long walks after tea, they have so much to talk over and I think Ralph is a very real comfort to her, he seems to give her strength and is taking his Father's place in the household, reading family prayers and doing other things like that which gives her the most intense pleasure.

Nita

. . . .

Ralph to Nita's Mother

Botolph House   29th July 1913

My dearest Mummy,

Here I am sitting out on the lawn at Botolph House with Nita beside me, in her long deck chair, sewing away at tiny garments.

124

We drove up to Botolph House and Nita was looking out of the window upstairs; we had such a happy happy meeting, and you would have loved to see her colour; she really has quite a bright colour, and looks most awfully well.

Your very affect.
Ralph

. . . .

Ralph to Nita's Mother

Swan Hotel, Mansfield   August 19th 1913

My dearest Mummy,

I am here for a few days about Pleasley business; mother is staying at a small cottage place my Father built at Pleasley, but Mr. Francis Smith our solicitor and myself are staying here.

Today we walked over the surface estate which is about 1200 acres of farming land, seeing the tenants and fixing up certain repairs that have to be done.

We are going back to Botolph House tomorrow; Nita seems to keep wonderfully well, though the discomfort of the last six weeks are necessary and unpleasant. We have got a small trap and pony, and we drive about together, so she is able to get away from the immediate surroundings of Botolph House which become monotonous after a time. Mullins is a great help to Nita with her sewing and they are both busy making innumerable unnecessary tucks in ridiculously diminutive looking garments.

My best love,
Ralph

. . . .

Nita to her Sister

Botolph House   August 28th 1913

Darling Sissiekins,

Ralph is going up to Scotland to shoot Grouse at Dunphail, Lord Elgin's Moor. He leaves on Saturday and returns the following Saturday and the next week gets two days' shooting at Wotton House, the Beaumont's, so life is becoming a little more lively for him.

Yesterday he had quite a thrilling adventure, the day before he lunched and played golf at Wotton House 10 miles away and while there met a Col. Cholmondeley who has just taken a beautiful place in the neighbourhood for 7 years. It turned out that his eldest son is a subaltern in the R.B., at present seconded to the Flying Corps. Mr. and Mrs. C. told Ralph that the son and 2 or 3 brother officers in the Flying Corps were coming over from Salisbury Plain in their Biplanes and intended landing in one of his fields, spend the night and return next day. He asked Ralph to go over to breakfast and watch their arrival, so R. borrowed Harry's car and chauffeur and took Gwen with him, they spent the morning there and saw the arrival of the 4 biplanes and met all the aviators. R. was fascinated as he had never seen any before and after coming home with Gwen decided to cut a tea party at the Vicarage and go back and watch the trial flights.

He took the car again and much to his joy Mr. C. the R.B. subaltern offered to take him up instead of the mechanic. Ralph honestly confesses that he was in a blue funk and found it most alarming. When they were 2000 feet up they were going 60 miles an hour and he felt as they swooped round and caught gusts of wind that they would turn right over. The noise of the engines was quite deafening, on reaching the ground some part of the machinery underneath caught in the furrow of a field and they nearly turned right over. The biplane was smashed and Ralph and the pilot only escaped being thrown out because they were well strapped in. R.'s knee was badly skinned. The crowd thought a bad accident had happened but they had a lucky escape.

10 minutes later another officer and his mechanic started off to Salisbury Plain to fetch repairing gear and tell the authorities of the accident, but started badly and failed to clear a hedge. The biplane was going at a tremendous pace and turned right over. Both men were flung out and when Ralph left some time later were still unconscious on the field. He had been talking to one of them a few minutes before and asked him if he ever felt the risks and the man said, 'Not a year ago but now I feel them every time I get into the biplane'. We heard by wire this morning that no bones were broken and both men had escaped with a severe shaking. The two biplanes are now wrecks but the engines are not damaged.

Love from Nita

. . . .

126

Botolph House   August 28th 1913

Darling Mumptykins,

I am going up to London for the day on Saturday to interview a permanent nurse who had an excellent reference from Lady Beatrice Rawson, the latter wrote and told me she was an absolute treasure and took charge of her very delicate boy when he was only three weeks old. She has lived with a Mrs. Walker for 6 years as Head nurse and brought up her three children from the month, she is 31 and a good sailor, I am offering £30 wages, while abroad £35. I do hope she suits, she sounds much the nicest of the many who applied between 30 and 40 altogether.

Nita

. . . .

Dunphail, Morayshire   2nd Sept. 1913

My own darling,

We had a splendid day yesterday. I shot better than I expected and I think I did my fair share in compiling the total bag of 87½ brace of grouse and 109 hare.

Your own
Ralph

. . . .

Nita to her Sister

12 Connaught Place   Sept. 30th 1913

Darling Sissiekins,

I am writing between my spasms as there is no doubt I will not be able to write to you later in the week. I have already written to George and there is a letter for mother inside the carnation catalogue I sent her. Nobody but the Nurse and Mullins know I am ill yet though it is 3.30 a.m. Ralph was at the theatre last night so slept in his dressing room so I was able to come down here, I disturbed no one. The pains are becoming more frequent and much more severe, the nurse has just gone to telephone for the doctor. I started them between 3 and 4 but have been awake since 2 so am rather sleepy. I'm trying my hardest to be brave but the spasms are unnerving. It's a great relief to think the 9 months are at an end and that the baby will soon be in the world.*

Much love from
Nita

* John was born that day.

. . . .

Ralph to Nita's Father

13 Connaught Place   October 18th 1913

My dear Daddy,

We go to Claydon next Saturday, I leave on the *Egypt* from Marseilles on the 14th Nov. and Nita follows on the 12th Dec. in the *China* to Bombay; she was coming out by a City Line boat to Karachi but they have suddenly stopped calling at Marseilles on the outward journey, so we had to change to P & O and take a ticket right through to Sydney from Marseilles via Bombay.

    Nita went to the doctor yesterday who passed her as practically all right again, which was good.

My best love your affect.
Ralph

. . . .

Nita to her Mother

Botolph House   November 6th 1913

Darling Mumpty,

It is so funny being down here again where I had such a long wait for John and where I sewed for him and thought about him so much. We brought him down last Saturday. Nurse and I had a first class carriage to ourselves and Master Ralph sat in state by himself in the next compartment and tried to disown us and all our paraphanalia as much as he could on the station.

    As well as a pram Eadith gave me two short frocks, the christening bonnet and a beautiful silver porringer, Charles I design, with a lid and

128

spoon. The lid has three knobs on top and stands on the table upside down holding the bowl. It is a beautiful piece of silver.

Lord Chelmsford has given John a solid and plain silver loving cup, a small edition of the exquisite one he gave Ralph. It has on the outside 'John Verney from his Godfather Frederic Lord Chelmsford'. Harry Lloyd Verney, Joan's husband and John's other godfather, sent John a most beautiful silver ink stand today. It has a silver tray with room for pens on both sides, 2 big silver pots and between them a silver box on the top with all this and Sissies' 1760 hot milk jug he could set up house tomorrow.

Very much love from
Nita

. . . .

Ralph to Nita's Father

Claydon House   November 11th 1913

My dear Daddy,

This afternoon at 2.30 p.m. John is to be christened, and a great event it is to us all at Claydon. I like to think that he will be christened in the same church as his father, and it is such a happy coincidence that it can be on this our wedding day.

... *Chapter Seven* ...

In November 1913 Ralph returns to India, followed by Nita and John. In April 1914 they go to visit her parents in Sydney and in June Ralph returns to his regiment. In August War is declared in Europe. His Regiment is ordered home and Nita manages to get back to England via the U.S.A. in time to have 12 days with Ralph before he goes off to the Front.

. . . .

Ralph to Nita's Mother

S.S. *Egypt*   November 14th 1913

My dearest Mummy,

Here I am all by myself on this big ship, with a photograph of Nita and John as a poor substitute for those two dear people. I left them yesterday at 10 a.m. and started from Victoria Station at 11 a.m. and after an uneventful journey got to Marseilles at 7 a.m. this morning.

. . . .

Ralph to Nita's Father

Imperial Hotel, Rawalpindi   December 31st 1913

My dear Daddy,

Nita and I are sitting in our room at this hotel, and John is next door with the nurse, all of us are as well as possible.

Poor Nita had a bad journey up here from Bombay; a train in front of hers was derailed and it blocked the line, so that Nita's train was 4½ hours late arriving at Lahore; her carriage, which was a through one from Bombay to Peshawar, ought to have been attached to the train leaving Lahore at 10 a.m. on Sunday morning, but as she did not reach there till 2 p.m., she missed that, and also the Calcutta Mail leaving Lahore at 12.30 p.m. and so was kept till 10 p.m. on Sunday night at Lahore, and did not finally get here till 8 a.m. on Monday.

As for me, I had tea, fires and flowers all ready here on Sunday afternoon, went to the station in my motor to meet them, and was absolutely amazed as well as bitterly disappointed, when the train arrived but with no wife or family for me!! Nita had wired to me as soon as she could, but as I had left barracks to see to things at the hotel, the telegram did not reach me till about 7 p.m. I at once telegraphed to the superintendant at Lahore to find out what had happened, as the station-master here knew nothing as to why the Bombay passengers by that route were not on the train. Nita had been told by the guard at 3 a.m. Sunday morning to pack up everything as she would have to change trains at the next station; she packed up all her bedding etc., and at 7.30 a.m. was told that it would not be necessary after all for her to change; it was bitterly cold at that time of the morning; such are the comforts of our luxurious train travelling in India!!! With her usual pluck she made the best of everything, and at Lahore went to the hotel and had a very good lunch and dinner there, of which they stood badly in need.

My love to you all yours always affect.

Ralph

. . . .

Nita to her Mother

At Kat, West Ridge, Rawalpindi   25th February 1914

Darling Mumpty,

Last week I only sent you a photograph, this week I have to give you the very good news that Ralph has been granted 108 days leave out of India from March 23rd so will go with John and me out in the *Mooltan* leaving Colombo on March the 28th. We go in the *China* from Bombay to Ceylon, and if we go overland from Adelaide reach Sydney on Easter Monday but I do not think we shall leave the boat anyhow until Melbourne. We want to avoid race week and its festivities.

. . . .

Wallaroy, Sydney   16th June 1914

My very own darling,

I have just left you having lunch with mother and George, there were so
many lumps in my throat I could not eat. Oh Sweetheart boy I shall miss
you so, every day we spend together makes separations when they come all
the harder.

    I hope little John will grow up like you and that he will make his wife as
happy as you make me. He is outside in his pram so unconscious of the
fact that his big playmate is leaving him tonight for so long.

Your very own
Nita

. . . .

Rawalpindi Club   July 2nd 1914

My own darling wife,

I got your very welcome cable soon after we arrived yesterday morning.
The word 'David' caught my eye at once as I was on the lookout for either
that or 'friend'. Oh my darling what can I say except that I am really
delighted but do hope you will take very good care of yourself and that you
will keep as well all through as you did last time.

    I am wondering so much if you will decide to go home any earlier,
perhaps the beginning of October instead of the end of that month. I am
not saying a word about it to any member of the family till I hear from you
but I know how perfectly delighted Mother and Gwen will be and how
anxious they will both be to have you at Botolph House. I know you found
it rather dull there before, but the place suited you so well that I am much
hoping you will go straight there and that I shall come and meet you there
as soon as I can get away from Colchester.

Ralph

. . . .

Rawalpindi Club   July 9th 1914

My own darling,

I think most of October will be taken up in getting ready to go home there
is always such a lot to be done. The Colonel is going to Kashmir for about
a month from August 25th. The Harmans are coming home with us on the
troopship but after about 8 months at home he will get command of the 1st
Bat.

132

I have not spoken to the Colonel yet about this Territorial Adjutancy but I spoke to the Boy about it this morning as he was asking me about a house at Colchester. The Boy said he thought it an excellent plan and he did not think the Colonel would have any objection to my sending in an application for it.

. . . .

Kuldana   July 12th 1914

My own darling,

The Colonel at breakfast this morning showed me an advertisement he had been sent about a house in Colchester so I told him about the territorial adjutancy and he has no objection to my sending in my name for it and he will recommend me for it, so I think I shall do that this week so as to have it in the War Office in plenty of time.

I am thinking of going up for the first part of my promotion examination in November next, Holes and Ted are going up for their examination then for the rank of Captain, if I do this we shall all three have to do it onboard ship on the way home because it has to be held on the same day all over the world.

. . . .

Kuldana   July 20th 1914

My own darling,

I am so glad you are going home on the *Mooltan*; you will like the Purser and the doctor so much, try and get at the latter's table. You will get home just 10 days before I reach Southampton and therefore about a fortnight before I get to Botolph House. I do not advise you to come to Southampton, especially under present circumstances. The Colonel says we shall all be able to get leave pretty well at once. I have said absolutely nothing at all in my letters to any one that could give a hint of David.

. . . .

Kuldana   July 24th 1914

My own darling,

I have just come back from my 2nd afternoon with F. Lee. Yesterday afternoon we did Military Law and I thought he was excellent but this afternoon he talked the whole time about the way to defend a village and I thought it a horrible waste of time.

This afternoon on my way back from Lee I caught up our Colonel walking with General Townsend* who took the place of General Cox.** The General told me he had this morning signed my application for the Adjutancy.

Your own husband
Ralph

* Ralph means Major-General (later Sir) Charles Townshend (1861–1924). In April, 1916, when commanding 6th Indian division in Mesopotamia, he was besieged and forced to surrender at Kut al Amara, thereby winning 'immortality' as 'Townshend of Kut'.
** General (later Sir) H. Vaughan Cox (1860–1923).

. . . .

Kuldana   July 26th 1914

This morning's papers seem to hint at a EUROPEAN WAR!! Austria and Serbia then Germany, Russia and France. But I do not think there is really very much chance of these alarmist rumours coming to anything, though Austria and Serbia might have a go at each other, if there were European complications there might be a chance of the Indian reliefs for this year being cancelled!!

This evening the Colonel is giving us another lecture on our military history for the examination. I think he hates Murree just as much as I do. I am going to play him at Squash this afternoon in the Squash tournament, he may beat me.

. . . .

Kuldana   July 31st 1914

We are all terribly perturbed at the cables today from London about the chances of a European War. All leave has been stopped, so Claude is not able to go home after all though he was actually starting the day after tomorrow. But he thinks he will go to Karachi as his boat does not sail for another 7 days in case by that time things may have calmed down and the order rescinded. But officers now on leave such as those in Kashmir need not yet be recalled provided that they were within 48 hours journey of their regiments. Of course we do not in the least know whether there is any chance of our being sent home now. Some people say that as we are the first regiment to go home this next trooping season we may be sent home now to take part in the European War if there is going to be one; other people say that all Indian Reliefs will be cancelled and that we shall be out here for another year.

Personally I am still optimistic and cannot believe that we shall be drawn into a European War and having seen something of War I cannot say that I am as anxious for it as some of these young boys here, though on

134

16. Lord Chelmsford as Governor of New South Wales.
Ralph is on his left. (see p. 93)

17. Miss Nita Walker.
(see letter of 2 August, 1909, *et seq*).

18. Senator and Mrs Walker at Hill View, April, 1910.
(see note to letter of 2 August, 1909).

19. Wallaroy, Sydney (see letter of 19 August, 1909).

20. Wedding of Ralph and Nita, Sydney, 11 November, 1909.

the other hand if orders came for us to go home as soon as possible to take part in it I confess that I shall be delighted to get away from the monotony of this place. This would be infinitely better than being left out here for another year while fighting was going on in Europe.

Your very loving husband
Ralph

· ·

Nita to Ralph

Wallaroy   Friday, 31st July 1914

My own sweetheart,

Really the war news becomes more serious every day and I wonder if David will be born in London after all. If we do fight we shall all lose a dreadful lot of money. When one thinks of the possibilities it makes one shudder. What will all the poorer classes do? Wheat has already gone up, so bread is dearer. I wonder one minute if you will be ordered home, and the next if you will be kept in India for perhaps months longer and then I wonder what I shall do in this contingency. I should prefer to go home.

· ·

Wallaroy   Saturday, August 1st 1914
                                                                    9.30 p.m.

The war news is even more ominous tonight. Germany having proclaimed martial law, she is also stated to have severed France telegraph wires and pulled up railway lines. Shares are going down here so father is buying in Colonial Sugar company shares as they have dropped pounds. I think I shall too if they go down more because they are almost the best out here and if father thinks it a good spek I shall follow it. I have enough money to do it. On second thoughts perhaps I had better not in case I am cut off from you and have to pay a transport bill!!

Nita

· ·

Kuldana   August 2nd 1914

My own darling,

Squidge has just rushed into my room with the news that Germany has declared War on Russia! I suppose this means that France will be at War

135

with Germany almost at once and then I do not see how we are going to keep out of it. If we are at War I do not suppose that the P & O ships will sail from England and you will not be able to get home. It makes one wonder when we shall meet again!! It is no good my offering you any advice at this distance but I am sure you will do whatever is best for David. If we are to get orders to move anywhere I should think they will come during the next week.

. . . .

Kuldana   August 5th 1914

My own darling,

We got the news this morning that War has really been declared and you can imagine the state of excitement here both among officers and men, we are ready to go anywhere at the shortest possible notice, but we are all most frightfully gloomy about our chances of leaving this country. We might possibly be sent to Egypt to take the place of troops there but I am very much afraid that is very doubtful. I cannot tell you how keen I am to go on service once again with the old 2nd battalion.

What we all dread more than words can say is our being left out here while our other two battalions are doing the fighting. Our best chance of leaving this country lies in the fact that we are the first on the roster to leave but I do not think any notice will be taken of that fact. The troops who are nearest the coast will probably be the first to go if any do go at all from India.

I keep wondering and wondering what you will decide to do. I should think that the War will not last more than 3 or 4 months but as you will probably not be able to get home during the War and as it will probably not be good for you to travel within 2 months of the expected arrival of David you may find it necessary to stay out in Australia for the event. I know you will hate this but I know you will consent to do what is wisest for your health on which my whole happiness depends!!

. . . .

Kuldana   August 6th 1914

My own darling,

At midnight last night an order was received for us to send one Captain to Kohala which is about 27 miles along the road to Kashmir to take charge of a temporary camp which is being put up there for about 400 officers who are returning from Kashmir, all of whom have been ordered to rejoin their regiments at once. I suppose Lee, Mcgriger, Bridgeman, Leigh and Constable are therefore all on their way back to us.

Squidge was woken up at 12.30 in the night and received orders to start for Kohala at 6 a.m. How he was going to get there I do not know, whether he was able to get hold of a tonga I do not know (I have just asked my bearer and he tells me that 'Walpole Sahib pony ride'.) He has also orders to report himself to Sir James Willcocks* who is on his way back from Kashmir. I can imagine the fuss and flurry there will be with 400 officers all trying to secure tongas to bring them back to their regiments!!! I expect that brute Danjibhoy will reap a nice little fortune over this.

Your own husband
Ralph

---

* General Sir James Willcocks (1857–1926) commanded northern army in India 1910; commanded Indian army corps in France 1914, but resigned owing to differences with Sir Douglas Haig.

. . . .

Kuldana   August 12th 1914

My own darling,

I should shock you horribly if I were to put down what our feelings are at the thought of being stuck here for another year at a time like this. The 3rd Division at Lahore are mobilizing but what for we do not know, everything is kept so secret, we feel that our only chance now will be for orders to come from home for certain regiments to be sent to Europe and this is not likely. Sackville-West came back two days ago from Simla and though he will not say anything definite because it is all supposed to be so confidential, yet he gave the 60th to understand that this 2nd Div. is to remain intact also the 1st Div. at Peshawar in order to keep the frontier properly guarded in case Afghanistan were to give trouble.

. . . .

Wallaroy   Wednesday, Aug. 12th 1914

My darling,

Every one is very busy saving and knitting. I started in earnest last night and have spent most of the day with knitting needles in my hands. Even

137

going into town in a carriage this morning with some parcels of wool. Nurse Gould who was in S. Africa for 2 years is asking every one to send her bags closed up and with the following list appended: 2 pairs pyjamas, 2 cardigans, 2 pairs of socks, a thermometer, enamel basin, several kinds of bandages and 12 yards of flannelette and calico, writing pad, pen and pencil, collar studs and toothbrush. I have forgotten the rest. These bags are to go to the Nursing Centres and as each wounded man comes in he is to be given one.

When she was in S. Africa she said the wounded used to come in with nothing but what they had on their backs, generally smothered in blood and very dirty. They ran out of pyjamas and other clothing and there was only one basin and one thermometer to every 60 men.

. . . .

Wallaroy   13th August 1914

Every one is pyjama mad. One seems to be surrounded by striped flannelette. I went over to see Mrs. Rich early this morning and could not find a chair to sit on in the drawing-room. She had about 4 dozen pairs cut out ready to send to people. Every one is busy packing bags. Sissie and I have undertaken to fill 4. I enclose a list of what I am putting in mine. They go to the base hospital and are given to the patients as they arrive. Every one you know is busy filling them, we hope to fill at least a thousand. There are rumours today that a force are going to New Guinea and start quite soon.

. . . .

Wallaroy   Friday, 14th August 1914

My darling,

You will never guess what I did today. I spent about 2 hours in a warehouse Paterson Laing and Bruce, buying great quantities of things for the bags I told you about. There is nothing like cheek and courage in this world. I pranced into Peapes asked to see the Head man or owner and was taken to a Mr. Millen who on hearing my name was Verney became most ingratiating. I told him I wanted his firm to cut me out pyjamas to be made up by different women for hospital bags, but first of all I wanted to get the material wholesale, but could not do this as a private individual, the merchants will only sell through a firm. So he offered to take me to P. L. Bruce if I did not mind working with him. We started off together to this colossal walking store in Wynyard Square. There I was introduced by Mr.

138

Millen to the Heals of the business as Mrs. Captain Verney!! and they were told to let me have anything I wanted, at cost price. Mr. M. and I shook hands and parted the best of friends. I proceeded to ransack the 10 storeys of P. Laing and B. huge warehouse. I carried away bales of material, ready made shirts, handkerchiefs, tooth brushes, pillow cases, towels, and I don't know what. The material Peapes are having cut out for me by a nice dark man who does all their cutting out, at a counter downstairs. He asked about you. On my way home with all my bundles I saw Mrs. Rich in her motor. She stopped my carriage and asked me to get in. So we transported all the parcels and then she told me that tomorrow 1,500 troops are leaving for one of the Islands. The Red Cross have no bundles ready yet and are nearly distracted trying to get them ready in time, they have only been given 24 hours' notice. Mrs. Rich took practically everything I had that was ready made and left me with hardly enough for my own 4 bags, so I foresaw another visit to the same place. Mrs. Knox came there in the afternoon and took what Mrs. Rich left, for the same purpose.

I see in tonight's paper that Japan has issued an ultimatum to Germany to clear out of her own part of China. Of course, this means War. No country could be expected to comply with such a demand. I rather wish Japan had kept out of it. G.B. is quite capable of fighting her own battles without her help and I foresee complications with the United States as she already shows signs of uneasiness in case Japan takes German Samoa which is opposite the Panama Canal.

Nita

. . . .

Kuldana   August 20th 1914

My own darling,

We heard more details last night about the landing of the Expeditionary Force in France and about the great reception they got at Boulogne also about General French's visit to Paris. It really was a most wonderful occasion as English troops have not landed on French soil except as enemies for centuries. We suppose that our troops are now in the thick of it somewhere near Liege, but we do not expect to hear much more news about them until the first big battle which may be taking place at this very moment.

We know that the German Emperor and his General Staff are now at the front and therefore the first real trial of strength is bound to take place very soon. We have definitely postponed our Gaff which was to have taken place next Tuesday because we none of us feel that we can go in for regimental concerts etc. when half the regiment may be fighting for their very lives in Belgium.

My idea is that our expeditionary force will form the left wing of the French Army. We are small in actual numbers, about 120,000 men, but I should think we must be very effective in quality and what makes an enormous difference our men are all keen to fight, just the opposite from all accounts of the German soldier. I cannot help feeling awfully sorry for the German private soldier who is a conscript and therefore compelled to fight against troops both French and English who, as far as we can judge now, are superior in almost every way. Certainly the French artillery is better than the German and I firmly believe that our more extended tactical formations, the result chiefly of lessons learnt in S. Africa, will enable us to destroy the masses of German troops with our machine guns just as a scythe cuts grass. To my mind it is really a question as to how long the German troops will stand being mowed down before they either lay down their arms or run! Am I altogether too optimistic?

Lord Kitchener is absolutely right to act as if the War will be a long one. If he makes preparations for a second or even a third Army to be sent to Europe in 6 months' time, should the War come to an end before that we shall have such a much stronger voice in the final settlement. Should the German Fleet be able to defeat our fleet and thus get command of the Sea our 2nd and 3rd Army will then be ready to defend our shores against invasion, so whichever way you look at it I think K. had no alternative but to act as if the War might be a long one.

. . . .

Kuldana   August 26th 1914

My own darling wife,

At about 2 a.m. last night the Colonel got a wire from Simla ordering us to mobilize and get ready to embark for England at an early date, with all our baggage, women and children; we suppose we shall perhaps be a fortnight at home, and then go on active service. I was very uncertain about the cable I was to send you, but on the whole I decided that you would wish to come to England, on the chance that we may be able to have some little time together before I go. On the other hand we may go off very soon after our arrival, but even then I thought you would feel happier to be in England than at the other end of the World.

We think we are going in the *Dongola*, which arrives at Bombay about Sept. 2nd and might leave again about Sept. 8th which would get us home about the 29th September and if you were able to catch this steamer on Saturday, which I am afraid would be a dreadful rush for you, you might be at home during the first week in October.

· ·

Ralph to his Mother

Kuldana   *Bergendal Day*   27th August 1914

My dearest Mother,

In reply to my cable to Nita asking if she could start on Saturday for England I got the following reply this morning: 'All sailing Saturday Oceanic Steamship *Venture* reach Honolulu tenth San Francisco seventeenth London twenty ninth Sept. cable your plans.'

I never knew anyone so capable as Nita. It never occurred to me that she would go home by that route but she will get home many days sooner than by the P & O which would of course have to go round by Gibraltar. In fact we ought to arrive about the same day if we leave Bombay about Sept. 8th. Her cable has thrilled me quite enormously because it makes it practically certain that we shall meet at home before we go on active service.

I feel an absolutely different man as I was getting most frightfully depressed about our chances of meeting. In fact I thought it probable that we would have left for Europe just before Nita arrived which would have been terrible. When I had sent her that first cable I could not help wondering if I had done right in doing so and thought that perhaps it would have been wiser to have left her in peace and quiet until she heard from me by letter. But her prompt and practical answer to it has made me feel quite sure that it was right to let her know.

· ·

Troopship *Somali*   Sept. 9th 1914

My dearest wife,

I must tell you in a few words about our march down to Pindi and our journey from there to Bombay. We left Murree at 2.30 p.m. on Thursday and we had quite a send off, all the Generals came to say goodbye to us and I saw Miss Louis Dowling and waved goodbye to her. We got to Trott about 6.30 p.m. where we were to bivouac for the night, but at 8 p.m. it came on to rain really hard so the Colonel gave the order to march again at 11.30 p.m. for Barraco, our second camping place; we marched all night with a most lovely Moon and clear sky and we reached Barraco at about 4 a.m. where we stayed all day, pretty tired out, it was terribly hot there. We started our last march at 2 a.m. and got to Pindi by 6.30 a.m. on Saturday. Puss met us about 2 miles out and told us that our troop train was to start about midday instead of 6 p.m. So we had to hurry up in order to do everything that had to be done in Pindi such as handing in our blankets etc. I got off duty about 9 a.m. and went for a bath and breakfast to the North Stafford officers' mess in the Mall. After which I went to the telegraph office and sent you a cable to Honolulu, though you will not be there till tomorrow.

We came to Bombay in two trains, in the first were the Colonel, Brockholes, Alldridges and No. 1 and 4 Companies. Claud Squidge and I shared a compartment, not one of those big ones but those shorter ones. Still we were not too uncomfortable. In the second train which was commanded by the Boy were the others, also Mrs. Harman. We reached Bombay at about 5 a.m. on Tuesday morning, the journey was not altogether without incident. Our native fireman fell off the engine while we were going about 30 miles an hour at 7 p.m. one evening, we stopped and went back and picked him up, our doctor attended to him and wonderful to say that he had only broken his collar bone and badly bruised himself.

At Baroda the Gaekwar provided tea and buns for all the troops so we stopped there and each man, woman and child got a mug of tea and a bun. The Gaekwar himself is in Scotland but this was done by his orders and one of his ministers was at the station to see that it was all done properly. I had a long talk to him and liked him very much.

When we got to Bombay we found nobody of any kind to meet us. We thought we were to embark on the *Dongola* but were not sure. We finally found a sergeant on the embarkation staff who to our absolute amazement told us that orders had been issued by the Admiralty the previous evening that no more transports were to leave till the 18th. This turned out to be correct and telegrams had been sent to stop us at Rutlam on the way but we had already passed that place. So here we are stuck out in the harbour just opposite the Taj Mahal hotel for 9 more days.

The reason apparently is that there is a German Cruiser somewhere between here and the East Coast of Africa and the Admiralty do not want to send out this convoy of troopships until H.M.S. *Swiftsure* gets here from Port Said to escort us. The Berkshire Regiment who are also on their

way to Bombay were stopped at a place called Deolali and are in camp
there for 10 days. I am so glad we reached Bombay as it is more amusing
here and also cooler out in the harbour. But this means that we shall not
get home till about Oct. 20th as we are not allowed to go more than 10
knots an hour. I believe we may be a convoy of anything from 10 to 20
ships, some of which are going straight to France with troops from India,
but we are pretty certain to come to Southampton.

The War news is much better these last two days, that the Germans
have had to take 1 or 2 Army Corps away from the West frontier to meet
the Russian advance on their Eastern frontier. This probably shows that
they are very nervous at the success the Russians have had so far and also
that they have not got any reserves which they can send out to meet the
Russians who captured 4000 Austrians and 100 guns from the Prussians,
driving the latter back on to the Konigsberg Fortress. There is no doubt
that the Russians so far have been victorious all along the line. The
Germans moved their troops from West to East in 130 trains, that means
70,000 men altogether. In my opinion this is most excellent news as I feel
sure they would not have weakened their force against the French,
Belgians and ourselves unless it was absolutely necessary. If only the
Russians can still continue their advance successfully I do not believe this
War can possibly be a long one. The German advance seems to have been
really checked at last and Austria practically has ceased to exist. She has
been frightfully badly beaten by the Russians. I do not see what is to stop
the latter now advancing as fast as possible from the South straight to
Berlin.

I may even be made a Major without having to take any exams!!!

Very much love I think of you and John on your long journey.

Ralph

. . . .

Nita to her Family

Oceanic Steamship Company S.S. *Sierra*   2nd Sept. 1914
At Sea near Pago Pago

Darling Family,

I've just sent you a wireless cable saying very well which means smooth
trip all very well but to tell you the honest truth we couldn't have had a
more ghastly time, not that it has been specially rough, but Nurse has been
seasick ever since we left the Heads, John has been seasick too and

altogether a very fractious nervy little person which we put down to his teeth and the unusual bustle and noises round him. The bugle which is blown 6 times a day upsets him for quite ten minutes afterwards. Nurse has been better today and yesterday. That is why I am able to leave John and write, she has eaten practically nothing since we left Sydney except dry biscuits, the cook's chicken broth in jelly form, the other Sissie gave us she finds too strong, and lettuce, tomatoes and radishes. I do not know which was the worst day, Sunday or Monday. We pitched vilely all Sunday so she never left her bunk. I hadn't time to wash but crawled up on deck with John wrapped up in a shawl, his face was a yellow green and he was too sick to cry. We sat up on deck nearly all day, a very grubby miserable pair, only descending for his bottles which he would hardly touch. The atmosphere in the cabin was appalling, Nurse was sick about every five minutes, there wasn't room either to turn round. The ship is so unexpectedly full, they are short of everything and the steward could only find one pillow for the two of us, this I gave Nurse and slept on the sofa with a bundle of clothes under my head and a dressing gown as the sole bedclothes.

. . . .

Nita to her Sister

Overland Limited, Extra Fare Train   19th Sept. 1914
Chicago – San Francisco

Darling Sissie,

We had a terrific rush in Frisco and only just caught this train, there was such a lot of bother about customs etc. Our compartment is almost bigger than our cabin and almost in the observation car so we spend the day there. Letters from Mrs. V. and Gwen were waiting for me in Frisco also cables from Wallaroy, Claydon and Ralph. The latter's regiment was delayed in Bombay so he won't be home until the middle of October. I'm so glad as I wanted to be there before him. The latest War news which we get almost every two hours at different stations is not so good, the Germans seem to be making a firm stand and the bloodshed is worse than ever. The food is more expensive than ever in this country. Boiled eggs 25 cents = 1/–, 2 poached eggs 40 cents = 1/8. No wonder thay have railroad kings. The stenographer who is clicking away at this machine just beside me has been the greatest use fixing up about some luggage which had to be left behind in Frisco because there wasn't room for it; we are carrying all the Australian mails so the baggage car is pretty full.

My passages were taken on the *Lusitania* sailing on Wednesday at 1.30 a.m. which meant going on board Tuesday night but I see in the papers today she has been requisitioned by the Canadian Govt. so I don't know what our plans are. We are not going to the Ritz Carlton it is too expensive, 5 dollars a day without food. I'd rather spend the money on something else.

We reach Chicago tomorrow morning and have 3 hours there.

Much love
Nita

. . . .

Ralph to Nita

H.T. *Somali*   Sept. 21st 1914

My own darling,

We sailed from Bombay soon after 11 a.m. yesterday. When we had got 3 miles out we took up our proper positions in this large convoy of about 33 ships. H.M.S. *Swiftsure*, the flagship, leads, then comes H.M.S. *Fox* behind her and to her Port then the *Dongola* and ourselves and then several lines of transports 6 abreast in two divisions. It really is a wonderful sight and crowds watched our departure yesterday from the Apollo Bunder opposite the Taj Mahal.

There will be No. 3 division when we meet the transport from Karachi but I do not quite know when or where that is to be [*sic*], somewhere this side of Aden. I believe we shall then be 48 transports. I should think this must be the largest convoy in tonnage that has ever sailed, though perhaps in actual numbers Napoleon's convoy of ships to Egypt may have been larger, but certainly this must be the largest convoy of steamships that has ever sailed.

Last night I was on deck reading signal messages with Holes when a ship appeared on the horizon. H.M.S. *Fox* was at once sent to find out what ship this was. This job took her about an hour and on her way back Holes and I read her signal message to the Flagship saying she was a Dutch boat bound for Tuticorin. This was about 10 p.m. Just then another strange light appeared on the horizon on our Port Bow. In a moment all lights were extinguished on the *Fox* and she went after this second ship. Holes and I could just see a small light from the *Fox* which was only visible

145

from this side. We watched the second ship and H.M.S. *Fox* getting closer and closer; when they were perhaps ½ a mile suddenly H.M.S. *Fox* flashed her searchlight straight on to her, it really was quite a thrilling sight. Of course she turned out to be a perfectly harmless tramp. But this trip will be full of minor excitements like that because of course this German cruiser the *Konigsberg* is known to be sailing about somewhere and this convoy offers her a wonderful opportunity if she has any dash!!

So every ship we pass at night is investigated by the *Fox*, both the Flagship and the *Fox* are cleared for action the whole time except that in the daytime there are awnings up over the quarterdeck. At night there are any number of signal messages being sent by lamp so I am always amused after dinner reading them.

. . . .

R.M.S. *Lusitania*   Sept. 27th 1914

My very dear husband,

It has never entered my head that you might be landed in France instead of coming to England until yesterday when I talked to a passenger, Sir Charles Ross,* who seems to be behind the scenes and to spend a lot of time at the War Office. He does not think there is any possibility of your getting past Marseilles, troops are so urgently required in France and embarking and disembarking takes so much time. I have been down in the depths ever since for oh I just long for a sight of your dear face and to feel your arms round me again.

I want almost most of all to see you and little John together. We have had such a long weary journey to get to you and now when it seems only a matter of days before we meet, all my hopes and plans must come to nought. You must be longing to know about the arrival of that fateful telegram.

It only reached me on the Wednesday night 26th August. When I opened and read it in the nursery I suffered the most terrible ten minutes of my life because I knew there was only one ship leaving Sydney on Saturday, the *Ventura*, sailing for America and according to the morning papers quite full. The Orient boat had been requisitioned by the Australian Government and the P & O leaving the next week would not get me to England until the end of October. So I had to catch the *Ventura* if I wasn't to fail you and I don't think I have done that yet darling since we married.

146

Father was in bed so I took the cable into the room and told him and mother quite quietly that I was leaving on Saturday, then raced down stairs and rang up the *Ventura's* agent. He spoke himself as it was after time and he was just locking up, he had to listen to a long explanation from me of the situation. I told him frankly he must find me a berth, I didn't mind in which class. He was very nice and said he could manage to fit me in but doubted if they had room for nurse and John, but would I call in in the morning.

I couldn't sleep a wink that night for I felt I couldn't face you without John and yet in my present condition it was a physical impossibility for me to look after him alone. At 8.30 thanks to Eadith's offer of the Rolls Royce I invaded the office and got what I wanted, the only cabin left on the ship. It was very diminutive, had no porthole and as far forrard as it could be. That day and the next were entirely taken up shopping for John, packing and saying goodbye to all the friends who flocked to Wallaroy at the most inconvenient times.

Everything was onboard in plenty of time on Saturday morning but John and I did not leave Wallaroy until 1.30. We said goodbye to father and mother there and were seen off by the boys, Sissie, Clo and Alec's family. They said goodbye at 2.30 but we didn't sail until after 4 as the ship had to be searched for Germans, 4 were found and left behind. As we sailed through the Heads I saw Sissie, Eadith and the Boys waving towels from our old point. I waved a nightgown of John's in return.

By paying an extra £7 I am thankful to say I was able to get another cabin with a porthole instead of that terrible black hole. The new one looked out onto the 2nd Class deck so I had my chair placed there and we used to be so nice and close when we wanted to take John into the cabin. When it got very hot we all slept out on this deck.

Marion our late parlourmaid at Wallaroy was in the 2nd class and the greatest help to me that first week as nurse was ill. I do not think I ever loathed a ship so much, we pitched from the time we left Sydney till we reached Frisco.

John's greatest friend on board was the deck steward whom he simply adored. When we had been onboard about 10 days I found out that he was not only in the Rifle Brigade but in the 2nd Batt. and remembered you joining perfectly. He was in the band and left the regiment in Cairo after being with it for 13 years. He asked particularly after Major Stephens who he thought one of the finest soldiers in the regiment. He was delighted to hear he is Colonel of the 2nd. Gillett is the steward's name but I don't suppose you would remember him.

147

We had an awful rush at San Francisco and only just caught our train. We had four days in the train breaking the journey at Chicago for about 3 hours. Then we went on in the 20th Century Limited, the millionaires' train and fastest in the world doing 180 miles in 2 hours. There was hardly any movement to be felt and I must say the Americans have got some reason for boasting about their trains, they are gorgeous and so comfortable. We had a delightful large coupé next to the observation car in the first train and an even more sumptuous one in the second train. John missed all the fresh air he got on the ship and the heat was most aggressive. The one drawback is the à la carte system for meals. It was such a bore having to calculate what the price of your breakfast or dinner was going to cost. 2 boiled eggs were 25 cents 1/−, 2 poached eggs 40 cents 1/8!! I thought it was just as well you were not with us owing to the heat and the fact that we got no exercise our appetites were very poor and we found two meals a day ample. Each compartment had its own filter of iced drinking water and boiling and cold water laid on.

Joscelyne hasn't started kicking yet, but I think she is very well. It is odd how history repeats itself. Kathleen and I are destined to travel at these periods and to travel without our husbands.

Eadith lent me £105 in cash before I left so I did not touch my letter of credit for £100 so you need not worry about money matters. Eadith will wait for the return of the loan. This trip has been very expensive but if you do come to England well worth it as it is the only way I could have possibly got to England in time. All the Orient boats have been taken off and the P & O passengers have to come all the way round.

I haven't told Nurse yet about Joscelyne but think I must soon. I didn't tell the family as I thought it would only add to mother's worries and it would be better to do it after I had got safely home.

* Sir Charles Ross (1872–1942) was Adviser on Small Arms to the Canadian Government during the First World War and inventor of the Canadian service rifle.

. . . .

Nita to her Family

33 Manor House, Marylebone Road   1st Oct. 1914

Dearest Family,

Nurse, John and I are all alone in this quaint flat. Mrs. Verney and Gwen having returned to Botolph House today.

148

We had a perfect trip across the Atlantic, sea as smooth as a lake and no signs of Germans but we had a bad fog for the first three days which made us a day late. We reached Liverpool about 11 a.m. of the 29th instead of the 28th. We got here at 4 o'clock and were met by Mrs. Verney and Gwen. [Claydon] Harry and Mr. Batty* came to supper. Harry is now a member of the Government, Under Secretary to the board of Agriculture so quite an important personage in Liberals' eyes. Joan came to lunch yesterday, John's 1st birthday and looked younger and prettier than ever. Harry [Lloyd] is constantly in waiting now as most of the household are at the front or drilling. He works from 4 p.m. till midnight at the Foreign Office and gets the War news first hand. All the tales of German atrocities to the Belgians are perfectly true, there is one child now at the Alexandra Palace who has had both hands cut off and an old man over 70 who is bent double because he had to walk before the troops and was prodded in the back with their bayonets because he was feeble and slow. Recruits are pouring in; it is considered quite a disgrace not to be represented at the front by some member of your family. Several mid-shipmen of 15 and 16 were killed when the *Aboukir*, *Cressy* and that other cruiser were sunk.**

I wonder if the following story has reached you. It is quite true. When we had those awful reverses at first and the Germans nearly got to Paris Kitchener went over to France and asked Joffre why he had not gone to French's rescue after French had sent so many urgent demands for help. Joffre denied ever getting them so they sent for the Chief of the Staff, a well-known French general, searched him and found the missing de-spatches upon him, they then searched his house where correspondence with Germany was discovered. His wife was a German and he had been a traitor to his own Army and Country. He was shot before the whole of his brigade and 5 other Generals dismissed. This was the reason we suddenly took the offensive and drove back the Germans. The French Army had been taught a lesson. I believe they were dreadfully chicken-hearted at first and simply fled from Namur when the first guns began to attack it. Our men have put a lot of grit into them.

Every one is looking forward to the arrival of the Australian contingent, they are all delighted we have done so much because the Germans predicted that our Colonies would seek their own interests if Great Britain was embroiled in War and never counted on such splendid loyalty. No one ever knows when regiments leave the country. They have no send-off or demonstrations of any kind. There is no doubt Kitchener is a marvellous organizer.

Rachel is down at Claydon, she is expecting another baby in January. Very very much love to you all from

Nita

* See footnote page 87.
** On 22 September, 1914, the German submarine *U-9* sank the three British armoured cruisers *Aboukir*, *Cressy* and *Hogue* in the North Sea. 62 officers and 1397 men of the 2200 aboard the three cruisers were lost.

. . . .

Nita to her Sister

The George Hotel, Winchester   23rd Oct. 1914

Darling Sissie,

No time for much as I've left my mail so late as I did want to give you news of R., but he has not appeared yet and Mrs. Stephens and I are growing too despondent. I'm sure the hotel people think he is a myth.

I went up to the station at 7 this morning and saw hundreds of soldiers with helmets and black buttons. I ran for all I was worth and nearly embraced the first, thinking he was an RR sergeant, but he was an Irish rifleman and told me he had come all the way from India with the same convoy as the *Somali*. She left there two days ago, he thinks bound for Plymouth. His ship went to Liverpool and arrived there last night I've written Mum some surprising news. I hope she won't feel hurt that I didn't tell her before, namely that there is to be an addition to the family in March, but I thought she would worry dreadfully if she knew about it while I was travelling. She will remember how I nearly had hysterics at dinner the night before I left.

Very much love from
Nita

P.S.   If it is a boy he is to be David. If a girl, I want you and Joan to be godmothers. You can decide on a name only not Emily I implore you!!   . . .

Nita to her Mother

Hursley Village   28th Oct. 1914

Darling Mumpty,

Ralph finally arrived on Friday 23rd about 10 p.m. All the mothers and wives were on the Winchester station, but it was very tantalizing. We only saw our belongings for about five minutes and then they marched off to the depot for tea and buns. Ralph was not allowed to stay with me at the hotel so I decided to come down here, late as it was, and he said he would try and breakfast with me. I went back to the George and packed my bag while the porter tried to get me a car but there wasn't one to be found in the town, there is such a demand. I was getting desperate as it was about 10.30 and this cottage is over 5 miles away when some officers who were returning to camp offered me a lift in their taxi so we started off a party of 5 in a small car stopping at the depot on the way to tell Ralph. My companions were very nice and most amusing and just as tickled as I at such an unconventional proceeding but there is no doubt War clears away a lot of fusty notions and conventions. We had a 5 mile drive and then alighted at this cottage, one officer preceding with an electric torch the others and I following with my luggage. It was just 11 when we managed to make my good landlady hear our blows and shouts and I said goodbye to my unknown and unseen escort whom it is not likely I shall ever recognize or see again. Next morning when I woke up it was pouring and I wondered if Ralph would think it worth while to come so far for breakfast especially as he did not know the way so I got up and dressed and at 7.30 accompanied by the youngest boy in the house aged 11 I started to walk to the camp. It is a good half-hour's walk and as it was teeming I stood under a tree and sent Freddy the last half mile for Ralph. He was so relieved to see me as it was quite impossible for him to get away and he did not know how he was to let me know. I had to come back alone and sit down to a solitary breakfast. After breakfast I telephoned to Nurse from the village post office to bring John out in a motor with lots of provisions such as fish, meat, butter, cakes and a *bath* tub, there has never been such a thing in this house! Ralph managed to come down for lunch. Mrs. Hayes cooks quite nicely and is so willing and anxious to make us comfortable. We have this sittingroom and a double bedroom at the top of a spiral staircase. Everything is spotlessly clean and she and her husband are quite the best type old-fashioned village folk. They have 6 sons! Ralph has a cold but is looking very brown and well and oh so glad to be home for a short time. He had to go back to camp before John arrived, so I took John there in the motor and Ralph lifted him out and carried him off to his tent. John was perfectly willing and not in the least shy, he very soon showed his preference for R.'s arms to mine. R. shares his tent with Capt. Powell whose bed was laid out on the ground so John had a great romp being rolled from one end to the other. He didn't mind how much he was tumbled about and had such rosy cheeks and such a sturdy air.

151

Ralph is busy up at the camp today so I am all alone in the cottage and do not expect him home until tea time. I walked up with him at 8.30 this morning. Tomorrow he has to attend a Divisional March. The whole division, 20,000 men, are going to march out 15 miles for inspection by the General. They are holding a Field day now in a field behind this cottage. The roads are blocked with ammunition waggons gun carriages and soldiers of every description. It is quite difficult work getting along and the guns are booming all the time, one might be near Ostende.

What treacherous creatures De Wet & B[eyers] are. I think Botha is splendid the way he is fighting for us.* The Guards have just been very severely damaged again. The 1st & 2nd Life Guards have lost most of their officers killed wounded or missing. Our third death has been reported, Captain Norman Leslie, the gay Lothario of the regiment, nephew of Mrs. Cornwallis West or Lady Randolph Churchill as she calls herself now, and 1st cousin of Winston. He only left us in India 18 months ago.

* De Wet (see footnote p. 12) and Fredrik Byers (1867–1938), then Attorney-General of the Cape, were opposed to the campaign against German South-West Africa, while Botha, the Prime Minister of South Africa, supported the imperial government. Beyers and De Wet headed a rebellion which Botha put down. De Wet was taken prisoner and sent to prison for six years.

. . . .

Ralph to Nita's Mother

Hursley Camp, Winchester
2nd Bn. Rifle Brigade

My dearest Mum,

We are all ready to go off on active service, and may go any day at a few hours' notice, but I do not think we shall go before towards the end of the week. Nita is simply wonderful; she bought such a lot of things for me before I arrived, that it saved me endless time and trouble during the day and a half I was able to get in London, when we stayed at my mother's flat.

We have taken 14 Great Cumberland Place, opposite the Marble Arch, for 5 months; it is such a nice little house and so handy for John going into the Park.

She will stay there also for the arrival of our 2nd baby!! in February, which will be very convenient; it is only a few hundred yards from Connaught Place, and we got the house for 6½ guineas a week, which is very moderate. It is much better for her to have a little home of her own, as it will give her some occupation, and she will be able to have her own friends to see her or to stay.

It has made the whole difference to us, having this cottage here, as I could not possibly have got into Winchester to see her very often; it belongs to a gardener and his wife, and they have turned out of their sitting and bed rooms, so as to give them up to us.

I usually have to start up to the camp about 7.30 a.m. and Nita walks up most of the way with me; I do not get back again till about 4 or 5 p.m. We are busy training all day and every day. When we do go, I expect we shall march the 12 miles from here to Southampton; Nita insists on staying here till after I have gone; she will then probably send John to Botolph House, and go herself to the flat, until she has got the house in Great Cumberland Place ready.

Nita is extraordinarily well, and her long journey across the world does not seem to have affected her in the very least.

What a wonderful little person she is!!! She is going to send out to me things for the men in my Company, as well as for myself; as it is, no soldier in the whole army is better equipped than I am with warm clothing luminous watch and compass, patent shaving apparatus, cigarette lighter pocket medicine case etc. etc. all of which she got ready for me before I arrived.

Your always affectionate son
Ralph

. . . .

Nita to her Father

The George Hotel, Winchester   November 5th 1914

Dearest Father,

It is a very long time since I wrote to you and I have many letters of yours to acknowledge. Ralph left today for the front, part of the 8th Division so that I feel depressed and lonely goes without saying. We both feel very grateful that we had 12 days with each other, we didn't expect more than three or four at first, and we had oh such a happy time together in the little cottage, quite the happiest 12 days of 5 happy years of married life.

Most of the Division went off yesterday and R.'s brigade the 25th were ordered to start at 3 but thank goodness the General changed his mind and they didn't leave until today at 10.30 a.m. Mrs. Mackay who lives close to Hursley lent us the car for the day so I was able to get John out

153

to say goodbye to Ralph. R. was allowed to come back to the cottage for the night so had dinner and breakfast with me and we walked up to the camp together at 7.30 and said goodbye at 9.45. I returned to the cottage and stood by the gate as the regiment marched past on their way to Southampton. Ralph was mounted. It poured and is still pouring with rain so they didn't leave in the best of spirits.

. . . .

Victorian, Southampton   November 5th 1914

My own darling wife,

We had a horribly wet march, and I am afraid I felt very depressed most of the way, but I am better now.

We came straight inside the docks and got onboard this boat about 3.30 p.m. I do not know when we start, but we do not expect to get to Havre till about midday tomorrow. So we shall have a good night's rest, though we cannot get any of our kit. I am in a deck cabin with the Boy, Turkey and Claud.

The Gov. make no arrangements at all about feeding officers on this ship so we have sent Serg. Barber on shore to buy us some food. I really think they might feed us on this short trip.

Dear Sweetheart, you were such a plucky little wife today, as I knew you would be. I do hope you get that motor car alright. I am now writing in the only saloon, and shall try and post it somehow here.

My fondest love to you and John; your dear letter is in my pocket now, I shall keep it with your photo.

I do hope you are not feeling too depressed; I am as well as possible and much more cheerful.

I love to think of the last ten days at the cottage, and agree with every word you say about them in your letter.

Your own
Ralph

. . . .

. . . *Chapter Eight* . . .

Life in and out of the trenches. A steady toll of brother officers being killed. The first Christmas Armistice, and Ralph gets leave after his daughter Joscelyne is born.

S.S. . . . .   November 6th 1914

My own darling,

I feel so much more cheerful today and can honestly say I am looking forward to all the interesting part of this show, I am sure a lot of it will be wonderfully interesting.

Sweetheart you were so wonderfully plucky yesterday and it made it so much easier for me. I want to think of you as happy and busy in London and comfortable in your new house.

We do not know our plans yet but expect to go into a Rest Camp for perhaps 24 hours, and then go somewhere by train, probably in cattle trucks fitted up with benches. I gave Couchman that wooly helmet which he was very grateful for, also chocolate to Geary and Ennis. This boat is really a cattle boat and usually goes to the Gulf of Mexico.

I gave a lecture this morning to my officers and sergeants about various things the Colonel talked to Company Commanders about earlier, such as straggling, importance of keeping the emergency ration untouched till ordered to eat it, billets etc.

. . . .

Nita to her Family

33 Manor House, N.W.   November 7th 1914

I enjoy staying with Joan and Harry so much and having the car at my disposal. Joan hears so much about the War from people in the know. French's secretary came over the other day and had a talk with the King,

Harry* saw him too and was told that everything was going simply splendidly for us at the front. In fact for the first time since the War began, just as we wanted; he couldn't make out why the papers didn't print more optimistic accounts.

Your loving
Mid.

* Harry Lloyd was Groom-in-waiting to King George V.

. . . .

November 8th 1914

My own darling wife,

I saw Bill Seymour yesterday in the distance, he is on duty here in connection with the troopships, also a chap in the regiment called Spencer, who was at Harrow with Harry and myself; he has just come back from the Staff College, and he told me that he thought that the Allies would be able to make a big advance during the next week.

He said that the German infantry are very little good now. He has not been at the front himself, but he has talked to a great many officers who have returned wounded, and they told him that the German infantry are allowed to get within 200 yards of our trenches and that we then open up on them with rapid fire and machine guns, and simply mow them down till it is quite sickening.

Your always affect, husband
Ralph

. . . .

Rutland Gardens   November 8th 1914

My own darling,

The news in todays papers is much the same. Capt. Gilliat has been killed, also Major Paley R.B. Sebbie Alison aged 17 who has just joined the Coldstream is missing, Mr. Alison will be worried. The North's ship was in that big Heligoland fight, his brother Major North has just been killed. Harry told us last night that a spy has been shot but it is not to come out in the papers as it might affect the Germans' treatment of our men in Germany.

Nita

. . . .

November 9th 1914

Such good news in the papers today, the Russians are sweeping the Germans before them and have crossed the border and are near Posen. Once Posen is captured there are no fortresses between it and Berlin. I was awfully sorry to see that Mr. McGregor's brother died from wounds on Saturday at his people's house in Cadogan Sq. It must be some consolation to his mother that she was able to nurse him and be with him at the end, he was only 19.

I have practically engaged the house parlour maid so will move in on Thursday. I expect a cook and between maid this evening. The Regina Bureau are sending me some.

. . . .

November 15th

The news today has been very good. Harry [Lloyd] came home to lunch and told us the *Emden* had been sunk by an Australian cruiser, the *Karlsruhe* chased onto some rocks, he thinks by the Faroe islands. Joan came back from Devonshire House with the good news that a German submarine had been sunk under the Firth of Forth bridge!

Nita

. . . .

In France   November 11th 1914

My own darling wife,

We marched a good 5 miles to the train, which was alongside the docks, and consisted of cattle trucks, roofed in, with wooden benches inside, each truck holding 40 men with their rifles and equipment, though sardines in a tin have much more elbow room than those 40 men did in a truck! We got to the train soon after midnight but found nobody there to meet us, so the Colonel rang up the telephone and demanded a staff officer who duly arrived. There was also only accommodation for 24 officers in three small first class compartments and we were 30 altogether. However, after a bit, with immense difficulty, this was remedied by attaching another first class coach with 3 compartments, so that we only had 4 in each carriage, as Teddy, Rosie and Monty bedded down in straw in a luggage van; it was so late when we started and so cold that we none of us slept much.

We travelled all day and the next night during which I slept splendidly, though I could only half lie down, as we were 4 in the carriage. It seemed so extraordinary to be travelling to the front in a first class railway carriage, reading the Morning Post! The country looked so peaceful, and no signs of War were visible anywhere.

We got to our destination early this morning, about 5 a.m., and detrained at once, and got the hot tea ready; it was not cold but there was a slight drizzle. We heard the first gun in the distance at about 7 a.m. on this our wedding day! We marched from the station at about 9 o'clock to a village 2 miles away, near where we are now billeted; I and my Company are in a delightful farmhouse, the men are in the farm buildings and the officers have been given the kitchen, a sitting room and a small bedroom with a large double bed, which will be occupied by me tonight!! So we are splendidly warm and comfortable and hope we may be left here for a day or two.

. . . .

14 Great Cumberland Place   November 12th 1914

My own darling Sweetheart,

Observe the address. I cannot realize that this is to be my home for the next five months. It all seems so strange and lonely. I came here this morning and was rather bored to find nothing had arrived from Winchester. I telegraphed to Judge to find out if the cases had left but have had no reply yet. I felt I must do something in the way of unpacking so went to the flat and collected all my possessions there and brought them here this afternoon and have been busy for the last hour unpacking and tidying away helped by my house parlour maid. The 'Tweeny' does not come until tonight and the cook on Saturday morning. I've put the maids on board wages until she comes and have my meals out.

. . . .

                                                            November 13th 1914

My darling Ralph,

I heard from Joan who always seems to get this sort of information from unknown sources that you reached the Front a day or two ago so you are probably participating in these fierce assaults round Dixmude. If I am right say 'Yes' in your next letter, if not 'No' means you are further south nearer Ypres or Armentières. I see by today's papers that the operations during the last few days have consisted mainly of heavy fighting to the north of Lys, the allies strength has been constantly maintained by reinforcements, our line has been maintained not without considerable losses.!!

On the whole the War news today is better. The Germans do not seem to be able to get past Dixmude though they seized it two days ago and the Russians are advancing rapidly especially in East Prussia, they have taken Johannisberg and are near Thorn further south.

. . . .

In France   November 13th 1914

My own darling wife,

Yesterday morning we spent in a short route march and a practice attack through a wood; there were a good many pheasants in this wood, and my bugler signaller and runner and myself managed to secure a wounded one, Puss Whitaker got another, and a third was caught by some other men in the Company! This is strictly against all orders, but I came back with one of them, a big fat cock pheasant, in my haversack, which we had for dinner last night! On our way back about 1 p.m. it was given out that arrangements had been made by the Brigade office for two motor wagons to be at their office at 2 p.m. to take about 40 officers up to the front to look at the trenches.

Our Colonel allowed Captains to go if they wanted to, so I bolted some bread and cheese, and rode over to the Brigade office by 2 p.m. There was no sign of the motors, but they did turn up about 2.45 p.m. While waiting I saw 5 motor ambulances, flying a small American flag, halted by the side of the road; I went up to one of them and had a long talk to the two Americans driving it; they turned out to be American medical students, who were studying in Paris when the War broke out, and they volunteered to serve with these motor ambulances, all five of which were given by a Mrs. Vanderbilt. They only stopped about a quarter of an hour and were empty.

We started off in these lorries about 3 p.m. just like a party of Cook's tourists, we most of us sat on the floor or stood up looking out for any signs of the War. We passed through one or two fairly large country towns, and saw the effect of shell fire; in one place the only building which was touched was the big church which had been completely demolished. It was curious to see the ordinary country life going on just the same, children running about the cottage gardens, women at work washing etc. After about 10 miles or rather more, we were going through the street leading out of town when we suddenly saw General Wilson* commanding the 4th Division, who used to command this Battalion in Egypt. We stopped and had a great talk to him, and he showed us all over the 2nd line trenches which were dug and still were being worked at by hundreds of Belgian refugees, who were forced to do this, but were each paid 3 francs a day for a certain completed task.

These trenches were only about 2½ miles in rear of the first line trenches, and they were only in case our first line had to retire for any reason; the trenches were about six feet deep and two feet wide and every ten yards or so there was a strong traverse for protection against enfilade fire. A high wire entanglement was in front. Of course these trenches were much better than the first line ones, and more elaborate.

Ralph

* General (later Field-Marshal Sir) Henry Wilson (1864–1922) had supported the Ulster cause during the Curragh incident in May, 1914, was made Chief of the Imperial General Staff in 1918 and was assassinated by the Sinn Fein in London in 1922.

. . . .

November 18th 1914

My own darling wife,

2 more letters from you this morning and 2 parcels; so very many thanks for the cap cover which will be immensely useful, also a pair of socks which I have got on now, sausages, cigarettes, a lovely knife and two refills for my lamp. Perhaps you would send me out one of these every week, as they do not last long, and the lamp is most useful. Also you sent me a towel which was most wanted, handkerchiefs equally so, tobacco etc.

I have done my first day in the trenches, and am now writing to you sitting in a dugout in some reserve trenches. The night before last I was ordered to take my Company out as a support to a regiment in the firing line trenches. About 1 a.m. while lying in a barn, I got a message from their Colonel that he would like me to come up into the trenches, so I went up and stayed there all yesterday, and rejoined my Battalion last night, as reserve Company, the other three Companies being in the firing line trenches now.

I simply cannot give you any idea of the dirt and mess one gets into in the trenches, which are made of clay-like soil and are deep and narrow;

passing along them, all one's clothes from head to foot get absolutely smothered in clay! The German trenches were only about 400 yards away from ours!

We have to do the reliefs in the trenches after dark. I have seen a good deal of shell fire but not very much rifle fire yet. Joe had a Corporal Green in his Company killed and one man wounded yesterday by bullets coming through the loopholes in the trenches. Those are our first casualties. I hope after 3 or 4 days in the trenches we may get 3 days in reserve in billets about 2 miles in rear, but even in these billets one often has to leave them in a hurry and take cover in trenches or 'funk holes' from shell fire.

. . . .

November 22nd 1914

As regards the part of the trenches we occupy, some of it is about 500 yards from the Germans and another part is under 100 yards from an advanced post which the Germans are digging, looking through the loophole one can see the earth being thrown up from below by the digger who is at the bottom. Two men were sent out the other night to creep up and try and find out something about this trench. They got out about 60 yards when they suddenly found themselves near another low trench invisible from our line, with a German sentry in it. He gave the alarm and one of our two men was shot dead, the other getting back safely, the one who was shot is still lying out there half covered in snow. We cannot get him back without risking other lives so have to leave him there. The Germans are very good at sniping and have shot more than one man dead by aiming at our loopholes. When on duty in the trenches every 2nd man has to be awake all night and during the day only about one in every ten are on watch. The trenches are very narrow and it is an awful job relieving or being relieved by another regiment. It takes quite two hours to do it and of course it can only be done after dark. During the day there is always work to be done in digging the trenches deeper or in digging small dugouts in the back or front faces of the interior of the trenches for the men to lie down in or sit in or light fires in. Every few hundred yards trenches are dug from the firing line back to the road about 300 yards or more in rear and it is by these communication trenches that one is able to get up into the firing line trenches. In some cases these communication trenches are not more than 3½ feet deep so it means stooping pretty low or else running the risk of a bullet. This morning in the farm we found 3 fat sows so we shot one with a revolver and the men are cooking bits of her now and using her fat to rub on their feet. We are all wondering if we are going to sit down on this line and try and starve the Germans out or break them financially. It will surely mean a long job. I should hate to have to sit on here all the winter and then continue the campaign again next summer, it seems so endless. I only hope the Russians do not propose to carry out a similar programme!! We hear that the kind of routine arranged at present is for each regiment to do 3 days in the trenches, 3 in billets like these, 3 more days in the trenches and then the 4th three days going back to the Divisional area so as to enable men and officers to get a proper wash and rest.

. . . .

November 23rd 1914

My own darling wife,

This morning in this cottage I have had no less than 3 lots of poor French inhabitants brought to me by my sentries; the first lot consisted of 3 old women who lived in a cottage somewhere close by, they had taken refuge from the Germans in a relation's house about 5 miles from here; these old women had walked in early this morning to try and recover some of their possessions, but I could not possibly allow them to go along the road to their cottage because it is not safe and is always being sniped by the Germans. So I gave them a cup of tea each and a slice of bread and jam and sent them back under escort to our headquarters.

The next to come was a man and his wife, a couple of about 35 to 40 years old; they used to have a small farm along this road. They had come today from a village about 4 miles to the rear, with a permit to allow them to see if anything had been left. They returned this way in half an hour, carrying a 2-handled basket containing all their worldly possessions, a few old clothes, an old hat etc. Their cows, their grain, chickens, household linen etc. had all gone; I felt so sorry for them.

The third party only came a few minutes ago and those were three women who lived in a small cottage farm close by; I have sent them under a guard with orders to allow them a quarter of an hour to collect any of their belongings; I am afraid this will be ample time for the purpose.

People in our villages at home, such as the Claydons, can have no conception what War means to the poor inhabitants; all these people are much the same as the Claydon people, having their small cottages or little farms; they had to clear out when the Germans came and are only now venturing to return to see what is left; in many cases their houses have been absolutely destroyed by shell fire, their food etc. taken for the use of the troops; because in an unoccupied house everything is looked upon as common property, and I do not see what other alternative there is, as the livestock would probably die of starvation, and the rest of their possessions be destroyed by shell fire. We do just the same; yesterday Teddy shot a big fat sow in this farm; we used her fat to rub onto the men's feet, and the men each had a bit of her to eat! There are a few cows still wandering about and I have told off two of my men to milk them and put them into some old broken-down stables; they have no owner as far as we know, so we make what use we can of them. Another big fat pig was killed this morning, and is being put to the same use. I cannot help thinking that if some of the people in England had to put up with experiences such as these in their own villages and homes, there would be no need for conscription, nor any lack of volunteers ready to train themselves for the defence of their families and their homes.

Those last three women have just returned in tears, carrying what they could in baskets or bundles; one of them used to have 5 cows, but she could not see any of them wandering about; they have walked over 5 miles over here and are now on their way back. We have to be so careful to guard against German spies that no one at all is allowed to be walking about without a passport or written permit; so it is not easy for these people to come here, even to see what is left of their own possessions.

Very much love
Your own husband
Ralph

. . . .

November 24th 1914

My own darling wife,

This morning 206 goat skins made up into coats arrived as a Government issue for officers and men, I should think they are excellent, we wear them under the overcoat and they come just down to the hip. We go back into the trenches this evening.

A patrol of one officer and 8 men of the Lincoln Regt. went out last night to the German trenches, killed a sniper on the way, and got right up to the main German trench, into which they fired; there were no German sentries, and they were all asleep. They had to retire pretty quick as there were only 8 of them but they must have frightened our German cousins!

Your mackintosh trousers are most awfully valuable now, I sleep in them and wear them all day over my puttees and breeches.

163

We get a government issue of rum nearly every day. I only care for it in my tea but it is not at all bad as a substitute for milk.

Another good ration we get from the government is bacon, we also get bread about 3 times a week. Occasionally very good tinned butter, bully beef, tea and sugar. So you see we have plenty to eat.

. . . .

14 Gt. Cumberland Place   November 26th 1914

My beloved Ralph,

Lady Chelmsford rang me up last night and asked me to dine, so I enquired for H.E. His regiment has reached India, they are to be quartered in Mhow. I looked him up in the Army List and find he is the junior Captain of all, only just escaped being subaltern by the skin of his teeth!

The War news today is almost too good to be true, a whole Division of Germans captured by the Russians and another expected to surrender; apparently they have got separated and cut off from the main Army by the Russians. We seem to have advanced a little near Ypres and according to this afternoon posters we have retaken Dixmude. Portugal has declared herself to be on our side but I don't think she will bring any troops into the field. People seem to have resigned themselves to a long and indefinite struggle, so I cannot hold out any hopes darling that you will be with us before David's birth.

This afternoon I could not resist sending off another parcel to you, mostly eatables that can be consumed straight away.

Nita

. . . .

In France   November 28th 1914

The Colonel wanted a small advance trench of the Germans' rushed the night before last, in order to capture it to see what was going on in it. Teddy with 3 men was ordered to undertake this job; he left our trenches at 1 a.m., it was very dark indeed and drizzling, he started from the Company next to me on the right and the whole Battalion lined the trenches; apparently he divided his party up into three, going himself with the centre lot; this trench is only about 100 to 130 yards in front of our trenches across some ploughed land. When a little more than half way across he was fired at, but nobody was hit; he gave the order to charge and was never heard of again. The trench was captured, only one other man being hit, nobody could find Teddy and word was sent back to that effect. The Germans, only about half a dozen, made their escape by a small communication trench back to their main line of trenches. Brockholes went out, this advanced German trench being held for the time being by us, and searched for Teddy with an electric torch; he was not in the trench, at least not in the part leading to this small outpost. Our other casualty was found by Brockholes in this communication trench and at first Brockholes thought it was Teddy but it was a man called Robinson who was killed. At last the party had to give up and return to our trenches, the Germans reoccupying their advanced post very shortly after our leaving.

What happened to Teddy nobody knows, perhaps in the dark he ran right over the trench and was shot, staggered on some yards and lay out of sight on the ground beyond. He could not have been seen by our men in this case. He is said to have run to his right but nobody is sure about it. All the ground our side of the German trench was searched carefully, there is just the chance that he was wounded and later on taken in by the Germans after they reoccupied their trench, in which case he would be a prisoner. When the enemy got warning from their own men running back, a pretty heavy fire was opened on our trenches, but we had nobody hit. You can imagine how depressed we all are at the result of this sortie, which was not worth the loss of so valuable an officer as Teddy.

General French has issued to our Army a special order in which after thanking his troops for their work in the trenches during the last month he expresses the hope that the hardest part of our job is over, and that possibly the end of the War may not be so very long delayed.

Our duty is apparently to hold as many Germans as possible on this side, while the Russians sweep across the country from the East. Should the Germans withdraw troops from here and thus weaken their line we should then advance and drive them back but if we are able to make them keep the stronger portion of their army on this side so as to leave the way more open for the Russians, we shall be doing what is required of us if we stay here for months to come.

In my letter to you this morning I mentioned that the enemy were shelling a part of this town. Little did I think that one of those shells had killed the Boy, and wounded Turkey Powell though luckily not very badly. They were apparently standing talking near the houses at the side of the street when a shell burst quite close; it killed Boy instantaneously and knocked Turkey down wounding him in the head, leg and hand; he has gone into hospital at a place about 4 miles from here, and will probably be sent home. We can badly spare two such officers as the Boy and Teddy in 48 hours without even being in action.

· ·

November 29th 1914

My own darling wife,

Tomorrow we go back for our 6 days in the trenches, with 3 days interval in support and after that shall probably return here again. Gray who was our Quartermaster Sergeant and is now my junior Subaltern is a very good man indeed and very nice too, but he finds it rather difficult not to say 'sir' when speaking to us and is still inclined to stand very much to attention when I speak to him! He is ever so much better than Pickering, who is in Turkey's Company, now commanded by Squidge. I am taking Gray into the trenches for the first time tomorrow and am sure he will be very reliable. Kemp is now Sergeant Major and is very pleased at his promotion. I have not got a Company Quartermaster Sergeant yet, so have told off Serg. Sparshott to do it for the time being.

· ·

In the trenches   December 1st 1914

My own darling,

I was on duty the first part of the night before last, and at about midnight we had a man killed, shot through the head through a loophole. Puss got up about 12.30 a.m. and said he was wide awake and would relieve me, so I went and lay down in what is now our Officers' Mess dugout, though I did not go to sleep.

About 1.30 a.m. Turnour came running to me to say that it was reported by some of his sentries that Whitaker had probably been shot; he had apparently been mending loopholes from the outside with a shovel with a Sergeant Bernard of 16 Platoon; when this was finished he asked the sergeant where his platoon was, and they went over and spoke to them.

This patrol consisted of two men who had to lie quietly in a ditch running straight from our trenches up to the enemy's trenches, the nearest of which was only 200 yards away. Puss only had a shovel with him, and had taken off his coat, so was in a brown woolen waistcoat, he had no revolver with him and was quite unarmed.

He apparently said to the sentries that they could not see very well from

166

21. Party at Government House for the Melbourne Cup.
Ralph is at the right hand end of the back row.
(see letter of 24 October, 1909).

22. Lord Chelmsford and his staff;
Ralph is seated, far left.

23. R.M.S. *Orsova*.
(see letter of 9 February, 1910).

24. Opening of the first Labour Parliament of New South Wales,
16 November, 1910. Ralph is on the left, holding his sword.

25. 'She caught two fish, one of 9½ and the other of 9¼ lbs.'
(see letter of 26 February, 1911). On the back of the photograph
it says that the fish weighed 11½ and 11¼ lbs!

26. 'Parliament was opened on the 16th inst
by the Lieutenant-Governor with the usual formalities.' Sydney, May, 1911.

where they were, and he started off up this ditch, not crouching or stooping, but quite carelessly and upright, and must have walked straight on close to the German sentries who were heard by this sergeant to give some sort of challenge and then about 5 shots were fired. Puss did not come back, so the sergeant at once sent in to report the matter to me. This was soon after 1.30 a.m. I came out and, after waiting about 10 minutes to see if Puss would crawl back down the ditch, I sent out one good man to creep up the ditch as far as he could to see if there was any sign of him; but he came back and reported he could not find any trace of him at all; it was bright moonlight at the time.

Yesterday evening, our General sent a note saying he was very anxious to secure a prisoner in order to find out what regiments of the enemy were in front of us. I therefore sent out another patrol up this same ditch, with orders to lie up there and try and secure a prisoner, dead or alive; they went out at about 6 p.m. and one of them came back in about 10 minutes to say that they had found Whitaker's body and that he was dead. Whatever happened, he simply threw himself away quite uselessly.

Ralph

. . . .

In Billets   December 11th

I paid out my men this morning 5 francs each, the first time we have paid them since leaving England but it is the first chance they have had of spending money.

I am thoroughly enjoying home comforts in this place and indeed it is so peaceful I said to Coote yesterday I felt as if it might almost be possible for you and Mrs. Stephens to come out here!

. . . .

In Billets   December 11th

This afternoon all the Company went over for a hot bath and apparently very favourably impressed the doctor over there with their cleanliness, as he reported that my Company were the cleanest lot of men he had yet seen at all. I can only imagine what the other Companies must be like!!

. . . .

In the trenches   December 13th

There are rumours that we are to make a big advance from here quite soon, if you read of our having done so you will know that it was a welcome change from the life in these damp and muddy trenches. My great news is that Ned Coke is to come to me as my second-in-command. I asked the Colonel if I might have him as we are such old friends. He will be such an enormous pleasure to me as a companion though I do not know how far he will be fit for this life after his 6 or 7 years in the city!! But it does make such a big difference to have somebody with me over 23 years of age to talk to. I hope he may arrive in a day or two.

· ·

In the trenches   December 16th 1914

My own darling,

This evening we sent out two separate patrols to occupy the German advance trenches; one went out under Bulkeley Johnson to the trench near which Puss was killed; it was unoccupied and nearly full of water; they found that shovel which Puss took out with him about 20 yards from the German trench. Mansel took out the other patrol to the trench where poor Teddy went to, and this was also unoccupied, but they found a grave just on the far side of it, with a wooden cross put up but with no name on it. I cannot help thinking this must be Teddy's grave, and that they buried him there that night.

· ·

December 16th 1914

My own darling wife,

We had another tragedy last night; about 10 p.m. Claude Percival was shot bang through the heart, and killed practically at once. He was apparently sitting on the bank of a new communication trench which was being dug from Bn. Headquarters up to Joe's Company on my right; a stray bullet got him in the back and went into his heart.

We really have had the worst possible luck so far, and I shall miss old Claude a good deal. This was simply a stray bullet, as he was 300 yards behind the firing line and it was of course quite dark at the time. Claude was superintending the work at the time and had just called to a corporal to give him some instructions. This of course makes me for the time nominally 2nd in command, but I am staying with my Company just the same, as there is no Captain for me to hand over to; anyhow I think I would just as soon remain with my own Company for the present. As you know I was rather specially attached to Claude, and shall miss him awfully.

· ·

Nita to her Mother

14 Great Cumberland Place   December 18th 1914

Darling Mumptykins,

You can imagine the excitement in England over the German raid on the
west [*sic*] coast. Everyone though deploring the loss of life is rather glad
about it because it is the one thing to wake England up and Yorkshire has
sent fewest recruits to Kitchener's Army of any of the counties in England.
This mail from Australia brought us news of Frank Newton volunteering
for active service; we all think it is so splendid of him but he wrote to Ralph
that he didn't volunteer for the first 20,000 because he thought unmarried
men without family responsibilities should be the first to go but when the
government asked for a second 20,000 he thought it was his duty to
respond, he would have always felt a cur if he had not. Kathleen very
loyally acquiesced and put no obstacles in his way.

There isn't such a thing as an able-bodied *gentleman* in London today
who has not either volunteered for the front or if he is not strong enough
for that for some useful service in England. I do not think any young man
would get a woman to talk to him if it was known he had not done one or
the other, he certainly would be cut in his club. Lord Chelmsford and men
of his age have responded nobly by going with territorials to India and
other parts of the Empire so as to release trained men for the front. Don't
you think it was splendid of Lord Chelmsford to go out as *junior* Captain
of the Dorset Territorials. Joan Thesiger told me on Sunday that most of
his senior officers are country tradespeople.

Young Harry volunteered but as he is now a member of the Government so a cabinet minister Mr. Asquith would not let him go. Harry
Lloyd, Joan's husband, is too delicate but works as a clerk at the Foreign
Office from 4 till midnight so releasing an able-bodied clerk, till he is on
duty at Buckingham Palace. Ellin Salmon's husband though 50 is going to
the front in January as 2nd in command of the 10th Batt. 60th Rifles whom
he left 12 years ago! The only shirker I have heard of is Mrs. Wallace
Nort's nephew Mr. Robinson who committed suicide a fortnight ago
because he wasn't passed for active service. I call him a shirker because if
he had lived he might have done someone else's work like Ernest Watt.
Mrs. Powell lunched with me yesterday, her husband was wounded when
Major Harman was killed, he is now in hospital in London. The explosion
she tells me made him very deaf as well as wounding him in the head, thigh
and hand but he is being patched up as quickly as possible to go back again

as they are so short of officers. Lady Barttelot came to tea with me last week and told me about Sir Walter, he was shot through the lungs and the doctor told him on the battlefield he hadn't a hope, he was thrust into a church full of dead and dying and left there for 3 days which was the saving of his life as it kept him quiet and gave his lung a chance to heal. He went before a medical board last week but they told him his lung was not well yet and that he couldn't go back for another month. Captain de Molyneux has just gone back after being laid up for weeks with a bad wound in the leg and abdomen. It is dreadfully hard on all these poor wounded ones that they should have to face the horrors of the War again but there is no help for it, men and officers particularly are so urgently wanted. I believe he went off his head at first as he was in that dreadful retreat from Mons, but it isn't true he has lost a limb.

. . . .

In the trenches   December 18th

Ned Coke arrived this morning and is now sitting in my dugout. We had a great meeting and this morning I have been showing him over the trenches and putting him up to all the tips.

Ned Coke told me that a friend of his whom he met at Havre had a letter from Miss Balfour, sister of Arthur B. who had had a letter straight from French himself saying that the war would be over in February and the troops back in England in March. Let us hope he may be right. I think very probably after we have been in billets this time the Colonel will want me to come as 2nd-in-command so as to share some duties with him, this had advantages as well as disadvantages, and I don't really know which I prefer. I am my own boss to a great extent as I am, more so than if I was doing 2nd-in-command to the Battalion, but in the latter job I should be living under a roof so long as we are in these trenches. Ned Coke finds it distinctly difficult to get along our deep and narrow trenches, he is so enormous! He keeps on begging me not to go as 2nd-in-command and leave him, as at present he feels so lost in this strange life but he will very soon get accustomed to it.

. . . .

In the trenches   December 19th

We had a restless night last night, Ned Coke's first one in the trenches. At 2.30 p.m. the Colonel sent for officers commanding Companies and explained to us that an attack was to be made on some German trenches by a Brigade on our right and that this Battalion had been ordered to make a 'demonstration' to distract the attention of the enemy from the real point of attack. We were supported by another Company from the Lincoln Regt. 4 platoons went out about 4.30 p.m. and took possession of the nearest line of the German advanced trenches, which were unoccupied; they opened a rapid fire from there, in order to try and make the enemy reinforce their trenches just in front of us which we were not going to attack. The artillery fairly bombarded the enemy's trenches on our right front, and an attack was delivered quite successfully as far as we know, but we have not had any definite news yet of what happened. The Germans set light to 2 or 3 haystacks which lit up the country for miles around, and the bombardment and firing continued up to about 1 a.m. when we got orders to resume our original positions in the trenches and to carry on as usual, an order we were all quite ready to obey. The artillery bombardment went on, however, nearly all night and in fact is still more or less going on now, so I should think the enemy have had a most uncomfortable time of it. Their guns have not replied at all or only very slightly indeed.

. . . .

In the trenches   December 23rd 1914

My own darling,

We go into billets tonight at L. where we were badly shelled some three weeks ago, but which has not been fired on much since. There was no attack of any sort last night, but all the same we spent a very bad night expecting one.

I told you in my last letter that an aeroplane had reported a force of the enemy massing at a village in front of us; at about 6 p.m. the regiment on our right reported that the Germans were pulling up their barbed wire entanglement which meant that they probably intended to advance through it themselves and attack our line. We had patrols out about 100 yards in front of us all night, and it was almost a case of standing to arms for most of the time. Each Company is given a Verey pistol which sends up a sort of rocket; I sent up two of these when it got dark in order to enable my patrol in front of me to see the enemy's trenches and try and find out if the wire was being removed in my immediate front; but they reported that they could not see any of the enemy working at it at all, though they could hear a great deal of movement going on in the trenches. However, hour after hour passed without any sign of the attack; in fact so still was everything that it made us all the more on the alert, as there is usually a total absence of firing on the enemy's part before they deliver an attack. I did not remain in the trench all the time but came back to my dugout with Ned, and we stayed in it for most of the time. Apparently the Indian Division some way to our right had been heavily attacked, and our 1st Division had been brought up in motor buses to their support.

That attack on the part of the Devon Regt. 3 nights ago seems to have done a great deal of damage to the enemy, combined with a very heavy bombardment from our own artillery; this was the night when two haystacks were set on fire; though we returned again in the morning to our original line of trenches, the Devons counted 120 killed of the enemy, as well as about 30 prisoners. Our guns certainly rained shells on their trenches with the greatest accuracy.

. . . .

In Billets   December 24th

. . . I have got a splendid piece of news for you which is that the 8th Division officers are to be given some few days leave each in January if it can be managed so you may see me home on a visit before the 2nd of next month!! I hardly dare look forward to it, but it is something to dream of and I really believe it may come off, unless there is a great change in the situation.

Tomorrow Xmas night all the Captains are dining at Batt. headquarters and we have sent contributions of food to make up a real good dinner, so while you are feeding off bully beef I shall be living on the (tinned) fat of the land.

Dodo Gilliat was in Freddy Blackers Company and was killed by a shrapnel bullet from a shell. Bingham Turner was killed the very first day he arrived.

. . . .

In the trenches   December 26th 1914

My own darling,

You ask in your letter about the sentries in my sketch of our trenches looking over the parapet, instead of through the loopholes. We have done away with loopholes altogether, except for a few iron plates with a hole in the middle, which can be used during the day; but at night we make the sentries stand up and look right over the parapet, and all the men have to shoot over the top of the parapet at night. The sentry's rifle lies horizontally on the parapet and he is supposed to shoot so as to hit the bottom strand of our barbed wire entanglement; the reason for this is that they are all inclined to fire high at night, or in the excitement of an attack, and that is of course useless, as all the bullets go over the heads of the enemy. When we had loopholes we found that the sentry could not keep at all a proper lookout, as he could only see a small piece of ground just to his front, but by looking over the parapet, which is comparatively a safe thing to do at night, he could see both to his right and left.

When we got here tonight, the Berkshires were full of the armistice which is still in force opposite us! Apparently it began by the Germans showing lights on top of their trenches, and at about 8 p.m. some of them came out of their trenches with lanterns, shouting out in English 'Will you play the game?' We did not fire on them, and a few men and officers went out to meet them. They arranged a local armistice and all today it has been continued; the Berks were walking about, as were the Germans, on top of the trenches, and they met on neutral ground half way between them. Apparently one German N.C.O. asked if he would be treated well if he surrendered, and on being assured that he would be, said that he would be on patrol in a night or two, and asked what he should do if he came to our lines to surrender; he was told to throw his rifle on the ground on being challenged and to hold up his hands; so we are keeping a lookout for him at night, and should he come along my men have orders to be careful not to fire at him; he said that about 50 of them want to surrender, but I am rather sceptical abut this; however, we shall see if anything comes of it.

We have also been ordered not to fire at all tonight, except in case of attack, and so there is absolutely no firing going on at all now; it sounds so peculiar, this absolute quiet; we are just as much on the alert, in case the Germans mean to play any nasty tricks, but personally I do not believe they mean to do anything of the sort, though the Colonel does not seem to be so sure about it. Our Brigadier appears to have been very angry about this armistice, but we are not taking any notice of his displeasure, and are not going to open fire until the Germans do.

One of the enemy told them that they would only have to stick it for another fortnight, as the War would be over by then, owing to the Russians having been so disastrously beaten! It must have been very interesting talking to the enemy in that friendly way, and I rather hope it may continue tomorrow, though we have had orders not to allow the men to show themselves too much, in case we might give some idea to the enemy how strong we are here.

We got a message from Brigade H.Q. last night about 11 p.m. to say that a deserter had come in and had given the information that a general

173

attack by the enemy was to be delivered along the whole line at 12.15 a.m., the signal to be the firing of 12 guns. We all stood to arms, but nothing of any importance happened at all; our artillery bombarded their trenches for nearly two hours, but there was no rifle fire at all. The wretched troops who had just gone into billets were had out and stood to arms from midnight till 7 a.m. for no reason at all. This morning as far as we are concerned the armistice of yesterday has been going on, we have been walking about on top of our trenches, and have been waving to the enemy who answered us by waving back! It really was extraordinary being able to walk about like that, the Germans doing the same, and neither side firing a shot.

The Colonel came up about 8 a.m. and made Coote fire three shots, which was the signal that the armistice was over, and this was answered by the enemy, but it made no difference at all and both sides have still continued it. I got up on our parapet and had a good look at their position through my glasses, and was not fired at once. We worked away at putting roofs onto our dugouts quite openly.

Your own husband
Ralph

· ·

2nd Bn. Rifle Brigade   December 31st 1914

My own darling wife,

Great news!!! I hope to start home in 3 or 4 days time on 7 days leave, so you may expect me to arrive home in London about Jan 4th or 5th.

One officer per Company and one officer from the Bn. H.Q. which will be Brockholes. Joe, Brockholes and 2 subalterns and myself will be the officers. The Colonel will go either the 2nd or 3rd batch.

This will give me 4 or 5 days at home! Isn't it perfectly glorious! The order says that the names must be sent in 72 hours before the leave is granted, so I suppose we cannot start for three days at least.

We go over to a place about 12 miles from here and are then motored over to Boulogne, starting at 8 a.m.; we are given free passes to London or anywhere else in the United Kingdom. I am so excited about it I can hardly write it down!!

I hope Mother and Gwen will come up to London to see me, unless you think I ought to go there for one night. One thing I have promised the Colonel faithfully to do, and that is to see Mrs. Stephens. Will you write to her to come up to see me in London, perhaps we could put her up for one night, we ought to ask her to do so, not the first night, but perhaps the second night of my leave.

Oh my own darling I simply cannot write any more; the mere thought of seeing you again within a week makes me delirious with joy. I daresay I shall not be able to let you kow definitely when to expect me but it will probably be on Jan 5th. If we get leave in 3 days time I shall have come straight from the trenches to you and shall be in a filthy condition!

Your own husband
Ralph

· ·

Battalin H.Q.   January 13th 1915

My own darling sweetheart,

When we got to Boulogne we found General Sloggett* who had a very nice chap called Black with him had two motor cars to meet us; Joe and his father went in one and Alldridge, Black and I went in the other. We got to St. Omer about 2.15 p.m. and had an excellent lunch, cooked by one of the Rothschild's cooks, who is paid £1,000 a year! This cook has been lent to Sloggett by this Rothschild. Old Sloggett does himself very well, he was very genial and kind and told me to come and stay with him at St. Omer whenever I could get away.

I am glad you did not come and see me off on the platform. I hate saying goodbye before a lot of strangers, and you would not have felt like making polite conversation to Mrs. Alldridge and the Sloggetts.

What a wonderfully happy time we had, my own darling sweetheart, and let us pray that we may meet again before long; we shall both always remember these last 6 days as well as our time at Hursley, as some of the very happiest we have ever spent.

I can't believe that there are many couples as happy as we are, or as devoted. When I look back on the last 5 years, I can't believe that there is any other couple in all the world who have done so much and seen so much together, I love you so very much more today than I did 5 years ago, though at that time I thought that was impossible! It has made all the difference to me, the last 6 days at home, as I can imagine you and our John so vividly now, and I can appreciate John so much more now than I could before.

I found Ned this morning at about 10 a.m. just getting up and cleaning his teeth between puffs of his pipe, first a brush and then a puff!

175

I am glad I said 'No' to that offer made through Mrs. Stephens of supplying the Battalion with Gum boots, because the Government have started giving them to us as a free issue, they have given about 60 pairs so far, and if they are reported to be very useful, more will be supplied, it will be a great boon if all the men were to be given these Gum boots free.

* Lt.-General Sir Arthur Sloggett (1857–1929) was Director General, British Armies in the Field, R.A.M.C., and Chief Commissioner, Order of St. John of Jerusalem and British Red Cross Societies 1914–18.

· ·

January 17th 1915

My own darling wife,

I had such a lot of visitors today, first Alldridge then Lawrence and Mansel came in about 3.30 p.m. and then Squidge and Joe. The latter two had a long talk to me about the Colonel, they both say he has got very irritable lately and very highly strung; they neither of them think Brockholes is the least use with him, that instead of trying to quieten him down he rather eggs him on; I am afraid Brockholes is rather young and inclined to dash forward without thinking, excellent qualities in a platoon commander perhaps, but not in the adjutant to a colonel like the Stiffen! I can't help thinking the Colonel always thinks of getting the Battalion mentioned in the papers or in Divisional orders for special gallantry etc. This War is so much too big a thing to try and score individual Kudos; to my mind it is no good any unit trying to attack separately, unless it is, by so doing, going to benefit the whole line.

If these small attacks succeed well and good, but no permanent result is obtained, and if they fail, everybody turns round and says 'What can you expect from isolated attacks but failure?'

Ned Coke, Joe and I are all very strong about this, and Holes consequently thinks we are all very much lacking in dash! But there are a good many non-dashers besides us according to his standard, e.g. Colonel Trevor who spoke very strongly about these isolated attacks to me yesterday. Perhaps Dashers like poets are born not made! I don't at any rate pretend to have been a dasher. Col. Trevor spoke with some feeling about this as it was his regiment, the Devon Regt., that lost heavily in the last isolated sortie about 3 weeks ago.

Joe etc. are anxious I should go back as second-in-command so as to act as a check to Brockholes! They think the latter has it too much his own way and that the Colonel allows himself to be run too much by him.

The news from Russia is distinctly good; she seems to be advancing in

176

three great Armies over 100 miles of front. As the paper says this must mean that Warsaw is safe, and also that Russia does not mean to have a respite during the winter months.

God bless you and John.

Ralph

. . . .

14 Gt. Cumberland Place   January 21st 1915
Thursday

My own darling,

I put on the outside of my envelope last night that I had just got your two letters telling me you were not to rejoin the company until this Friday in billets. You wrote me pages about the Colonel's irritability and Holes' anxiety to cut a dash. I rang him up to tell him you would be in Estaires tonight and he asked for news of you. I said you were better etc. then he said Does Ralph say anything in his letters about the Colonel's nerves and irritableness. I am afraid I lied and said No, but that you mentioned when you were on leave you thought he looked very worn and then Holes expanded and let himself go on the subject and said he thought he was getting dreadfully nervy and that a week's leave would be the greatest boon. He said the Colonel was awfully loyal to those above him and was torn in two because the Generals kept urging him to do things against his better judgment and the night the Devons lost so heavily he was told by the General to attack the trenches; he didn't like the idea of doing it and knew if he did he would lose half the battalion, but he felt he must obey orders and pretend it was his own wish. Holes went on to say that you and Ned Coke and Joe Sloggett did not realize that it was not the Colonel's wish to venture on such a mad attempt, but he knew of those official messages which reached the Colonel urging him to do something and how miserable the Colonel was about it and how it was that owing to him nothing did happen as he persuaded the General that it would be madness. Capt. Brockholes talked most warmly on the subject as if he had almost read your letter to me and was answering its accusations.

Nita

. . . .

177

My own darling wife,

Yesterday afternoon I spent a very interesting 2 hours in a loft at the top of our Battalion H.Q. with a young subaltern in the Artillery who was observing the effect of the fire from his battery. We wanted the artillery to get the range of a track past the corner of a wood, about a mile and a quarter to our front; we telephoned to them the spot on the map and the correct bearing by the compass; this subaltern arrived and his job was to watch the burst of the shells, and to send back by telephone to the guns as to whether they were too high or too short, or too much to the left or right.

The Guns were firing from close to this place and of course could not see at all what they were firing at; they got the range as near as they could by the map and also the direction, a few of our men were strung out from the end of our telephone to the bottom of the ladder leading to the loft for the purpose of passing orders or messages; I lay down beside him in this loft in the straw with my glasses, and we looked through the end wall of the loft, which has been broken to pieces long ago by the enemy's shells.

The message would come 'ready to fire' and then 'fired' and after three or four seconds the sound of our gun more than a mile behind us; we would then watch for the burst of the shell, each of which so he told me costs £2.16.0!

We were looking right over 'D' Company's trench and between the shells we could see Gray sniping at one of the German loopholes, and watching the enemy with the help of a man looking through a periscope; we then saw the head of a German appear to the left of the loophole Gray was shooting at, and shortly afterwards a German periscope appeared sticking up over their trench. Gray of course did not know we were watching him and told me this morning he had not seen the enemy's periscope at all. We have two men at a telescope up here all day now and they act as an observation post and report at once to us if they see any of the enemy moving about. In this way, and we have three of these posts altogether in our line, we hope that it is quite impossible for the enemy to collect any large body of troops in front of us during the day, without our knowing it; also if they intend to attack us by night we should still probably be able to see reinforcements assembling during the day and thus get good warning.

The Colonel ordered four telephones from a man at Hull and he is having them sent to No. 14 by Saturday night, and will call for them there and bring them back with him, so you might look out for them and see that they are read for him.

· ·

In the trenches   February 2nd 1915

My own darling wife,

Tommy Pilcher's amusement at night now is to go out towards the German lines and stick Union Jacks on their barricades; he also put one up on a ruined house in front of his Company's trenches which used to be occupied by the Germans. I think the flag on their barricade is about 50 yards or so in front of their trench.

A colonel of the Gunners came through this morning to see me about trying how long it would take to get supporting artillery fire. So I wrote out a message asking the battery in our rear to open fire with 4 rounds only at a certain point just opposite to us; it took 8 minutes only from the time I wrote the message which was telephoned to the Battery who of course did not know that a test was being made. This Colonel, whose name is Goff, wanted to see our two Redoubts on our left and right, so I took him along and showed them to him.

· ·

In the trenches   Fenruary 3rd 1915

My own darling wife,

We had a great joke against Squidge last night. Monty Stopford had a large sparklet syphon sent out to him with two boxes of cartridges for it each about 3 inches long. We used two of these to make soda water and then it suddenly occurred to us that they were quite like miniature shells, so we got a small piece of that yellow slow match stuff which is used in those cigar lighting contrivances and fixed it beautifully in the ends of these two empty sparklet cartridges. We packed them standing upright in an empty little tin box which used to contain proper fuses for the real bombs.

I wrote out the message to the O.C. 'G' Company as follows. 'Herewith two experimental bombs to be tested and reported on. Please supervise test personally and report to me in writing by 9 a.m. tomorrow.'

We sent this up to Squidge by one of the H.Q. runners and his receipt for 2 bombs was brought back by him. This morning at the 10 o'clock conference no report had been received from Squidge so I said suddenly

179

to Holes as if I had just remembered it 'You have sent on that report about those bombs to Brigade H.Q.?' to which he replied 'No, because Squidge had not sent it in yet.' Squidge hurriedly went to the table and wrote out his report, how the first had landed in water but the second failed to explode though the fuse could be seen burning quite plainly.

Anyway the joke was a huge success and old Squidge enjoyed it as much as anybody.

. . . .

14 Gt. Cumberland Place,   Thursday February 4th 1915

My beloved Ralph,

I am frightfully tickled over Ellen and a sock episode! You remember I told you in a previous letter how Mrs. Stephens returned one pair sent by Gwen measuring 13 inches in the foot and 12 inches round the ankle. I measured some of Gwen's next lot and extracted two more pairs just the same size and sent them to her asking that they should be made smaller, Gwen got them just as another pile were sent in and extracted 3 equally large, 6 prs altogether. She was going to give them back to the women but your mother wouldn't hear of it and told her to send them to Ellin, she would replace them by sending Mrs. Stephens through me 6 pairs made by a Blind asylum. Ellen rings me up last night and says she has had the most preposterously large socks sent to her by Gwen, no man could possibly wear such things or get his boots over them, she is returning them by Aunt Margie on Saturday to Gwen!! I fairly chuckled at my end of the telephone but 'lay low and said nuffink'. I did tell her that I was very glad she was making the complaint and returning the socks because I have had to do the same so often and was sure Gwen thought I was unnecessarily fussy.

. . . .

In Billets   February 5th 1915

When I got back to the Mess I found a letter from you written just after Sir Charles Ross had told you that very likely we should be stopped at Marseilles and how you had to catch the *Ventura*, the only ship leaving Sydney which would get you home in time to see me and you add 'I had to catch the *Ventura* if I wasn't to fail you, and I don't think I've done that yet, darling, since we married.'

My own wife, that is putting it in much too mild language, no soldier has ever had a more loyal loving and capable little wife than I have got, and you will always know that not only have you never failed me but that you have given me ample cause to remember with very real and devout gratitude Nov. 11th 1911 when we were made man and wife.

Sweetheart, I don't often write about it, but you know what I feel about you and I know what you feel about me; well do I realize that the gloriously happy marriage ours is and always has been is due to your unselfishness and also to your being such a capable little wife; I sometimes wonder what system is followed by the Hand which guides our destinies; take all the splendid young men who have fallen during the War; I honestly feel ashamed sometimes to think that I am still alive! I have every hope and belief that I shall be spared to return to you safe and sound at the end of this ghastly war, but why should I be spared when such glorious men have died? I never talk of these things, not even to Ned, but anyone who has any serious ideas in his head at all must sometimes wonder why one is spared and not another.

I know well my own sweetheart that you would not allow yourself to be overcome with sorrow for John's sake and also for the sake of the child that is yet to be born; I shall never be able to approve of the attitude of my own mother as regards my father's death; in my opinion one ought not to allow oneself to be permanently overcome by what after all is inevitable, and by what is merely a changed state of existence, for I do believe that this is so.

. . . .

Colon-Sergeant Daniels* to Nita

'D' Company   Thursday
2nd Bn. Rifle Bde.   February 18th 1915

To Mrs. R. Verney

Dear Madam,

Pardon me for taking this liberty, but I feel I *must* write and thank you on behalf of the Non-Commissioned Officers and Rifleman of 'D' Company, for your very great kindness, which has been shown to us, by forwarding articles of all kinds of clothing etc. during the very severe weather we had. I cannot really express by writing, the feelings of the N.C.O.s and Men in the Company, and above all the grateful look on the men's faces when they receive the presents.

One can hardly believe how touching it is for a soldier (just at the moment he fancies a drop of milk in his tea, or a nice taste of cake, and a cup of cocoa) to receive such a present.

I can write from personal experience Mrs. Verney, as I can stand *any* kind of hardships, and hard knocks, but these acts of kindness are what really touch a soldier's heart, whilst on Service.

I must admit that it's not quite so bad now as it has been, but even now, at the best of times, it's not too good. We shall be very thankful for a change in the weather, as that's the most trying of all. We cannot speak too highly of the arrangements of the Battn. Staff in general, as everything that's possible to be done for the good of the men, has been and is being done, and we are all living in *very* great hopes that the War will not last through another winter.

In any case, that we shall come out at the end 'Victorious' goes almost without saying, when we hope to have an Everlasting Peace.

Again thanking you on behalf of 'D' Company for your continual kindness and thought,

I remain

Yours obediently,
H. Daniels, C/Sgt.
'D' Company

* C.S.M. Harry Daniels (1884–1953) won the Victoria Cross at the Battle of Neuve Chapelle on 12 March, 1915. On 21 July he was granted a commission and retired in 1930 as a Lt.-Colonel.

. . . .

In the trenches   February 19th

I got your letter of the 16th yesterday.

I had already read Winston's speech and thought it excellent too. I spent yesterday evening in the trenches reading the full text of Gen. French's last despatch date February 2nd and I am bound to own I found it a depressing document. It seemed to me to be merely a summary of unfortunate incidents, always the same story of a gallant fight to take the trenches of the enemy, possibly successfully, only to find the position untenable with both flanks 'in the air' and then a retirement back to our original line with considerable loss to ourselves, with a supposed greater loss to the enemy, or else the position reversed, our trenches having been taken from us. At first we regained them the same night after heavy fighting and resumed our original line. Then again the despatch is so grossly unfair in what is mentioned in it, for instance take the case of poor Teddy Durham's show; this was a total failure really. Teddy and about 20 men, it is true, captured an advanced trench of the enemy's but failed to kill or capture a single German, and we lost one man killed and Teddy killed or a prisoner. On the other hand a subaltern of the Worcester Regt., who got a D.S.O. for it the following morning, went out with about a dozen men, captured an advanced German trench, found about 20 of the enemy fast asleep (luckily for the Worcesters) and killed them all. You cannot compare the success of these two small sorties, yet Teddy gets mentioned in this despatch and there is not a word about the Worcester subaltern. Take again Sir Edward Hulse, whom I told you I met the other day, who got mentioned for going out, firing a great many rounds into a part of the German trench and returning with what is recorded as valuable information as to the number of Germans in the trenches! Again no mention at all of that very gallant attack of the Devon Regt. just on our right the first night Ned joined me, in which they took two lines of German trenches at immense cost to themselves, though of course as usual the position proved untenable and they had to retire back in the early morning to their original line, but it was a most gallant show and the Devons lost, as far as I remember, about 180 killed and wounded but no mention at all of that. Bye the bye, Roberts was the name of the Worcester subaltern.

Then again there was a very gallant engineer subaltern attached to the Devons who took out a lot of bombs and went along the front of a line of the German trench throwing these bombs into it as he went along, no mention at all of this. Take the military chaplains who are mentioned as having shown 'conspicuous gallantry'. I can only talk of what I know on this part of the line, but I have never seen any parson in or near any of the trenches. One or two come to Laventie and they are much in evidence at Estaires. I am sure they are doing good work but hardly worthy of being included under the heading of 'conspicuous gallantry'. Then the Indians who, from all accounts, ran like hares, especially the Gurkhas. They were, of course, very heavily attacked but I have never heard that they were a great success, largely, no doubt, owing to the climate. Still they get very much lauded up to the skies by French. One more thing which annoyed all of us a good deal: 'Since the date of my last despatch I have had ample opportunity of inspecting all units under my command and am immensely impressed' etc. etc. Of course, he has never been anywhere near us, except when he came to Estaires with the King. [About 4 miles from them.] Nor have we seen any member of his staff. I shall be anxious to hear what is the opinion in England of this despatch which, after all, is the future official history of the war, as Wellington's despatches are of the Peninsular Campaign and Waterloo.

. . . .

We had a tremendous jest last night about rockets. We have been given 4 rockets to be sent up by us two at a time, in case of attack to warn the artillery. We were ordered in 'D' Co. to send up one as an experiment at 9.30 p.m. and the Colonel came up to witness it. We were at dinner when this order arrived. I disclaimed any knowledge at all of rockets and Coote also said he had never sent one up in his life. On which Ned said, 'Good Lord, I've sent up thousands on Diamond Jubilee occasions and others! Coote, you must have sent one up at the time of the Diamond Jubilee?' 'I don't remember having done so,' said Coote, 'and I was only seven at the time.' Anyhow, Ned said he would send up one himself he knew all about it. The Colonel, Holes (adjutant) and Monty Stopford all turned up to see this great experiment. Gray, Coote and myself all stood round as well. The rocket is tied on to a long stick which is supposed to rest on the ground and which goes up into the air with the rocket. Instead of resting it on the ground Ned or the Coote (both deny it stoutly) stuck it about a foot deep into the sticky muddy bank at the back of the parapet so that it stood up nice and firm and straight. These rockets are lit by means of a stick of slow match stuff about two feet long which splutters away and which is pushed up through the bottom end of the rocket tied securely to this long stake which was fixed into the muddy bank. Ned lit his spluttering slow match and applied it to the rocket which burst into sparks and smoke but could not rise at all, so safely was its stake embedded in the mud. The consequence was that the rocket, instead of bursting about a hundred feet or more up in the air, burst most splendidly just above our heads, emitting the most disgusting smelling fumes and showers of blue sparks all round us! The Colonel made a bolt for the narrow door of our mess hut. Holes and sentry disappeared behind a sandbag wall; Ned, clearing everything and everybody out of his way, caught Gray in the chest with his elbow, sending him with considerable force into the bottom of a wet and muddy ditch where he sat under a positive shower bath of sparks and smoke. I ran for my life about 20 yards down the parapet! The Coote, with a white face, appeared from behind a large roll of barbed wire and we all, including all the sentries and men, went into such paroxysms of laughter that the Germans answered us with cheers from their trenches. It really was too screamingly funny for words. We were all coughing and spitting from these beastly fumes. We asked Ned if he always sent up his thousands of rockets like that, but he assured us that 20% of fireworks acted in that strange manner always. The second one was a great success. We stood it up in an iron bucket; it burst beautifully over enemy's lines. All this time

Ned was still holding on to his spluttering rocket-lighter which simply would not go out. We stamped on it and swore at it without the smallest success. At last he threw it far away into the open where it continued to fizz and splutter for quite a long time. We retired to our mess and got rid of the smell of the fumes with the help of a bottle of Kummel which Coote had brought back from leave! This rocket joke came just at the right time because Ned was in the depths of despair at not getting any papers and was gloomily picturing us fighting the Germans for 5 years without a single letter or paper of any kind.

Later.

I will add a line to tell you of the very sad thing that happened this morning. General Johnny Gough* was coming over to lunch with the Colonel who went to meet him; as far as I can make out on their way back, the Colonel took Johnny Gough a little way round to show him something connected with the parapets and Johnny Gough got badly wounded in fact dangerously wounded in the stomach. There was nobody else there with them and the Col. came running back to Batt. Headquarters to fetch the doctor and a stretcher; they took him to Daddy Sherston's hut ('A' Co.) as it was the nearest and they hope to move him after dark back to the first aid post and thence by ambulance to hospital. I'm afraid he is very badly wounded. The Colonel has been with him ever since; you can imagine what an awful shock it must be to him. They were, of course, the oldest of friends and one was best man to the other. I know very little about it at present but will let you know how he progresses.

* See footnote p. 13.

. . . .

February 21st 1915

There is better news of Johnny Gough today. Sir Anthony Bowlby,* a great London surgeon, saw him last night at Estaires. His brother, Hubert Gough,** telephoned through that the report was a hopeful one. This news has done the Col. a lot of good he was in a terrible state last night about it, and did not come round the trenches at all till early this morning. He and Gough were on their way to Headquarters and the latter asked to stop and have a look at the Aubers Ridge in front of us, so they went a few yards off the road and stood behind a cart. A sniper saw them and hit Gough first shot, when the doctor and stretcher-bearers arrived he blazed away again but did not hit anybody, so it was awfully bad luck that Gough was hit first shot. He had been offered the command of a Division in K's army but Douglas Haig asked him to stay on as his Chief of Staff so Gough did not accept the Divisional command.

* Sir Anthony Bowlby (1855–1929) was then the Advisory Consulting Surgeon to H.M. Forces, France, with the honorary rank of Major-General.
** General (later Sir) Hubert Gough (1870–1963) was at that time commanding 2nd Cavalry Division.

. . . .

In Billets   February 22nd

A telephone message reached us last night just before we left the trenches to say that Johnny Gough was not at all well, and had had a very grave operation, adding 'All concerned have been informed.' We did not show this to the Colonel till we had all left the trenches. This morning another message arrived to say that Gough had died about 5 this morning. The Colonel went over to Estaires in a motor; the Battalion will probably be going to the funeral this afternoon. Isn't it a dreadful tragedy?

As regards to being mentioned in despatches, it seems to me to be almost automatic because all our Brigadier-Generals in this Division have been mentioned in French's despatches this time and, as far as our own is concerned, Lowry Cole* hardly ever comes near the trenches at all, so his 'distinguished conduct in the field' must refer to the field round his house at Laventie! It is rather a farce also the way all the Headquarters Staff are mentioned but still that has always been the way, the British Infantry do all the fighting and get very little in the way of rewards. Gen. Capper** who has had by no means a good reputation in his 7th Division got a K.C.M.G.! Old Sloggett, generally known as Naughty Arthur, got a K.C.B.

* Arthur Willoughby George Lowry-Cole (1860–1915) was, in fact, killed in action three months later.
** Major-General Sir Thompson Capper (1863–1915).

. . . .

14 Gt. Cumberland Place   February 23rd 1915

I won't send this off until I can tell you whether you have a son or a daughter! How nice of the Colonel to say you will get leave when the second leave is given. I am very sorry you should be one of the last to hear about our little one. Kathleen and the family in far away Australia will probably know before you. I went up to the nursery a short time ago and told John I hoped to give him a wee bubba to play with before he went to bed!

Much love for the present my own precious husband. It is a great thing to be able to suffer for you. I do hope I shall give you what you want, a little daughter.

Ever your very loving and devoted
Nita

. . . .

Nita's Nurse to Ralph

Dear sir,

Just a line from me to say your little daughter is fairer than John and a replica of her pretty little mother, 7lbs. 4oz. in weight and has a good strong voice. She only took three hours to come but everything was ready and we were all on the spot. Three hours has passed and everything is going well. Your wife sends her love and I am writing this at her bedside but she must be kept quiet and cannot write herself.

She herself is glad it is a little girl.

Yours faithfully
A. Steele

. . . .

In my Dugout   February 26th 1915
                                                  7.30 a.m.

I am so awfully happy. The telegram arrived with the letters last night in the trenches about 6.00 p.m.

I first of all opened the telegram and saw that it was a daughter. Next I opened Joan's letter which informed me I had a second son! I hastily opened your letter and found that it is a girl, so I had no doubt but that Joan's error was probably due to a mistake on the telephone.

It was the very greatest comfort to me getting Dr. Wallace's postscript and Nurse Steele's at the end of your letter. When I opened the telegram I called out 'I have a daughter,' on which Coote took up our flare pistol and said we must send up a flare in honour of the occasion! So we went outside and shot off a flare over the German trenches. We had port for drinking her health after dinner.

Later.

At the conference this morning the Colonel asked what the name of the daughter was to be so as to have it as a password for our patrols tonight.

187

But instead of Joscelyn I suggested John, so 'John' is the password for all our patrols in the Battalion tonight.

. . . .

In Reserve   March 8th 1915

My own very darling sweetheart,

I thought of you every minute I was awake on my return journey, what a happy week we had, and it is such a comfort to me to know that you are so well, also Joscelyn, and I can't be grateful enough for having had this week's leave, it has made the whole difference. I shall think of Joan having tea with you this afternoon at about 4.30 p.m. I found no less than 5 envelopes addressed in your handwriting waiting for me on my return!

Oh my sweetheart, the parting was as hard as ever, but pray God a time will come before long when we can be together again with no parting hanging over us; still it was well worth it, having a whole week with you at home, and I feel I have made the acquaintance of my daughter and feel sure that we shall get on very well together! John was a perfect little son and I feel sure he will really be a comfort to you while I am away.

I found a letter from Aunt Margy and also one from Harry waiting for me, about Joscelyn. What a good idea it was to have the Christening as we did, and I know how pleased Mother was that we had it while I was at home.

... *Chapter Nine* ...

In March, 1915, Ralph is wounded in the battle of Neuve Chapelle and spends his convalescence staying with his family, relatives and friends in England. He gets appendicitis and is passed as unfit for further Active Service and is invited to become Military Secretary to Lord Chelmsford on his appointment as Viceroy of India.

· ·

Nita to Ralph, undated

Answers from Ralph

Please don't answer unless absolutely able to.

Darling we are so anxious to know the answers to the following questions, perhaps you will just put Yes or No beside them.

1.	Are you suffering great pain?	*No*
2.	Have you been suffering great pain?	*No*
3.	Were you inoculated against tetanus?	*Yes*
4.	Are you likely to be on your back some time?	*Yes*
5.	Are you likely to get to the War again?	*Hope Not*
6.	Did the bullet go straight through?	*Yes*
7.	Has the bullet been extracted?	
8.	Have you been under chloroform?	*No*
9.	Did you get any letters from me at B?	*No*
10.	Did you get more than one telegram from me?	*2*
11.	Is there anything you want specially?	*Only to see you*
12.	Can we bring you fruit and papers?	*Don't know*
13.	Are you headachy?	*No*
14.	Is anyone else wounded besides Capt. Burton in the same Battalion?	*Capt. Mansel*
15.	Were any killed?	*Don't know*

Delighted letter
Delighted to be here
Am feeling very well, longing to see you, hope to see Mother tomorrow.

Your own
Ralph

....

Nita to her Mother

14 Gt. Cumberland Place   March 12th 1915

Darling Mumpty,

I have just had a postcard written by a Dr. Chavasse and signed by Ralph which says 'Slightly wounded in the right thigh and am getting on well, shall probably be in London in a day or two. Will communicate with you as soon as possible. Ralph.'

It came last night but Nurse Steele didn't give it to me till this morning so Ralph may very possibly be in London this very minute. I can only sing a Te Deum of joy that he is wounded and out of those dreadful trenches for perhaps weeks to come. I feel I have so much to be grateful for as he evidently got wounded in that big fight in the neighbourhood of Neuve Chapelle and Aubers which has been so prominent in the papers the last two days.

....

Ned Coke* to his Mother

March 15th 1915

My dear Mother,

I will try and give you as clear an account as I can of the battle of Neuve Chapelle.

The intention was to capture N.C. and get on to the high ground beyond it. This task was allotted to the 8th Division. The 7th Div. on our left were to seize Aubers and the Indians the Bois du Biez. We started off on the night of the 9th. At 7.30 a.m. on the morning of the 10th our guns to the number of 500 opened a terrific bombardment on the German trenches and carried this on for half an hour. At 8.5 a.m. the attack

190

commenced and we took Neuve Chapelle without much difficulty. Meanwhile the 24th Brigade on our left got hung up by the fire of our own artillery. But for this we could have pushed on and reached our objective. The next day the Indians attacked Bois du Biez, got into it, but were shelled out of it. The 7th Div. made another attempt to get in but found the Germans very strongly entrenched. That afternoon the Germans brought up more guns and a Bavarian Division arrived. The next day, the 12th, was the most awful day we are ever likely to experience again. It has left an indelible impression on us all.

The Germans started shelling us with 100 guns including several 'Jack Johnsons'. They began at 5.30 a.m. and continued until 4.30 p.m. not the ordinary shelling but firing as fast as they could load. Our casualties were naturally very heavy, this territorial battalion alone lost 6 officers and 145 men in the bombardment. The men were splendid.

The General was wounded and most of his staff killed. No words can say what it was like. The sight of our own bombardment and a subsequent German bombardment leave a memory which will cling to us for a long time. At 2.0 p.m. on the 12th the Rifle Brigade and the Royal Irish Rifles were ordered to take *at all costs* a German trench. They were told to rush it. The trench happened to be 500 yards away with a deep ditch full of water between them and the enemy. They were heavily enfiladed by a Brigade of machine guns in the Bois du Biez, and 3,000 Germans in front of them was a very strong force.

They tried once and were all shot down. Stephens (Col. commanding 2nd Batt. Rifle Brigade) went to the General and expostulated; the General said orders came from higher authorities. Again they tried, and again they were mown down – absolute murder. Poor Gilbey was killed and five other officers, and six wounded. The battalion is decimated. The telephone wires were all broken by the German bombardment, and all communication ceased. The staff lost their heads.

March 13th. Orders were received to consolidate the position already won. Once more the 7th Div. attempted to get on Aubers Ridge but could not get on.

March 14th. We remained where we were digging hard and being heavily shelled. Very cold at night and difficulty about getting water. Wounded and dead English and German everywhere. At 6.30 p.m. we 25th Brigade took over advanced position of 23rd Brigade where we are at present having dug ourselves in. The Battle is dying down.

On the 12th the Germans counter attacked with a regiment. They were mown down and left about 500 dead on the ground.

We captured about 1,000 prisoners and killed a great many Germans but I rather doubt their losses are as great as ours. How are we to replace these officers killed? Some of my greatest friends went straight to certain death and they knew it. What a tragedy it was – if only one of the incompetent staff had been up to see the ground before issuing that senseless order, 'Regardless of cost'. They were not going to risk their precious skins, they were about 5 miles away.

I was very pleased with this territorial battalion; they did extremely well and were much praised. The weakness is the N.C.O.s and officers; they are useless. They don't attempt to assume responsibility. It is awful hard work for me. One has to be everywhere. It was madness to attempt the attack without fresh troops behind. We got the Germans on the run and if fresh troops had come up to help the 24th Brigade and carry on the pursuit we should have had a great victory. As it is here we are after 6 days' fighting, having gone through the greatest German bombardment on this Western side without practically any sleep – still in the trenches. Do the staff realize that the men, though wonderful, are not superhuman. The staff work throughout the whole battle was deplorable. We have taken Neuve Chapelle, a tiny village, captured a mile of country, at what cost? Two Divisions are decimated. The strongest battalion in the 4th Army Corps is 400. The Scottish Rifles are commanded by the Sergeant Major, and so on throughout the 7th and 8th Divisions. Why one is alive is the marvel and, if alive, not gone mad during those awful days. Nobody here will ever forget the 12th March. The staff said the Germans could not bring up extra guns. On the afternoon of the 11th they had at least 100 extra with ammunition. They have been keeping their artillery ammunition for an occasion such as this. Now they must take us out and reorganize the two Divisions, yet I do not know who there is to take our places. The casualties were so heavy the medical arrangements broke down. Wounded were left out for days. I hope the authorities think one mile of France is worth the destruction and decimation of the best Divisions out here. They went into battle absolutely up to war strength.

Poor Lady Gilbey, I must write to her. He was such a friend of mine. Do tell her what I feel about it. He was splendid. Though wounded, he insisted on going out to bring in the wounded and was shot in the head. He did not suffer. Ralph Verney was wounded at the beginning of the battle and was spared the horrors of the rest of it. Do see him and tell him what I think of the whole show. I have not a moment at present to write either to him or to Lady Gilbey. Do see them for me. She will be absolutely broken-hearted. Beyond being awfully tired, I am quite well and cheerful.

We are supposed, according to the General Staff, to have killed and taken prisoners 4,000 Germans. This does not include the wounded; and of course we broke right through the German lines. If only we had had fresh troops there would have been some compensation for the very heavy losses.

* Edward Coke (1879–1944), son of the 2nd Earl of Leicester, was then a captain in the Rifle Brigade.

. . . .

Ned Coke to Ralph

My dear old Ralph   23 March

I cannot say I was distressed to hear you were wounded and saved all the terrors of the next three days. The battalion did very well but the whole success was thrown away by deplorable staff work. The cavalry, who were waiting, ought to have been dashed through and it would have been a real victory. The casualties were enormous – about 550 officers and 6,000 men. I will not go into the various phases of the battle as you have read the paper reports, which are more or less true. The Terriers, which I was adjutant to, did extremely well. They had heavy casualties, losing 8 officers and 300 men. My successor has appeared now the battle is over and I am back in command of D Company. The Coote was wounded and we lost about 40 men (in D Co.). Large drafts have been poured in, dozens of very young subalterns. We are still in the trenches but come out tomorrow night. We go to . . . for a few days' rest, then we go back to F Lines and probably have another push from there against Aubers. I do not know whether we can stand another show. March 12th was too awful. We were bombarded by Jack Johnsons from 5.30 a.m. till 4.30 p.m. Men and officers blown to pieces. I've seen sights that I shall remember to my dying day.

I very much doubt whether the German losses are as great as we made them out, but they lost very heavily in their counterattacks. Poor little S is sitting in a cellar with me now. He is shattered and at one time completely broke down. I am not surprised. It was too awful. It was far worse than anything one could have imagined. There were no troops behind us, and after all these terrors we had to do 12 days in the trenches. Where is Kitchener's Army? Is it never coming? Oh to get away from this holocaust of dead bodies everywhere, German and English. Poor Eric and Biffer, how one misses them all. Holes exposed himself needlessly. Poor little

Tommy Pilcher. What a tragedy it all is. Daddy Sherston, Squidge, Paul Kennedy, who arrived after the battle, and I are the only Captains.

I can see you in your pink silk pyjamas, masses of flowers and an admiring crowd of ladies. How I envy you, but dear Ralph how thankful I am. I was in an agony when I heard you were wounded, and the relief when I heard you were all right. How long is this ghastly business to last? Trench warfare is absolute peace-soldiering to what we have been through these last ten days. The night is rendered hideous by people yelling in their sleep. My nerves will not stand another show and I am sure nobody else's will. Every General is cursing every other. The cavalry were waiting at Rouge Croix and were never sent. Rawlinson and Allenby, I believe, are to be sacked. Carter, 24th Brigade, has been sent home, likewise Capper, 7th Division.

If the cavalry had been sent at 3 p.m. on the 10th the Germans were fairly on the run and we should have got Lille. They gave the Germans 12 hours to bring up very big reinforcements and over 100 guns and then made futile attacks against them which led to these appalling casualties. Was the awful cost worth it? One mile of country including a village in which there is not one brick standing upon another. The Germans' machine guns played the devil, the 2nd and 3rd days one could not advance against them, they mowed down line upon line.

. . . .

Nita to her Sister

14 Gt. Cumberland Place   Friday, March 19th 1915

Darling Sissiekins,

You must all be longing for details about Ralph. He is going on splendidly in that gorgeous hospital in Park Lane. He arrived there on Sunday night and his mother went to see him next morning for an hour. He was suffering much from shock and nerves. Apparently the wound was not serious but he had had a trying time. He is still unable to tell us about it but we gather that the bombardment by our artillery began at 7.30 and lasted till 8.0. The R.B. and another regiment who were hidden behind a breastwork charged the German trenches at 8.0. Ralph was wounded 25 minutes later and lay for 3 hours unattended except for a field dressing put on by his orderly who stuck to him all the time and came back with him to the first aid station at 11.30. From then till 3.30 next morning Ralph was in a series of ambulances, waiting sheds and trains and was jolted and rattled over cobblestones along French country roads, always being stopped to let more serious cases pass. Poor Capt. Burton, who was shockingly wounded in the head and has since died, recognized Ralph from his stretcher and called to him. R. was taken to No. 7 stationary hospital in Boulogne on Thursday morning and stayed there till Sunday when he crossed over. He was dreadfully fatigued and miserable. They X-rayed him on Monday morning and operated that afternoon. The examination was most successful – no bones touched, arteries or nerves damaged, but he has two large holes where the bullet passed through and they have inserted a tube to carry away the pus, it will remain in for 3 weeks or a month. Dr. Shields says it will be 3 months before he can march. My one prayer now is that the war will be over before then. His nerves have had as much as they can stand.

On Tuesday I would not be kept from him any longer but was carried downstairs into Joan's motor and carried from the motor into the hospital and back again an hour later. It did me all the good in the world seeing him.

Nita

. . . .

Mrs Couchman to Nita

March 30th (1915)

Dear Madam

Your kind letter to hand, I should be very grateful if you could send me any news of my son Sydney.

I have no details, some one (in the trenches) wrote and told me Sydney was seriously wounded on the 16th and that is all I have heard.

I have indeed felt anxious since then and shall welcome any particulars you are able to send me.

Sorry to hear Captain Verney has been wounded, please accept my sympathy.

Yours gratefully
C. Couchman

. . . .

14 Gt. Cumberland Place ·   April 1st 1915

Dearest Father,

Ralph is having a thorough rest in the hospital and is not at all loath to lie in bed all day. His hair has become very grey but he looks well, though his digestion troubles him a good deal. I have got a more accurate account of the battle now. He was not hit by any of those Germans who were surrendering and who his men were anxious to bayonet, as they were all unarmed. The bullet came from the Germans further along in front, who were trying to check our advance. Thank goodness it came when it did, within 25 minutes of the attack, as the rest of the day and the next two days, particularly the 12th, must have been too ghastly. I am sending Mother Capt. Coke's account. When you have finished with it perhaps you would let me have it back. I want to keep it for Joscelyn as he is her godfather.

Little Tommy Pilcher was shot through the head while leading his men.

Mr Gilbey, too, died heroically. He continued to advance though shot in the arm and cheek. He was finally hit in the mouth. Poor Mr. Brockholes exposed himself needlessly while standing behind a parapet talking to two Colonels and was shot through the head and fortunately knew nothing. He died next day still unconscious. Capt. Burton lingered for a week and then died of bronchitis as well as from his wound.

. . . .

Nita to her Mother

April 5th 1915

Darling Mumpty,

I have got Ralph safely home and am enjoying myself immensely! He goes to the hospital daily to have his wound dressed and then we drive for an hour round the park which is so jolly just now.

He came home from hospital quite unexpectedly. I went to see him at my usual hour and found him being dressed to come home so I came with him. I sent 80 more pairs of socks to the men. They can never have too many but no other kind of woollies are wanted now and I do hope won't be wanted again for years to come.

. . . .

Nita to her Mother

Botolph House, Claydon   May 5th 1915

The 2nd Batt. are in the thick of the fight for Aubers Ridge. Poor Colonel Stephens has managed to get away (I don't know how) for his mother's funeral. She died quite suddenly from a stroke. I am still sending out socks and other things and am also looking after a prisoner in Doberitz, Germany, a rifle-man – sending him weekly parcels of food. We have 380 prisoners from the 4 battalions and Mrs Tom Morriss is distributing them amongst friends.

We can send our parcels through an American agency; they are so badly fed and so miserable. I am thinking of keeping another supplied out of the Wallaroy funds. It only costs 3/– a week and I've a large sum in hand.

. . . .

Nita to her Mother

14 Gt. Cumberland Place   May 30th 1915

Darling Mumpty,

Everyone is very depressed in London. We have had so many disasters lately. 2 battleships torpedoed in two days at the Dardanelles, a terrible train disaster and another ship full of explosives has sunk at Sheerness with a loss of 500 lives. Young Harry is going to enlist in something if his post in the Govt. is taken from him. There have been so many changes this week and so many older men thrown out of the cabinet that he expects one of them will be given his job, in which case he will have to enlist, much as he hates it. He has no alternative as he is young and strong and every man is so urgently wanted, Rachel will not stand in his way.

We expect a Zeppelin raid in London next month. I have provided all my household with masks and anti-gas solution as the Government believe the bombs as well as being incendiary will be filled with poisonous gases like those employed by the Germans at the front.

We have been given orders to keep all doors and windows closed so as the fumes should not get in.

Nita

. . . .

June 10th 1915

Dearest Father,

Kathleen has quite settled down* and makes Gwendolen 10 years younger in spirits. Ralph is still waiting for a daily summons from the hospital. It is very trying as it keeps us from making any plans. Aunt Margy has lent us a delightful house on Holyhead Island called Rhoscolyn until the end of July. The children and nurses go there about the 19th June and R. and I hope to join them sometime in July. It is very bracing and wild, hardly any one else on the island. We think of leaving them there and then going for a motor tour in Ireland as it is so close. R. ought to get 2 months' sick leave after the operation. Our future plans are very undecided. We are thinking of trying to get this house from next October to April as there does not seem to be any chance of the war being over by then. We are not going to make another big offensive movement until we have got our asphyxiating gas ready. Ours is to be even more deadly than that used by the Germans. It is invisible and will paralyze the enemy at once. They will become like statues just in the poses they were when the gas reached them. Doesn't it seem too terrible for words? But we must protect our men by taking some retaliatory measures.

You would be very much astonished if you could see and hear the enthusiasm about Lloyd George.** Only a year ago he was the most reviled person in the United Kingdom, now he is the most popular. Conservatives are all acknowledging he is the soundest man in the new cabinet. Last night at the Coliseum he got more applause than anyone else, even than Kitchener. I think the latter is not such a hero as you would imagine. He is held responsible for this terrible lack of high explosives which we've so badly needed at the front for months past and he is becoming such a terrific autocrat. This strong coalition government has been formed partly to try and keep him in order. He is absolutely heartless about the number of lives sacrificed and not only that is so terribly unjust. A long list of honours was sent him by French the other day covering some months and several big fights – altogether over 2,000 names. When he saw it he said, 'What nonsense, I'm not going to give all these honours' and took a pencil and scored a line through every second name! This is a fact. The man who gave him the list told Capt. Coke about it. He is, after Kitchener, one of the most important Generals at the War Office; the

Quartermaster General of the Forces, the man who is responsible for feeding, clothing and transport of our whole army. Capt. Coke's naval brother told him that it is quite true what Winston said. All the battleships at the Dardanelles with the exception of the *Queen Elizabeth* are old surplus ships that would have been turned into firewood and scrap iron if there hadn't been a war so there is nothing to be depressed about excepting for the loss of life when they are sunk by mines, etc.

Since the disastrous fighting on May 9th there hasn't been another big attack. Then we lost 2,000 in our brigade of 4,000, the 2nd Batt.'s share being 650 and not an inch of ground grained. Rachel's brother has been wounded 3 times and is just returning again. If Ralph hadn't to have this operation he would have been back next month.

Everyone is longing for the war to end. It is the one topic of conversation, that and Zeppelins, but alas no one can see any glimmer of light; we are only half-way through the tunnel.

Don't pass on what I write about Kitchener. It is no good disturbing the general public's faith in him. French is merely a figurehead. His Chief of the Staff, Robertson, is the man who is really doing the work out there.

Much love to you all
from Nita

* On her return from Australia.
** Mr Lloyd George was appointed Minister of Munitions on 25 May, 1915. He had been Chancellor of the Exchequer since 1908.

. . . .

Nita to her Sister

14 Gt. Cumberland Place   Thursday June 24th 1915

Darling Sissiekins,

Ralph had his appendix out this morning and is going on very well. I spent from 9.30 till 11.45 a.m. waiting for news and felt too wretched in a rather dark waiting room. I sat with him for an hour this afternoon but he was very drowsy and hardly realized I was there. I was nearly overpowered by the smell of chloroform which clung to him.

. . . .

Claydon House   October 20th 1915

Darling Mumpty,

I am sure the cable we sent this weekend will give you great pleasure.

Ralph had his board on the 13th and to his utter amazement was given 3 months more leave. None of us can believe our good fortune yet.

As Harry and Rachel and their children are to be all the winter at Claydon House and Kathleen and her babies with R.'s mother and Gwen at Botolph House we thought we would pitch our camp somewhere in the neighbourhood and succeeded in getting a very nice house on the outskirts of Winslow 4 miles from Botolph House. It belongs to Lord Addington. His father died last June and he is at the front but his mother is charming and lived in this house until a year ago when she moved into the Dower House as it is larger and her married daughter wanted to bring her family to stay.

Our 6 babies have great meetings on the Claydon House lawn, 4 are running about and are much the same size. Joscelyn and Ralph look on from their nurses' arms. Ralph Bruce is hugely fat and very stolid, his face looks bigger than Ralph's or mine.

. . . .

Nita to her Mother

Seven Gables, Winslow   November 25th 1915

Darling Mumpty,

I wrote you a long letter from Broomhall and didn't finish it but put it in an envelope. One of the maids there packed my things and I am much afraid either overlooked it or posted it. If the former it may be there still, so I had better write another and give you the same news.

[Claydon] Harry, Ralph and I travelled north on Thursday night with Victor Bruce, the youngest son, who is in the 11th Hussars. We had a very comfortable journey there and arrived at Broomhall in time for breakfast. The men went off shooting directly after and Lord and Lady Elgin and I joined them after lunch. Next day more members of the family turned up, so we were a very large party. Lord and Lady Elgin, Lord Bruce (R.A.) the eldest son, Capt. Bobbie Bruce, 11th Hussars and his wife, Capt. David Bruce, Seaforths, Lieut. John Bruce R.N. and 2nd Lieut. Victor Bruce, 11th Hussars, Lady Veronica Bruce, Rachel's eldest and only unmarried sister who is now a hospital nurse, a Mr. Bruce, Lord Elgin's brother, and his daughter Miss Janet Bruce, both country cousins and very dull.

Altogether there were about 50 in the house including the beaters and loaders who Lord Bruce brought with him from Perth, men from the R.A. Lord Bruce was at preparatory school with Ralph and Harry. He is such a heavy lump, always reminds me of the Scarlet Pimpernel as he always has his eyes half closed and a stupid vacant expression on his face. He is really very clever and businesslike, but intensely shy.

. . . .

December 29th 1915

Ralph's board is on the 13th of next month he has no idea what will be done with him.

18 Queens Gate Place
London, S.W.

. . . .

Lady Chelmsford to Ralph

January 15th 1916

My dear Ralph,

I have just received a cable from my husband in which he says, 'I desire Ralph Verney as military secretary. Have telegraphed Kitchener. Will you ask Verney?' So am writing to tell you from him how very much he wishes to have you on his staff and how much we both hope that you will be able to accept the post which I know you will fill most adequately. It would also be a great pleasure to me to have Nita out in India where she would be a very great help.

I do not think you need be anxious about the climate for your children as Simla is cool all the year round and it is always possible to leave them there during the hot weather. My husband always said he intended to have you as his military secretary if he ever became Viceroy of India! and I do not think you will find it easy to go counter to his 'desire'! Come and talk it over with me on Monday.

Yours sincerely
Frances Chelmsford

. . . .

And so Ralph went again to India to serve Lord Chelmsford for 5 years as his Military Secretary – but that is another story!

... *Index* ...

Ranks and titles shown are the highest mentioned in the book: the persons concerned may be found in the text under a lower status, or none.
The Verney family tree is at the front of the book. To aid identification in the index, the relationship to Ralph Verney (R.V.) is given in brackets after each name.

Hewitt, Sir G., 65
Holman, Prime Minister, 111, 112
Hulse, Sir Edward, 183

Imperial Light Horse: in Boer War, 50, 55
India: R.V.'s service, 59–61, 123, 130–43 *passim*

Jenkinson, Lieutenant, 44, 45, 49
Joffre, General, 149

Kays, Colonel, 40
Kekewich, Major-General Robert, 52, 53
Kemp, Vecht-General Christoffel, 52, 53 *n*
Kidston, William, 74–5, 77, 78, 79
King's Royal Rifles *see* Rifle Brigade
Kitchener, Field-Marshal Lord, 6 *n*, 140, 149, 198, 199
Kitchener, Lieut-General Sir Walter, 6, 12–13, 17, 18, 26, 28, 36, 39, 52–3, 55
Kruger, President Paulus & Mrs, 11, 27
Kruger's Post (S. Africa), 26, 27, 28

Laing's Nek (S. Africa), engagement at, 9, 10
Lamington, Lord, 65, 66
Le Hunt, Sir George, 85
Leicester Regiment: in Boer War, 24, 25
Lincolnshire Regiment: in France, 163, 171
Lloyd George, David, 198, 199 *n*
Lowry-Cole, Brig-General Arthur, 186
Lydenburg (S. Africa), activities at, 22–34
Lyttelton, General Sir Neville, 6, 13, 18, 26, 56

MacDonald, Miss, 99, 100
McGowan, Premier, 108
MacGregor, Sir William, 87
Madden, Sir John, 74
Mansel, Captain, 168, 176, 189
Masserene, Lord & Lady, 116
Milman, Mr & Mrs Hugh, 88, 89
Mounted Infantry: in Boer War, 44–54

Nel's Spruit (S. Africa), relief of, 32
Neuve Chapelle, battle of, 190–3
New Zealand: Ralph & Nita's visit, 109–10
Newton, Captain, 69, 87, 92
Newton, Frank, 93, 112, 113, 115, 116, 169
Newton, Kathleen *see* Verney, Kathleen
Nightingale, Florence, *preface*, 122 *n*, 124
Nightingale, Parthenope (*later* Verney), *preface*
Norfolk Island: R.V.'s visit, 105–6
Northcote, Lord & Lady, 66, 68, 74, 84

Percival, Captain Claude, 134, 142, 168
Philp, Sir Robert, 75, 77, 78
Pilcher, Lieutenant Tommy, 179, 194, 196
Pole Carew, Lieut-General Sir Reginald, 21
Powell, Captain Turkey & Mrs, 151, 165–6, 169
Pretorious, Andries & Mrs, 30–1, 32 *n*, 40 *n*

Queensland: R.V.'s tours of, 70–1, 80–3, 88–91

Rawlinson, Colonel Henry, 50, 52, 53 *n*, 55

marriage, 111–12, 113, 114, 115
during war, 169, 186, 198, 200
Ralph's letters to, 2, 22–4, 42–3,
57–8, 87
Verney, Margaret (née Hay Williams;
aunt), preface, 9, 96, 113, 117,
118, 119, 124, 198
visit to Australia, 114, 115, 116
letter from Ralph, 41–2
Verney, Maude (née Hay Williams;
mother), preface, 98–9, 117–18,
119, 120, 149
Verney, Morforwyn (cousin), 19
Verney, Nita (née Walker; wife):
marriage to Ralph, 93, 94–8
in Australia & NZ, 103–4, 106,
109–10, 115, 131–9 passim
return to England, 141, 143–5,
146–8
and children, 127–9, 132, 143–4,
148, 186–7
during war, 148–53, 156–9, 164,
169–70, 180–2, 186–7, 189,
194–200

relations with Verney family,
98–9, 100–1, 113, 117–19,
124–6
Verney, Parthenope (née Nightingale;
step-grandmother), preface
Victoria, Queen: death, 33

Wade, Prime Minister, 108
Walker, Dame Edith, 94, 97, 114,
128, 147, 148
Walker, Nita see Verney, Nita
Walker, Senator & Mrs, 94, 95, 96,
104, 115, 116
West Australian Regiment: in Boer
War, 39
Whitaker, Captain Puss, 142, 159,
166, 167
Willcocks, Sir James, 137
Wilson, Field-Marshal Sir Henry,
160
Worcestershire Regiment: in France,
183

Yarr, Dr, 60, 64